A.I. Photo Manipulation

Foreword

Like it or not, A.I. is everywhere and is here to stay.
It can be seen as the enemy and a threat to all our roles, jobs
and creativity, or it can be seen as just another tool to allow us
to create and produce things we could only have previously
dreamed of.

My view is to embrace it, learn it and use it.

I ventured into A.I. photography whilst designing cover art for
my latest music album. I needed it to look professional and
grab attention with a modern, even futuristic feel.

The photos in this book were all taken of objects around my
house and garden.

You will find the original photo, totally unedited, followed by
several versions of it having been processed with A.I.

It's a fun and creative process that still needs a keen eye for
detail, colour and design.

I hope you enjoy the images.

If they evoke thoughts, feelings, emotions and even inspire you
to be creative then they have been successful.

- Ant -

Contents

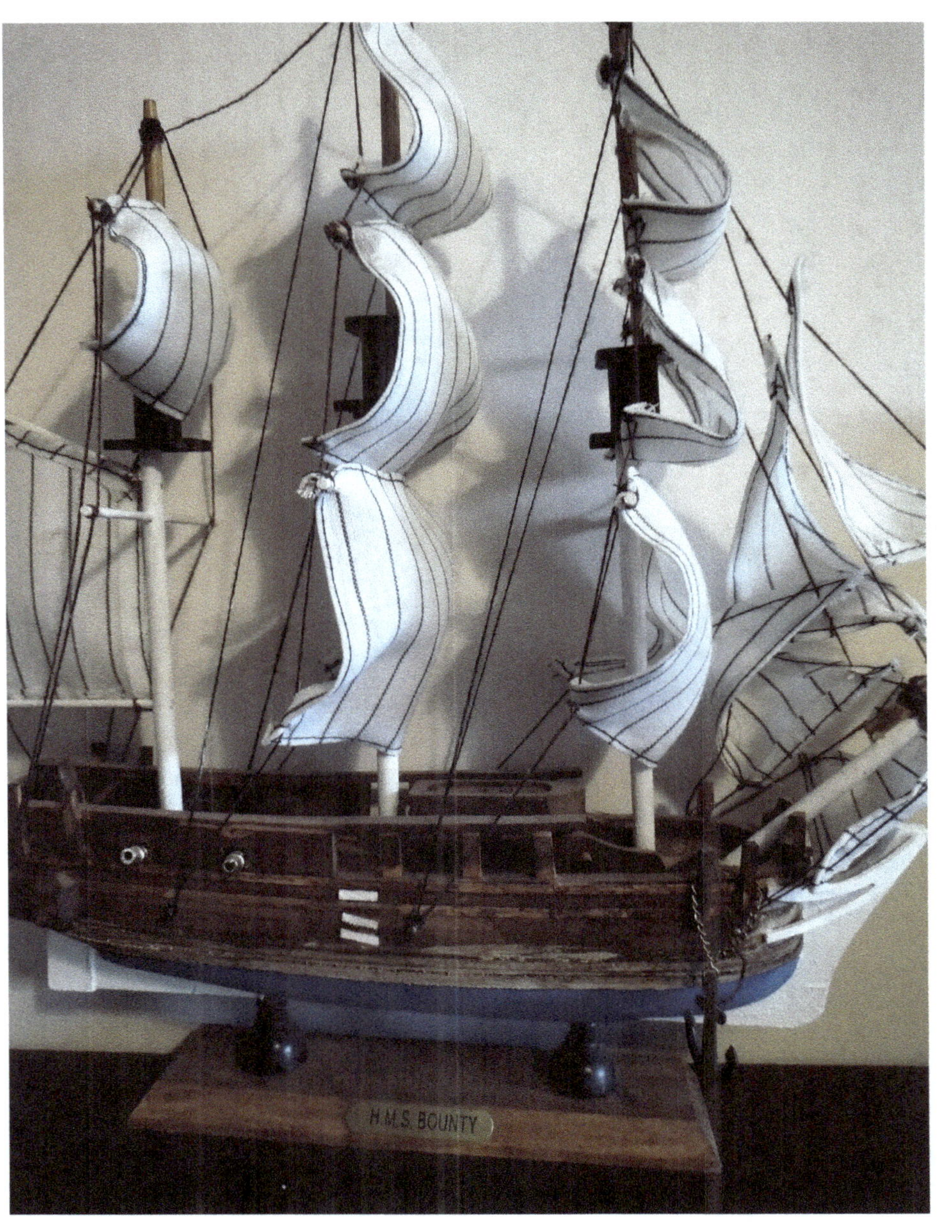

Bounty model ship

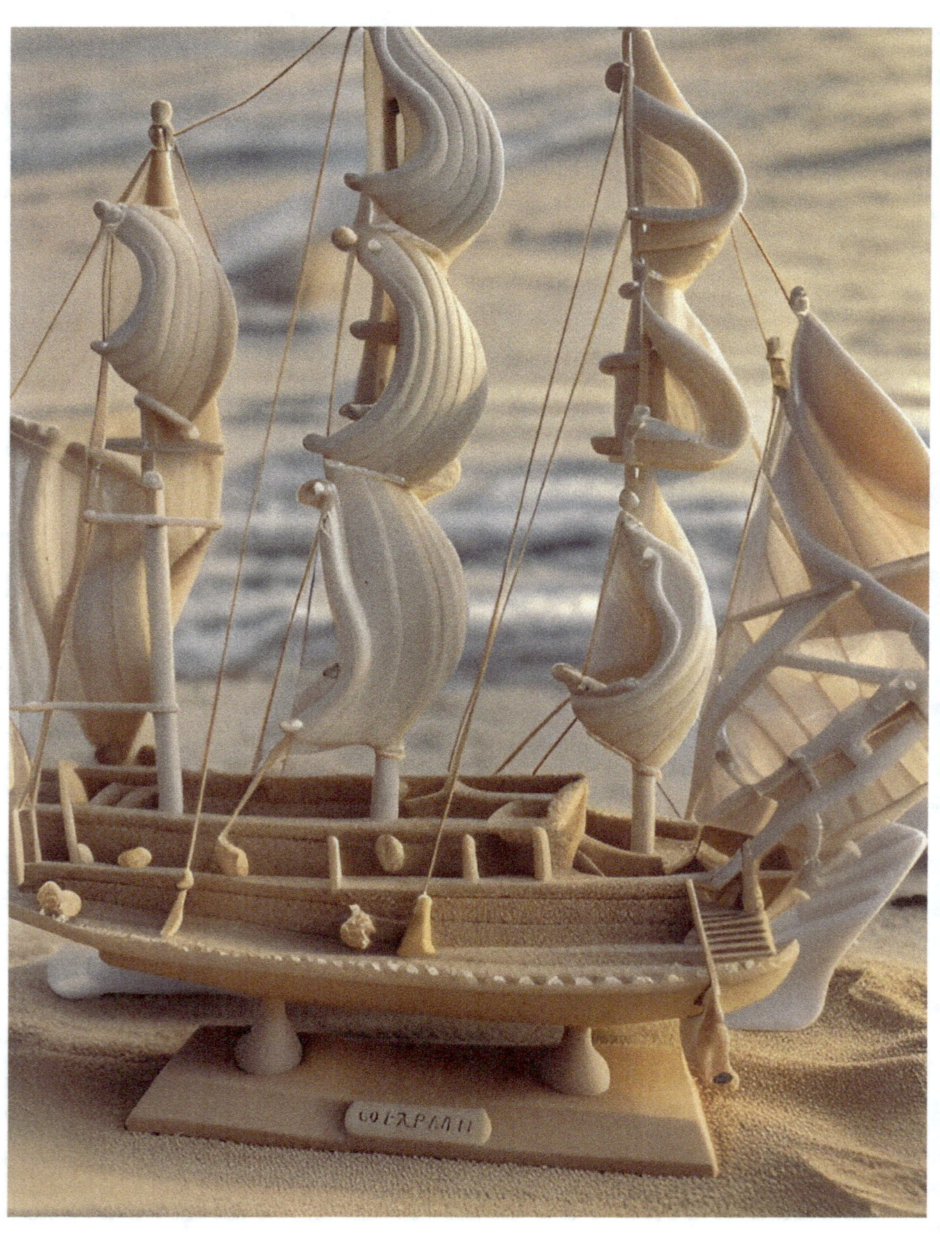

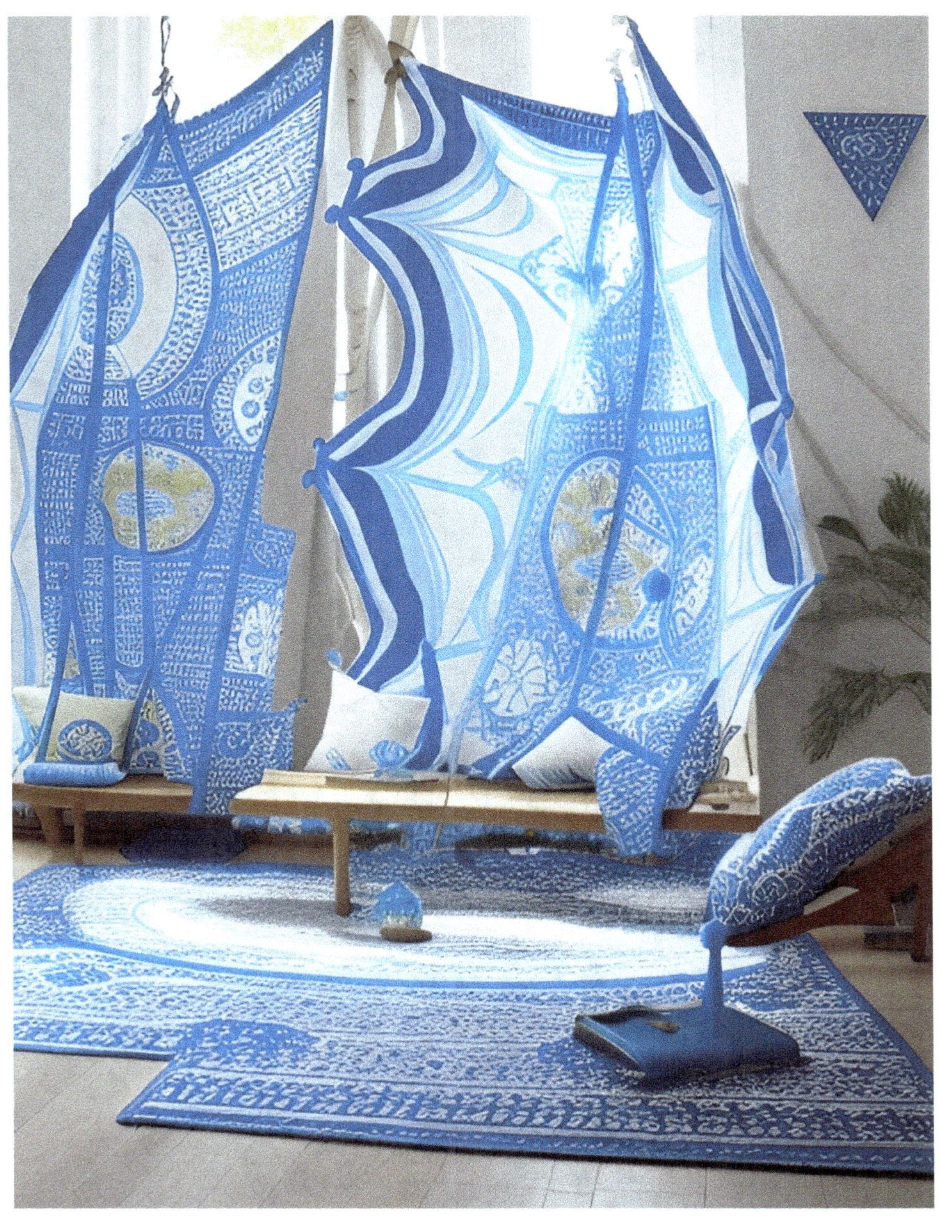

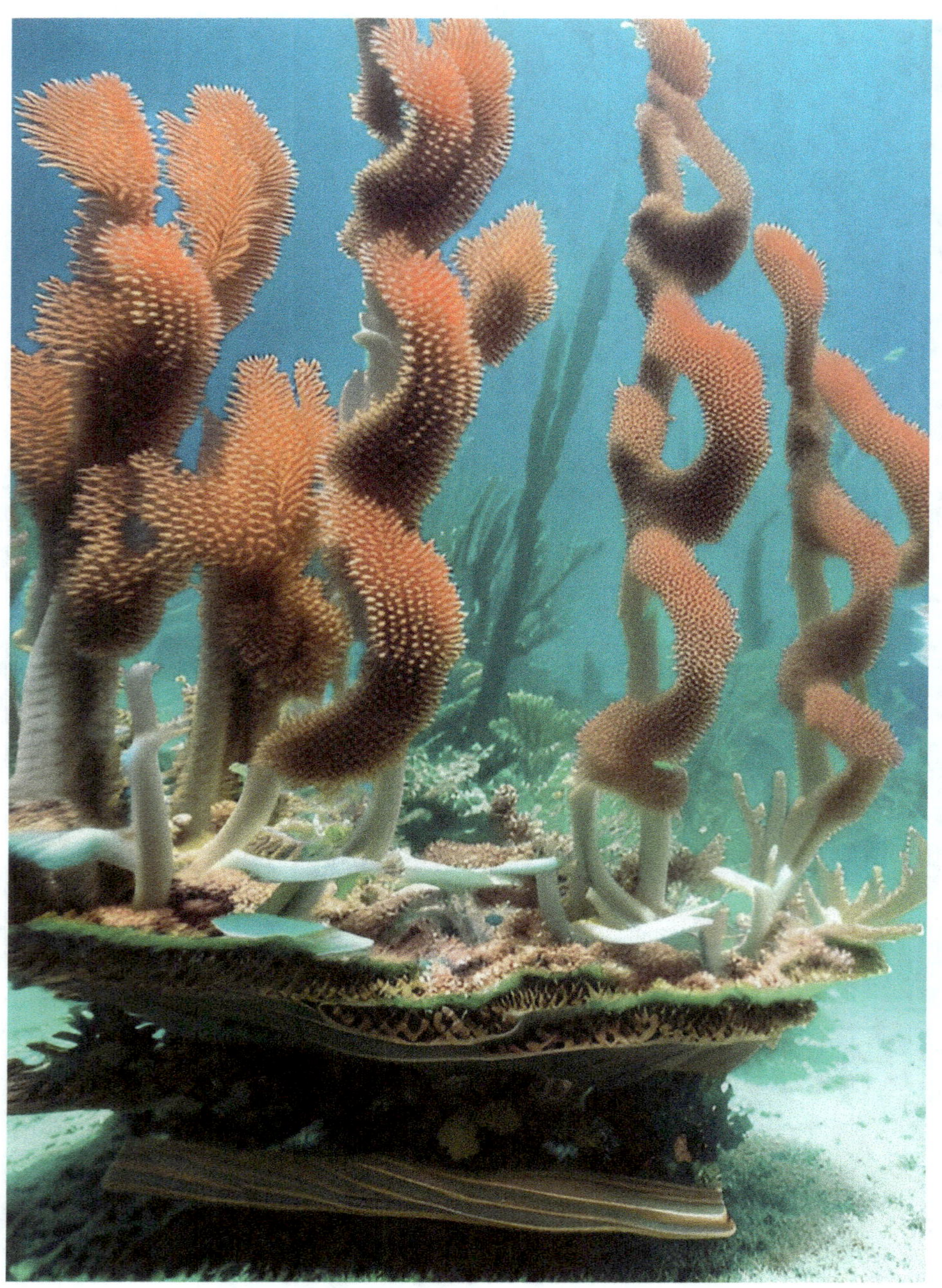

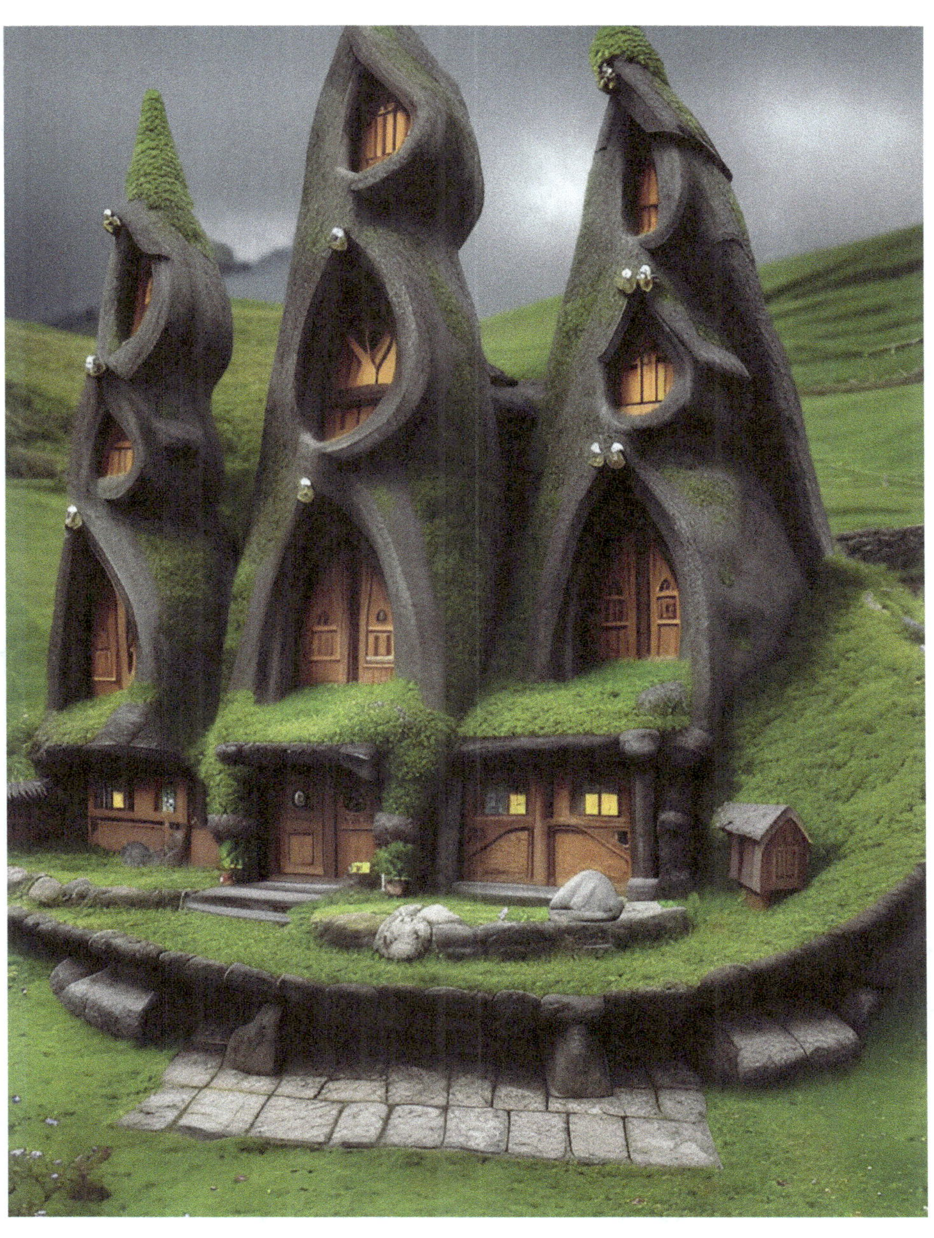

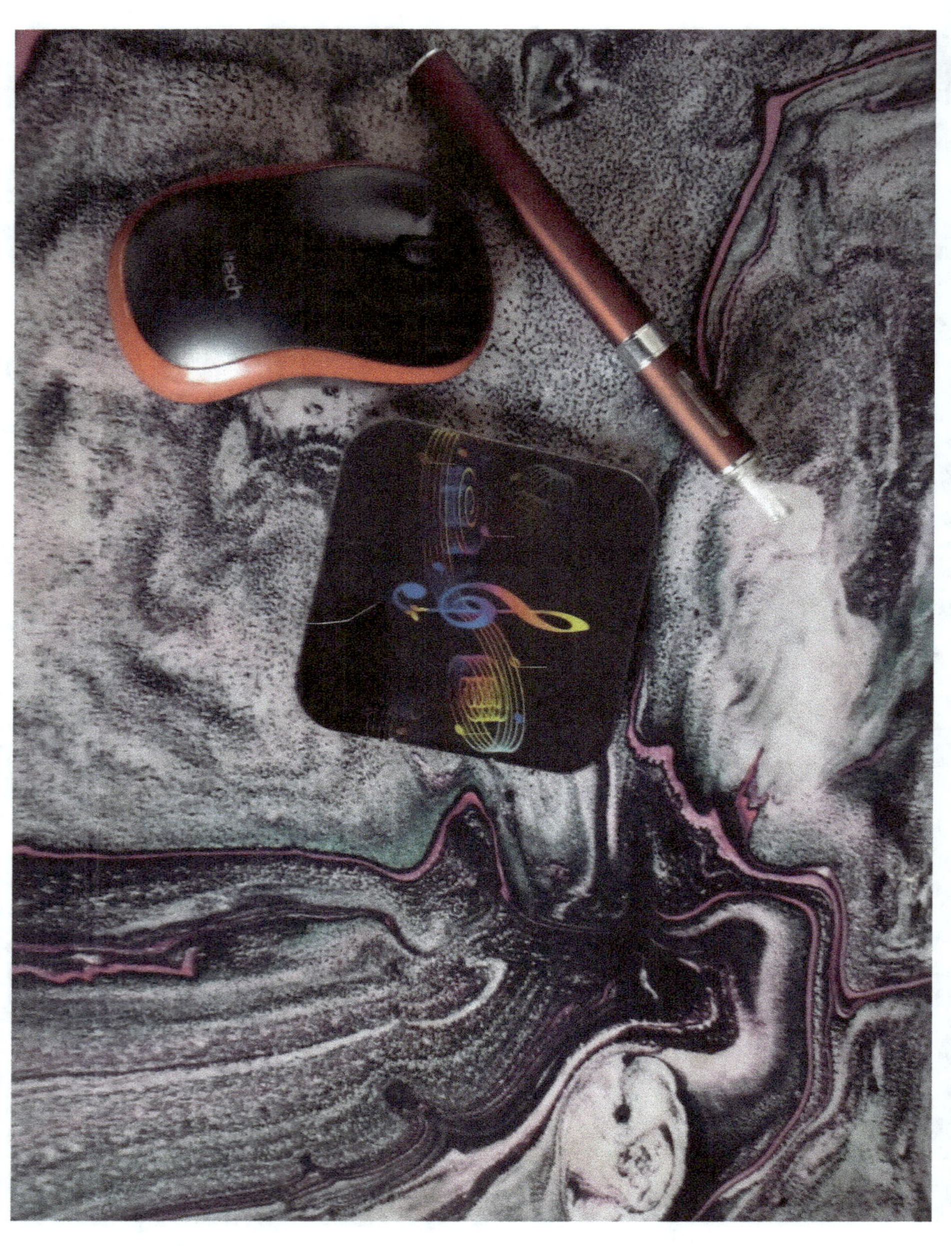

Coaster, Mouse and vape

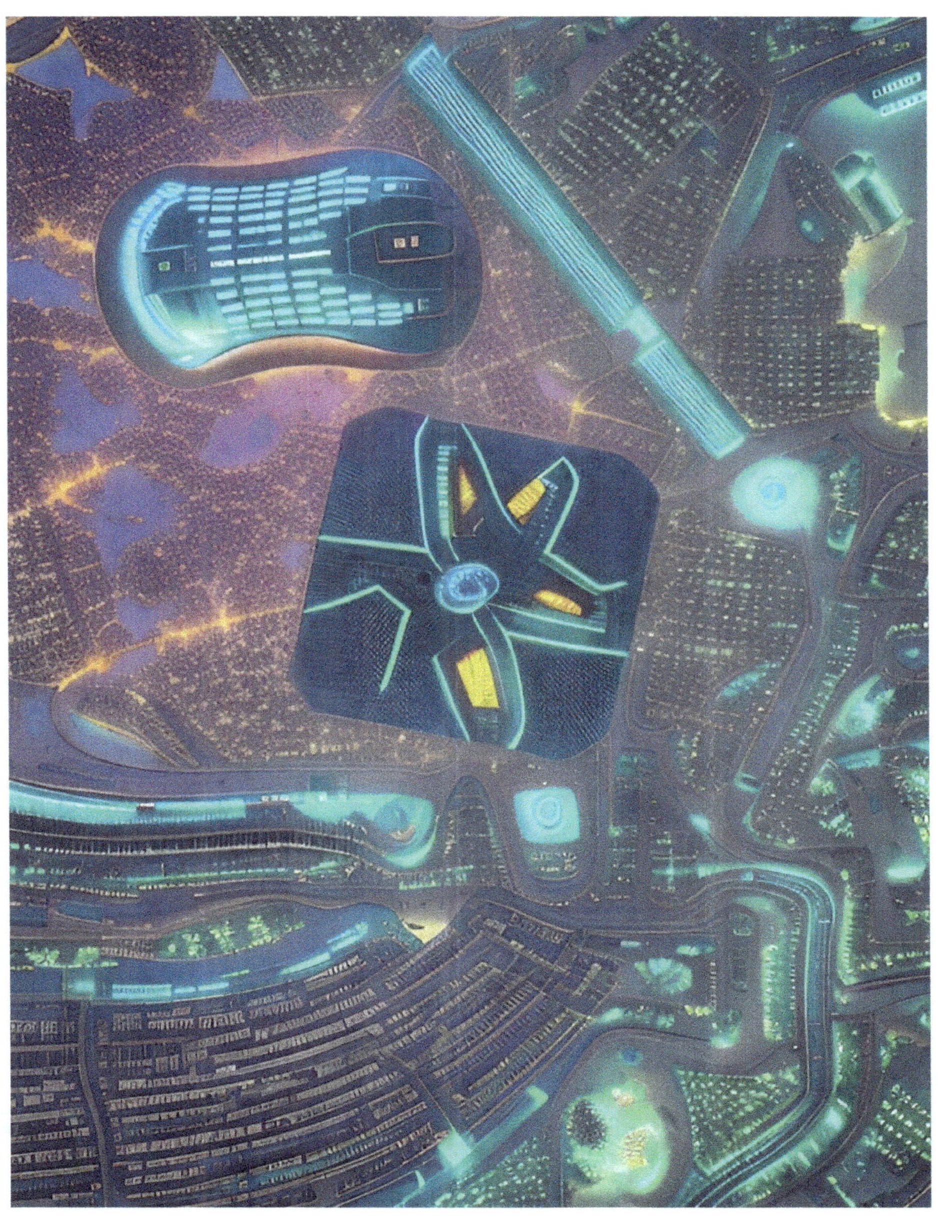

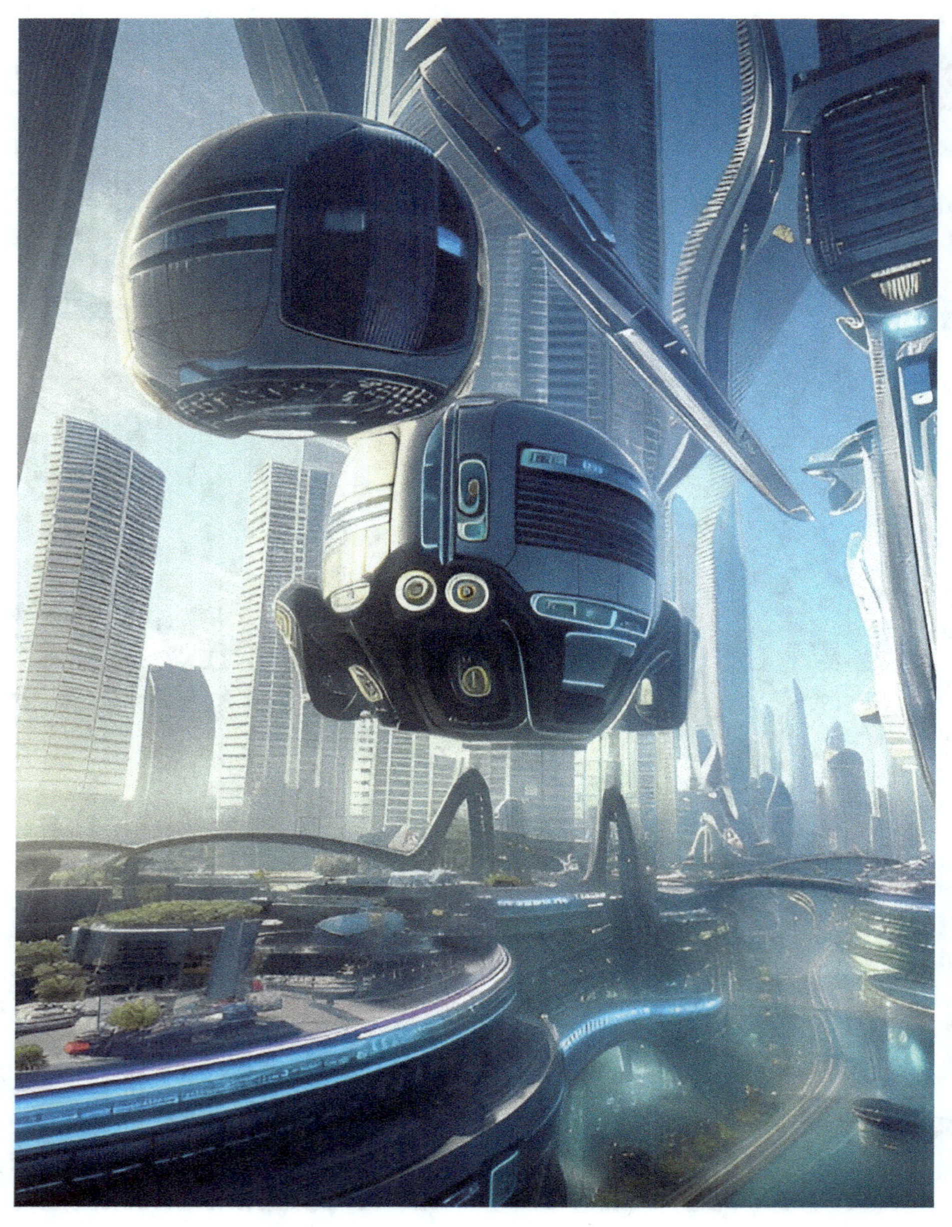

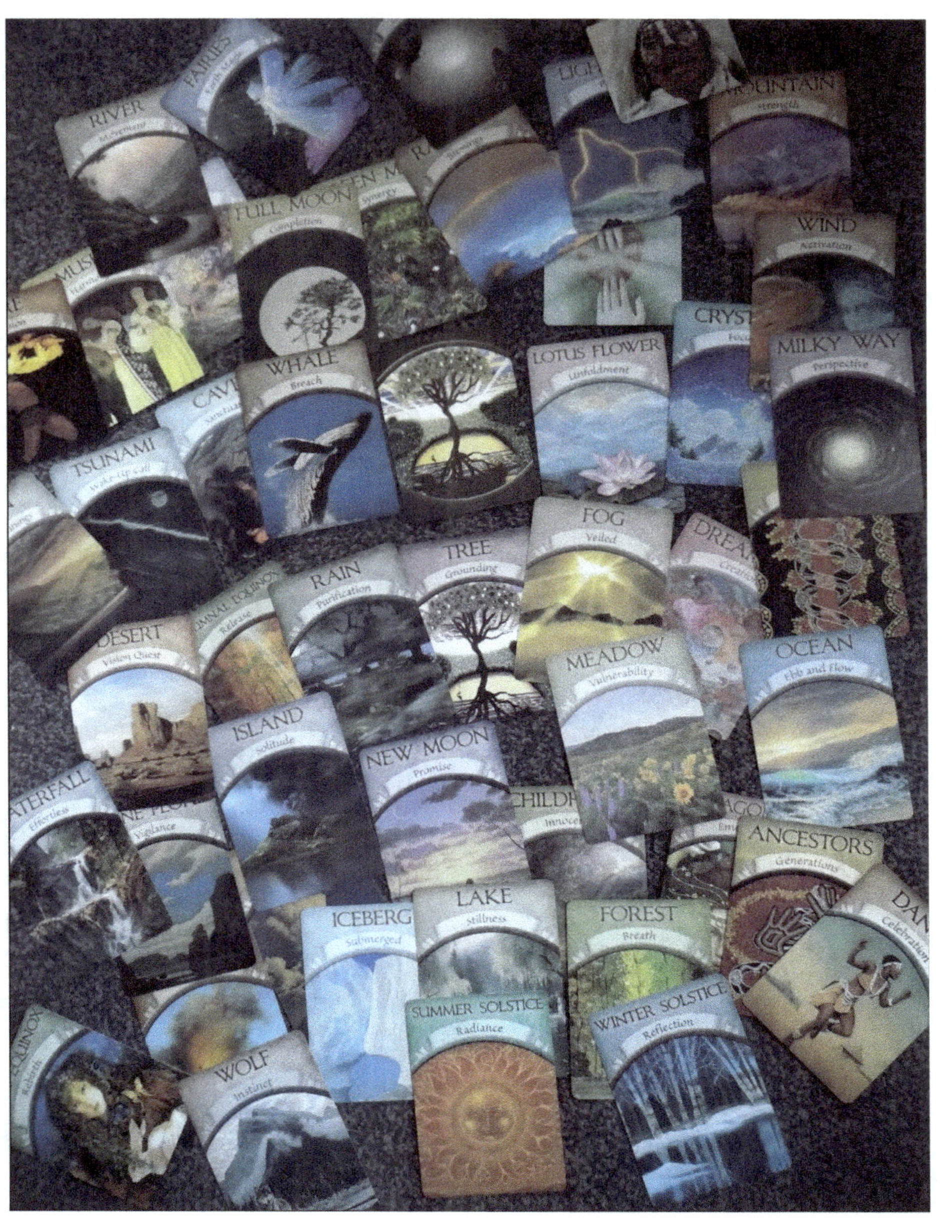

Meditation cards

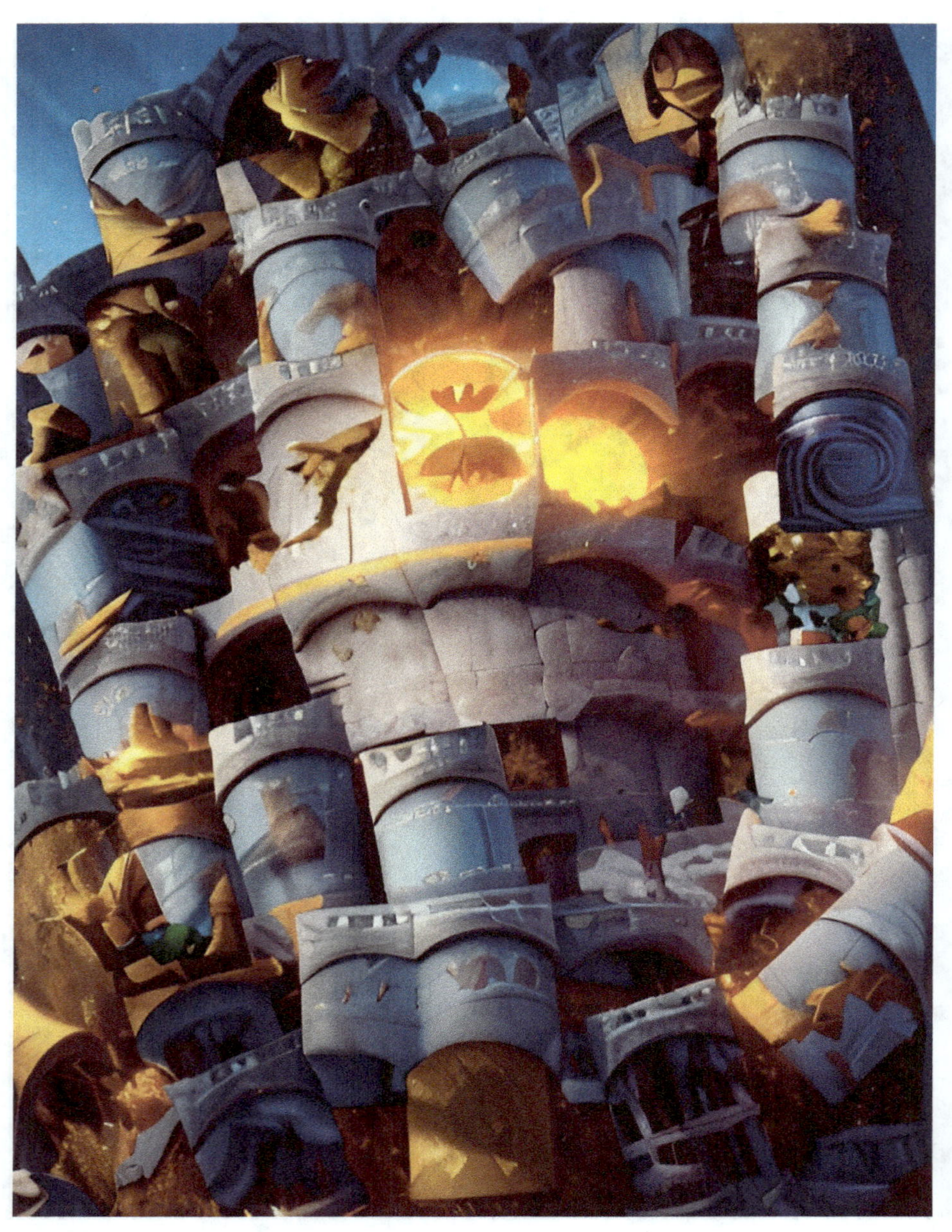

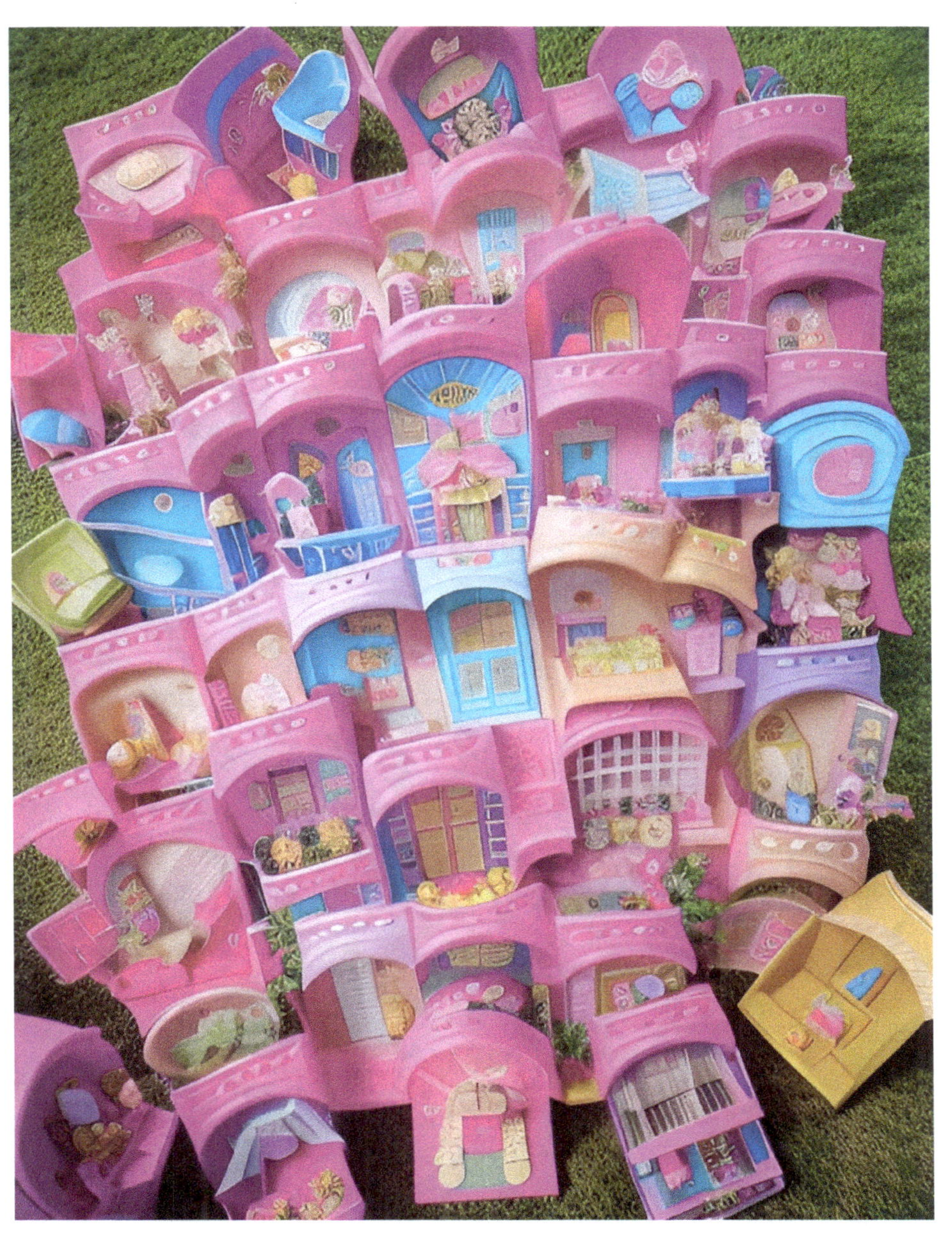

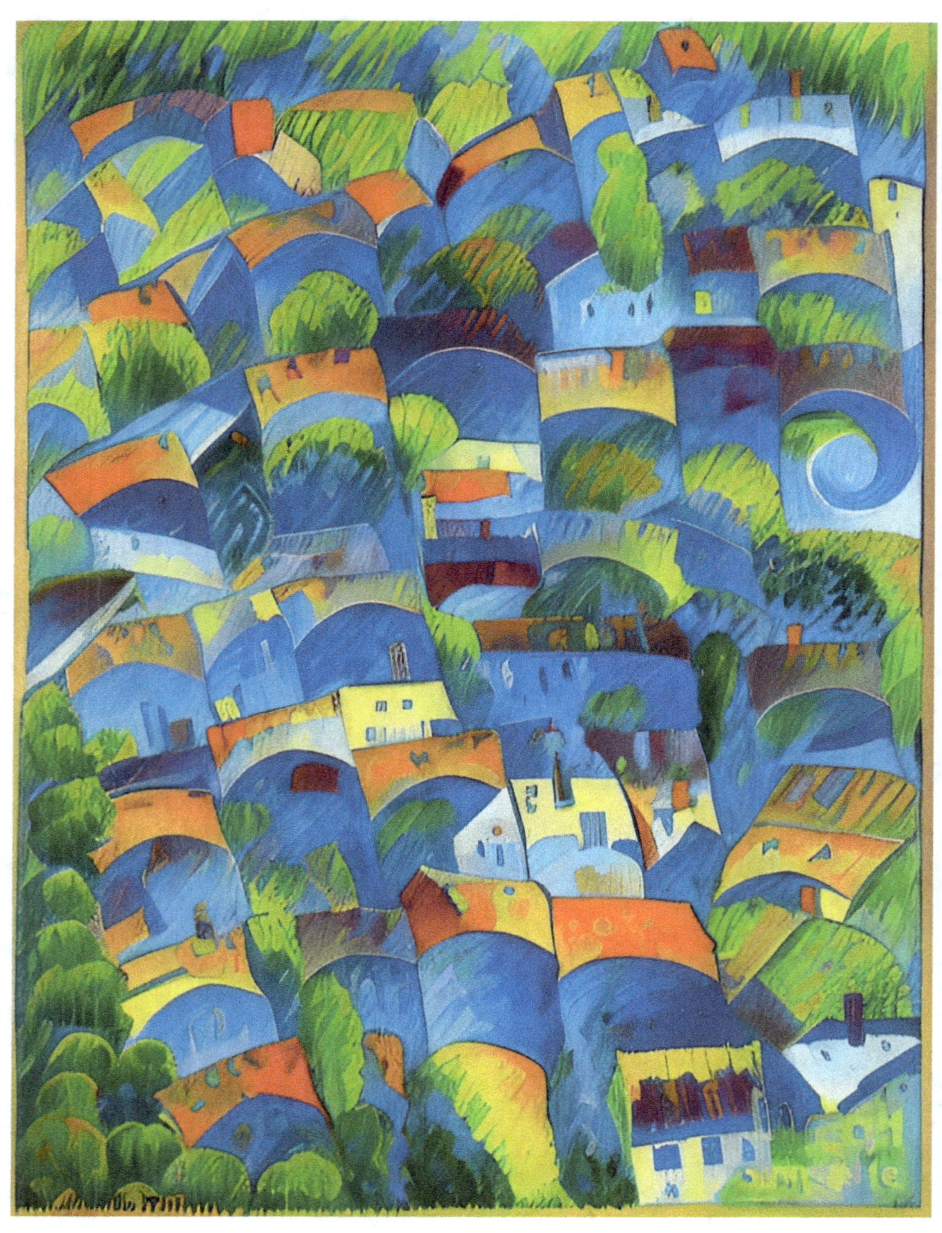

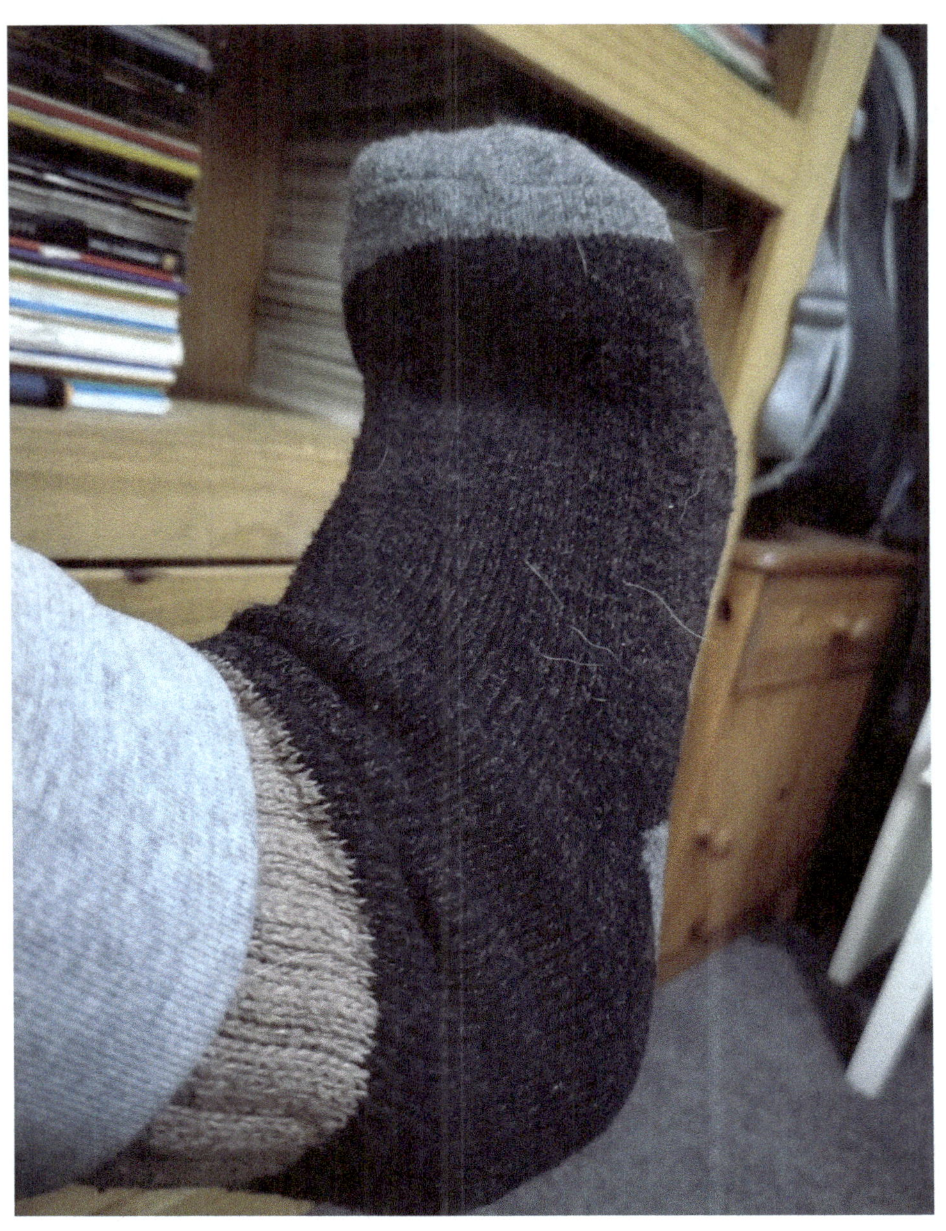

My sock

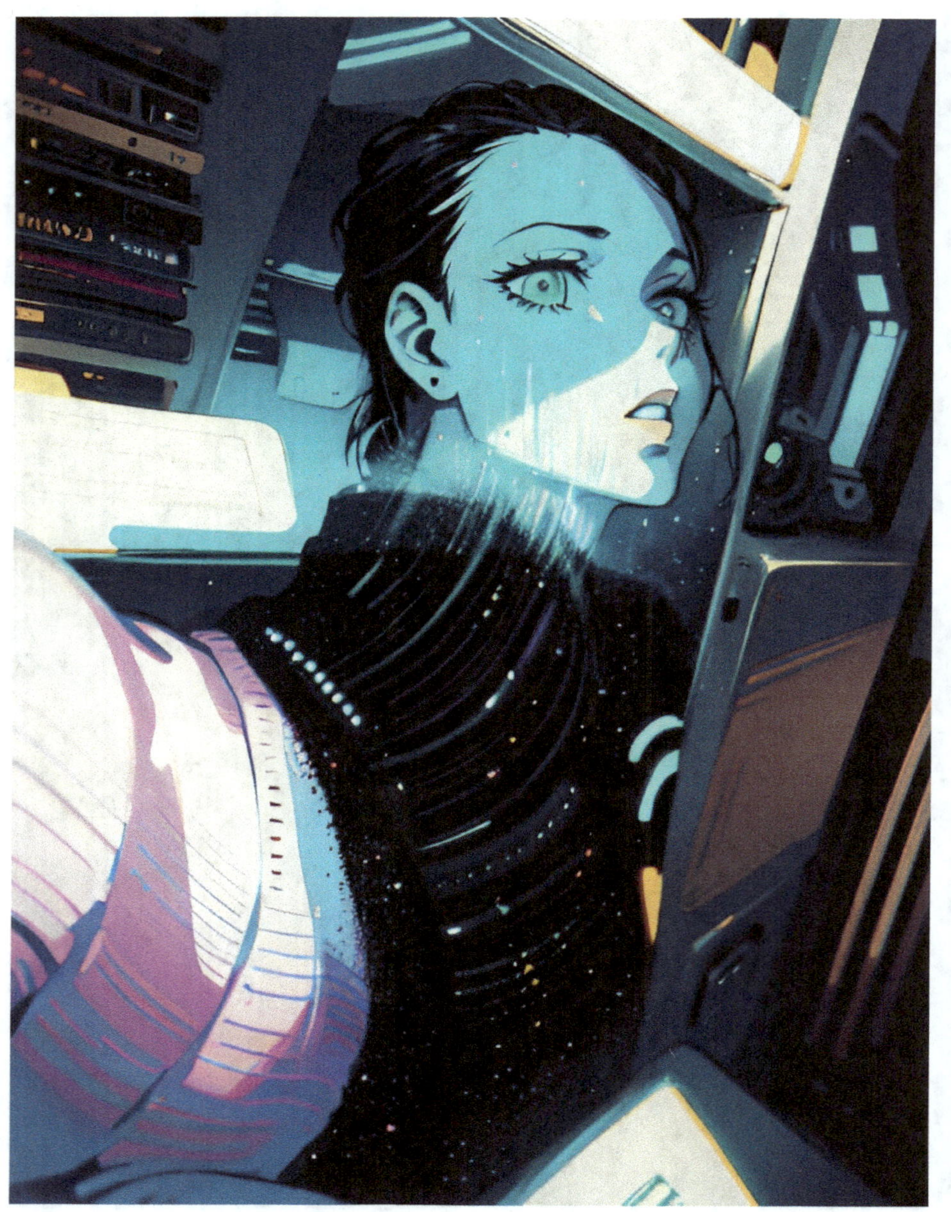

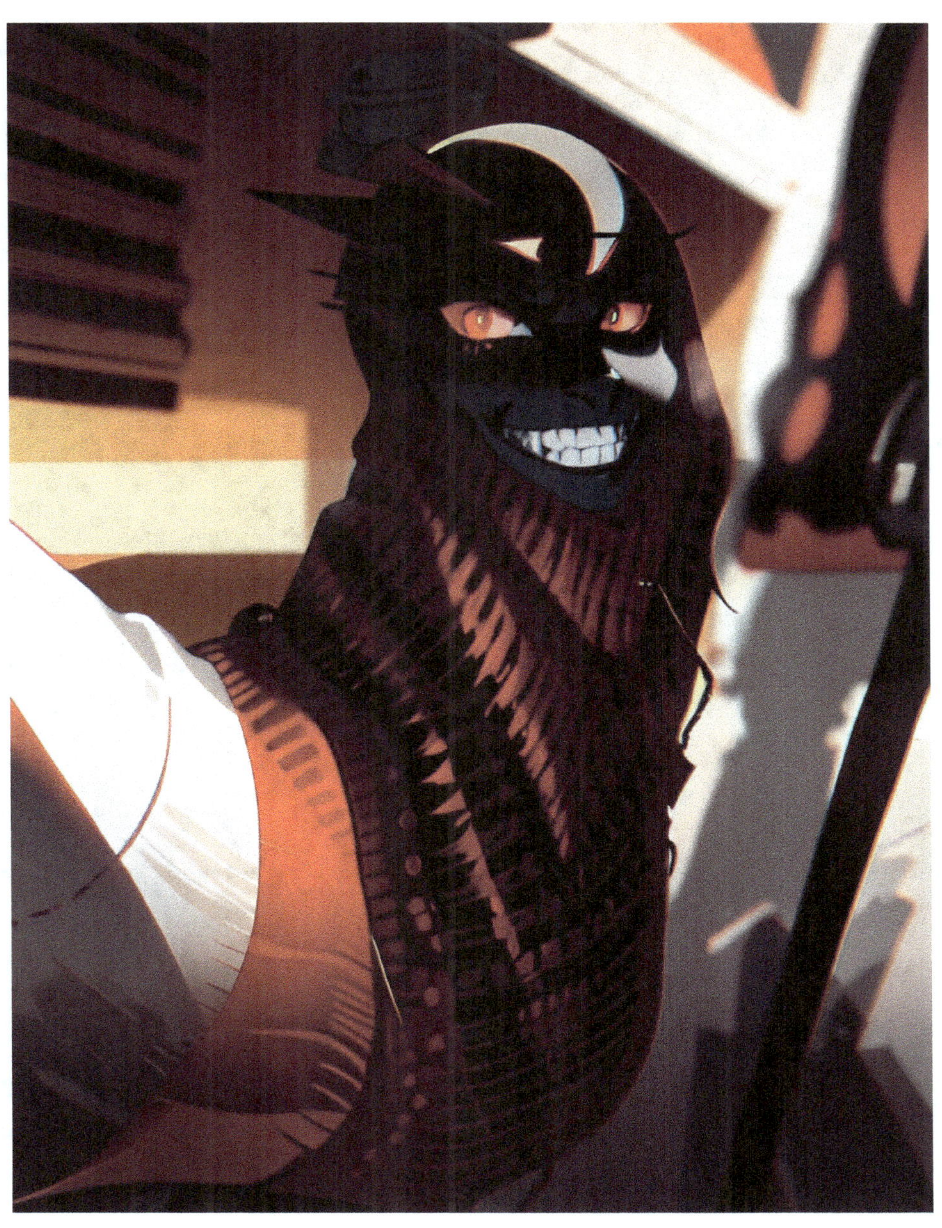

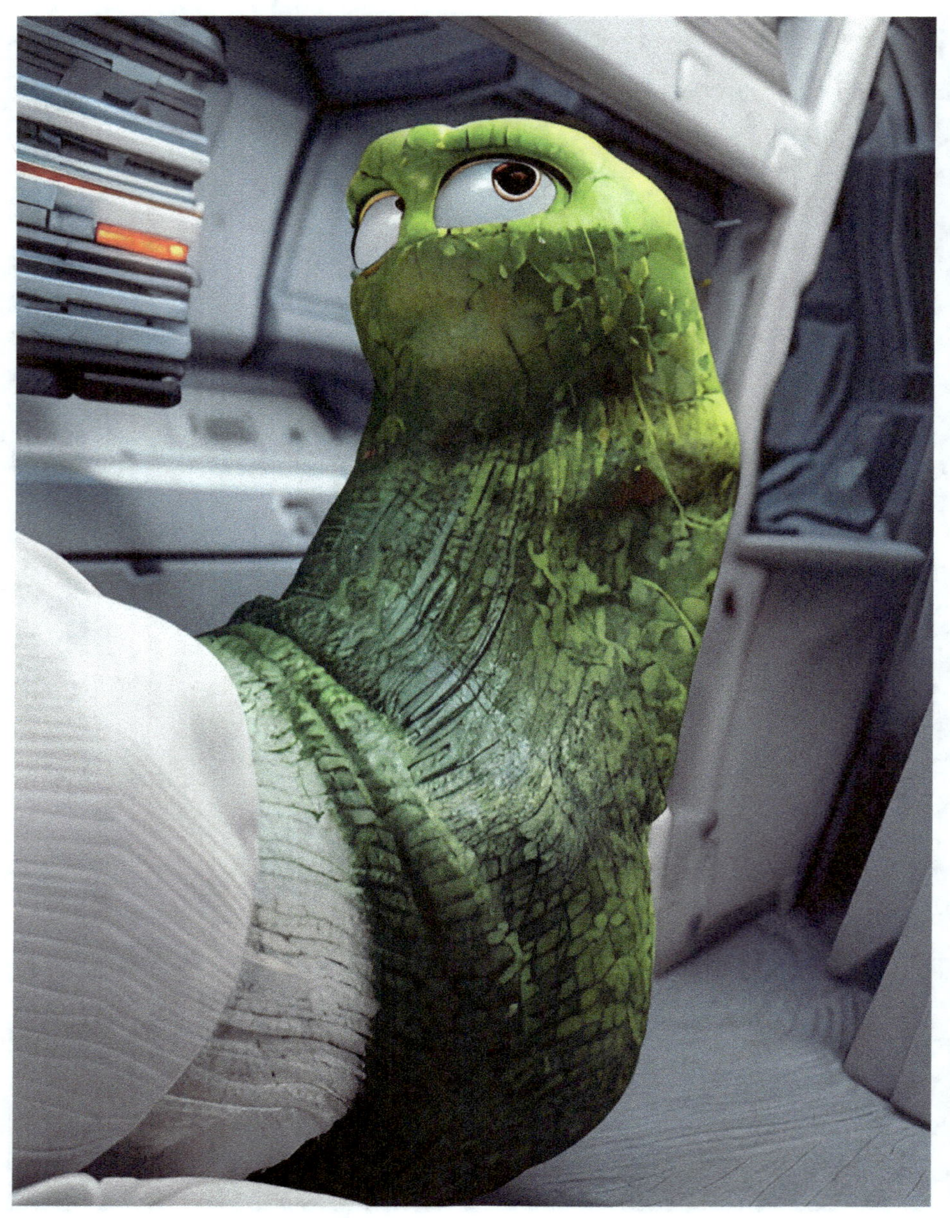

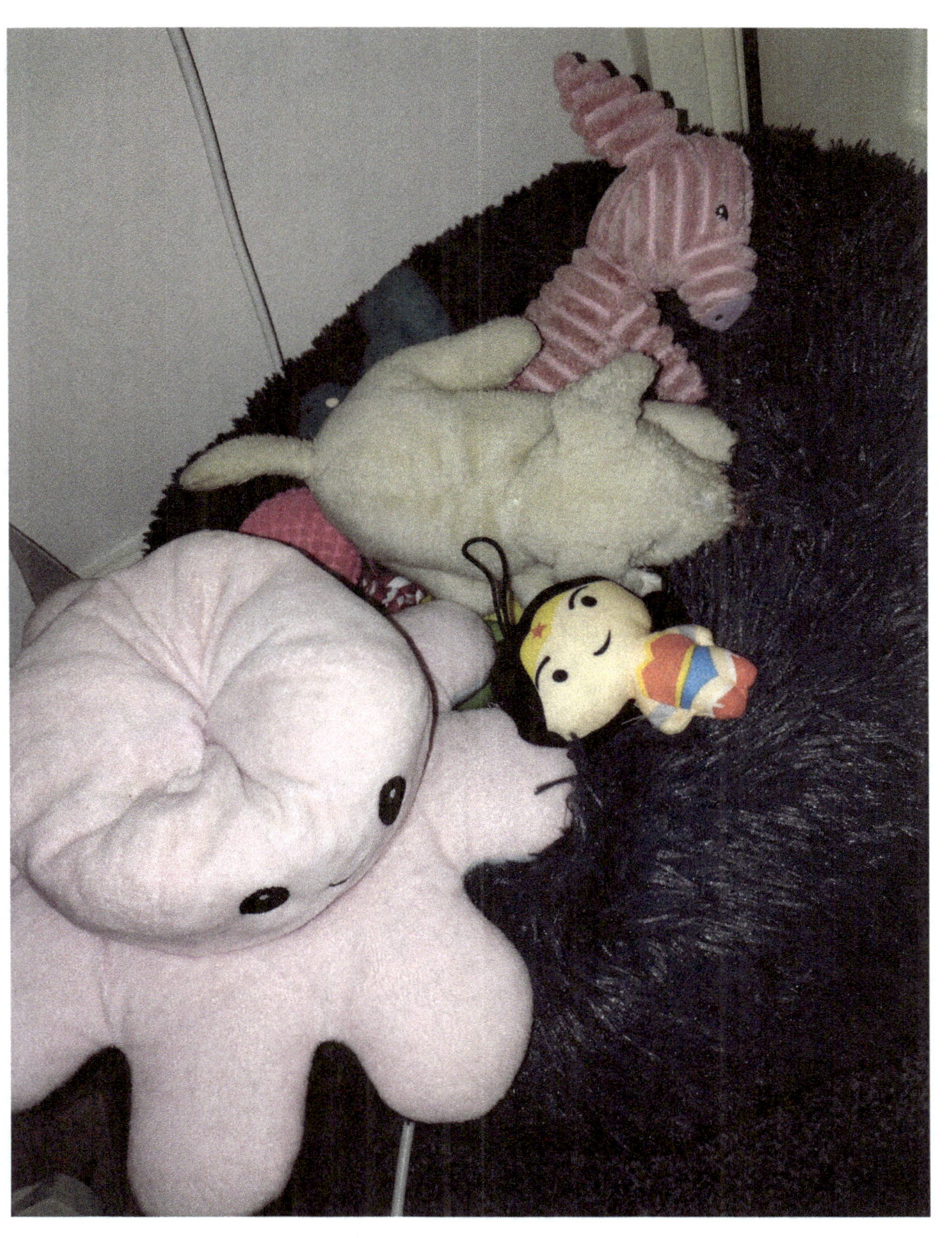

Dog toys

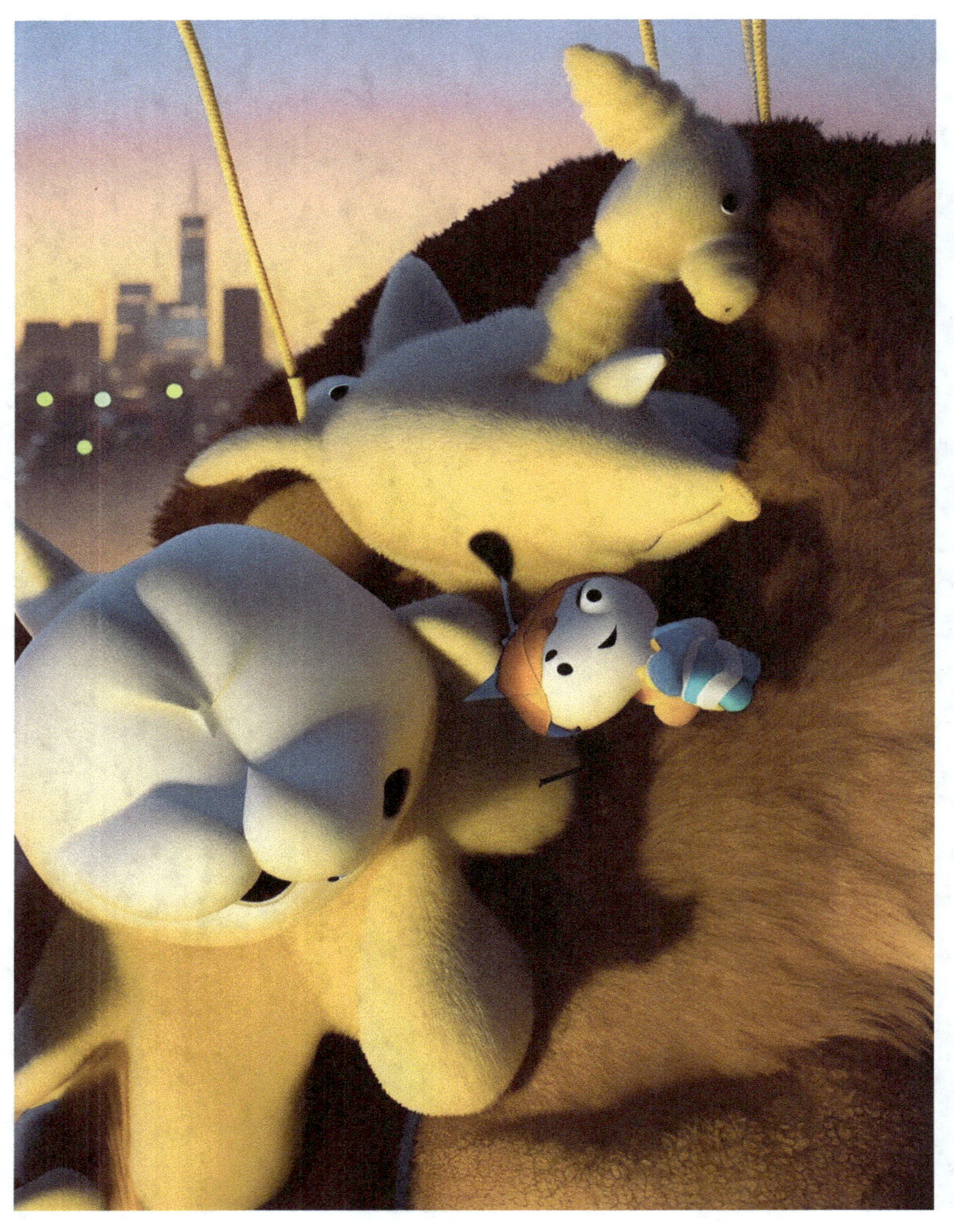

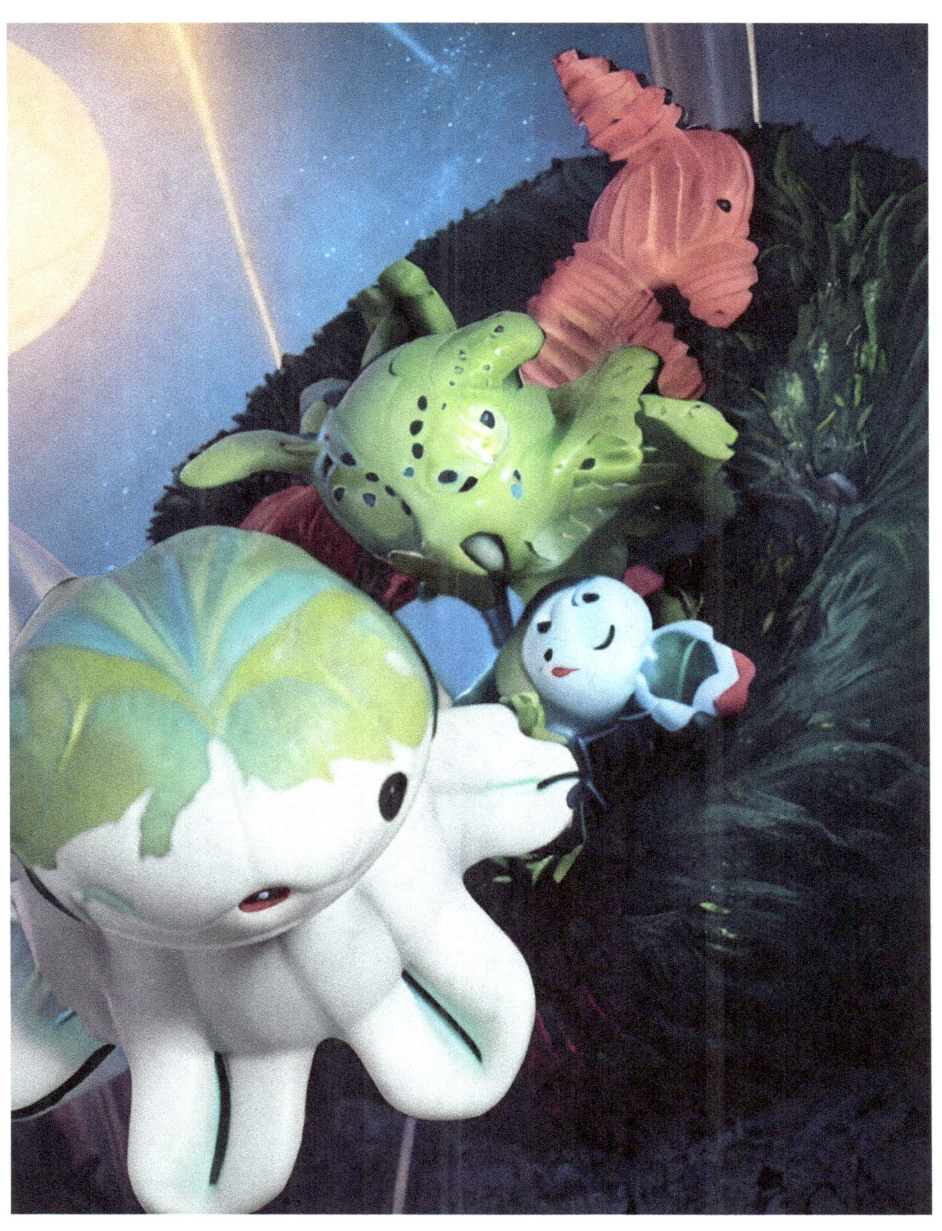

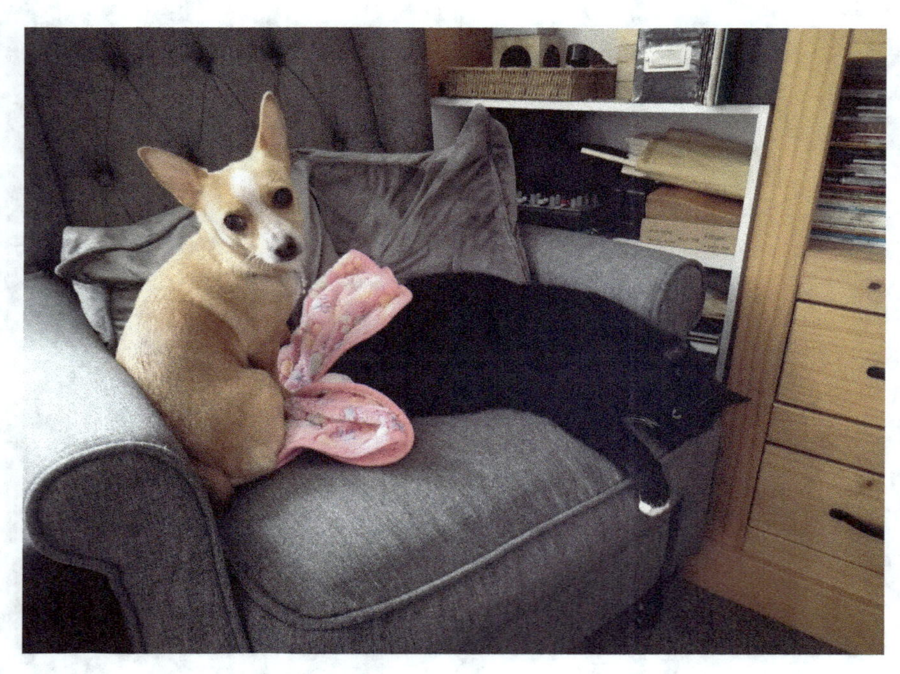

Dog and Cat

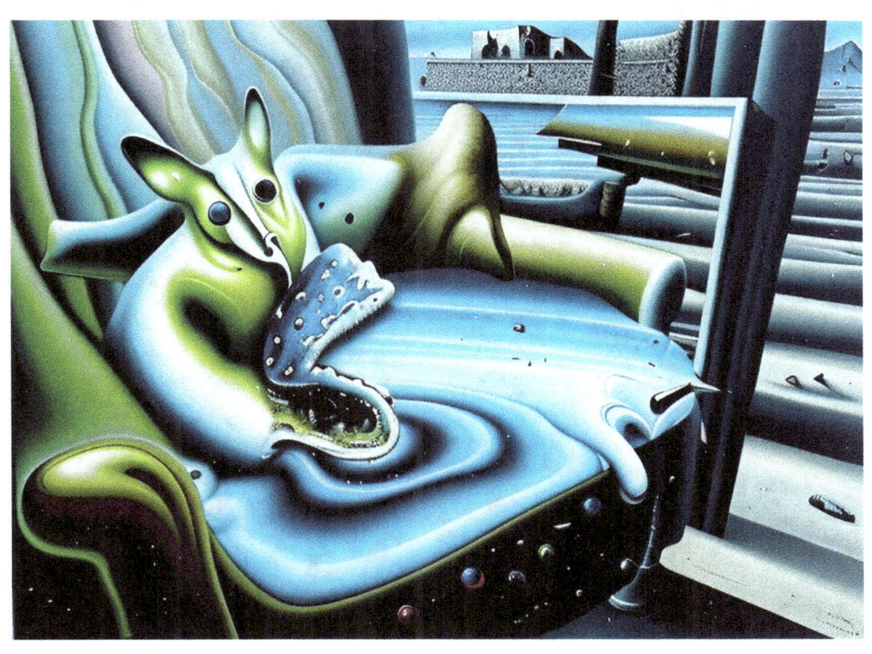

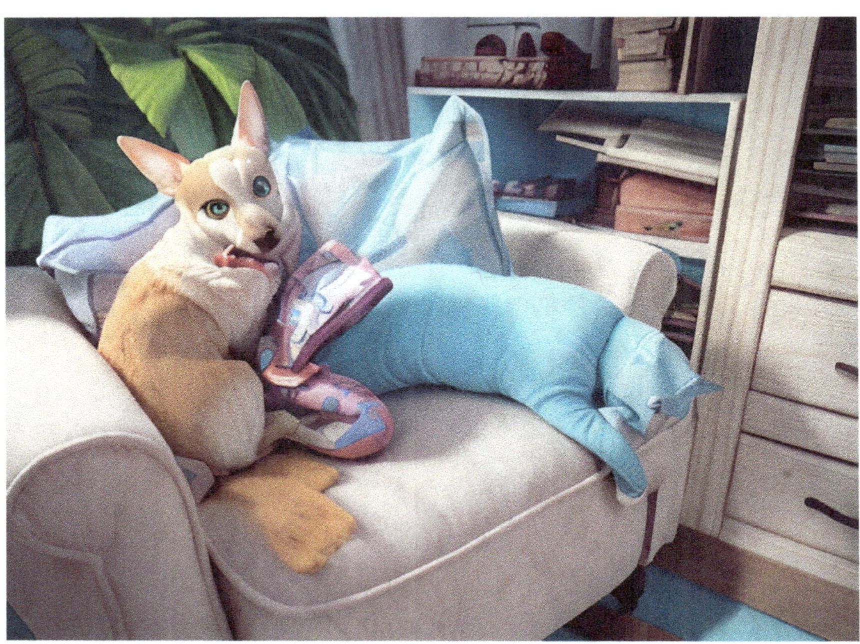

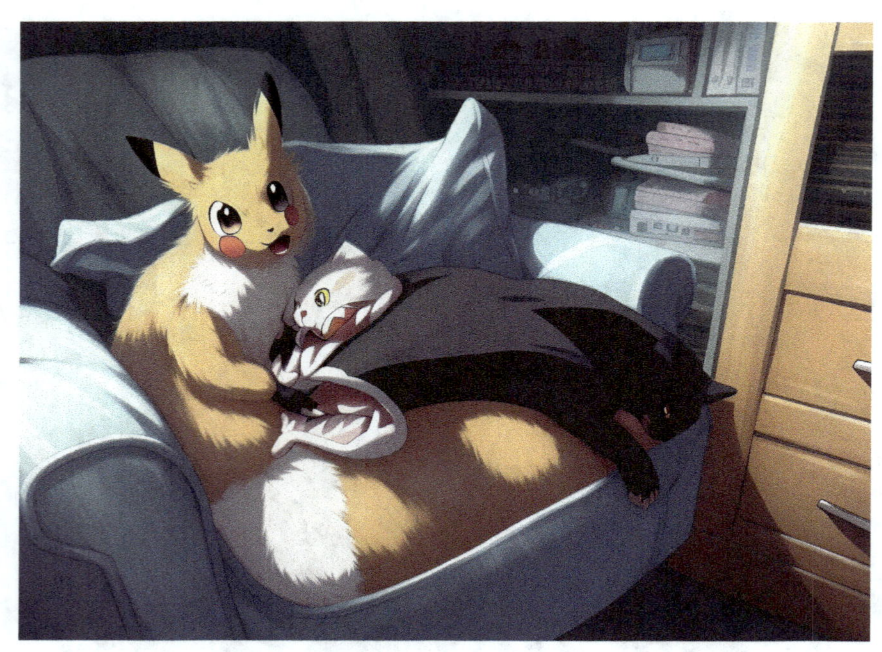

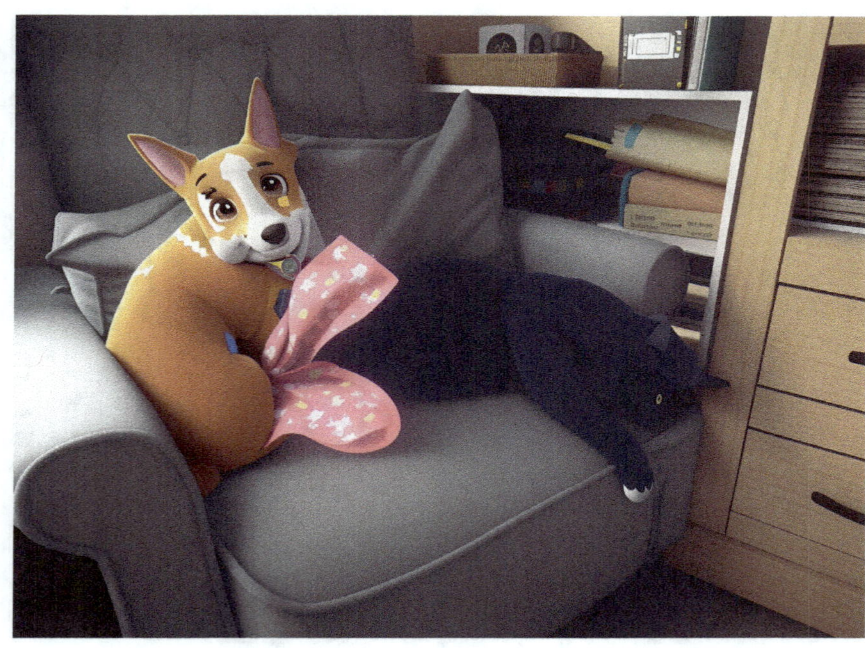

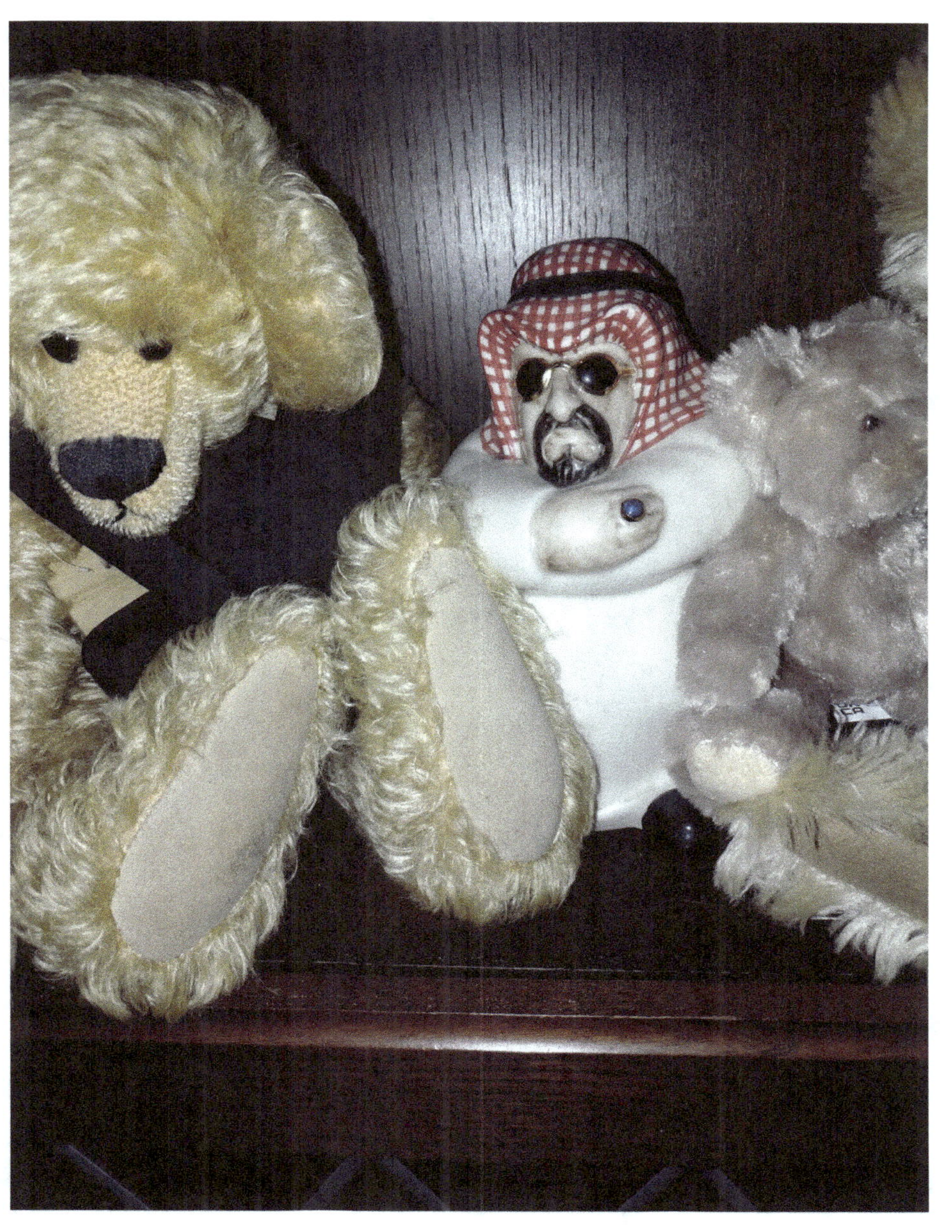

Arabian Bears

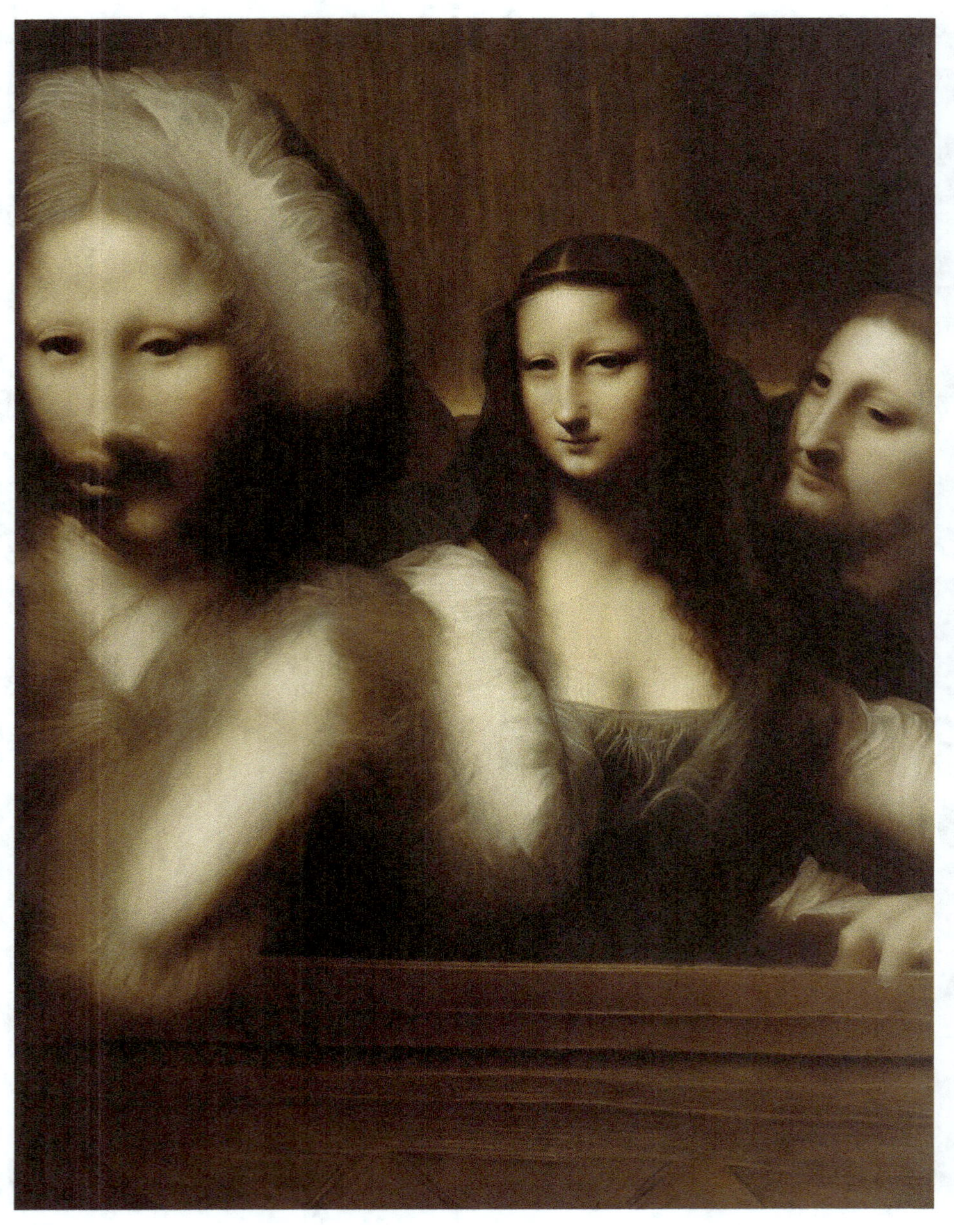

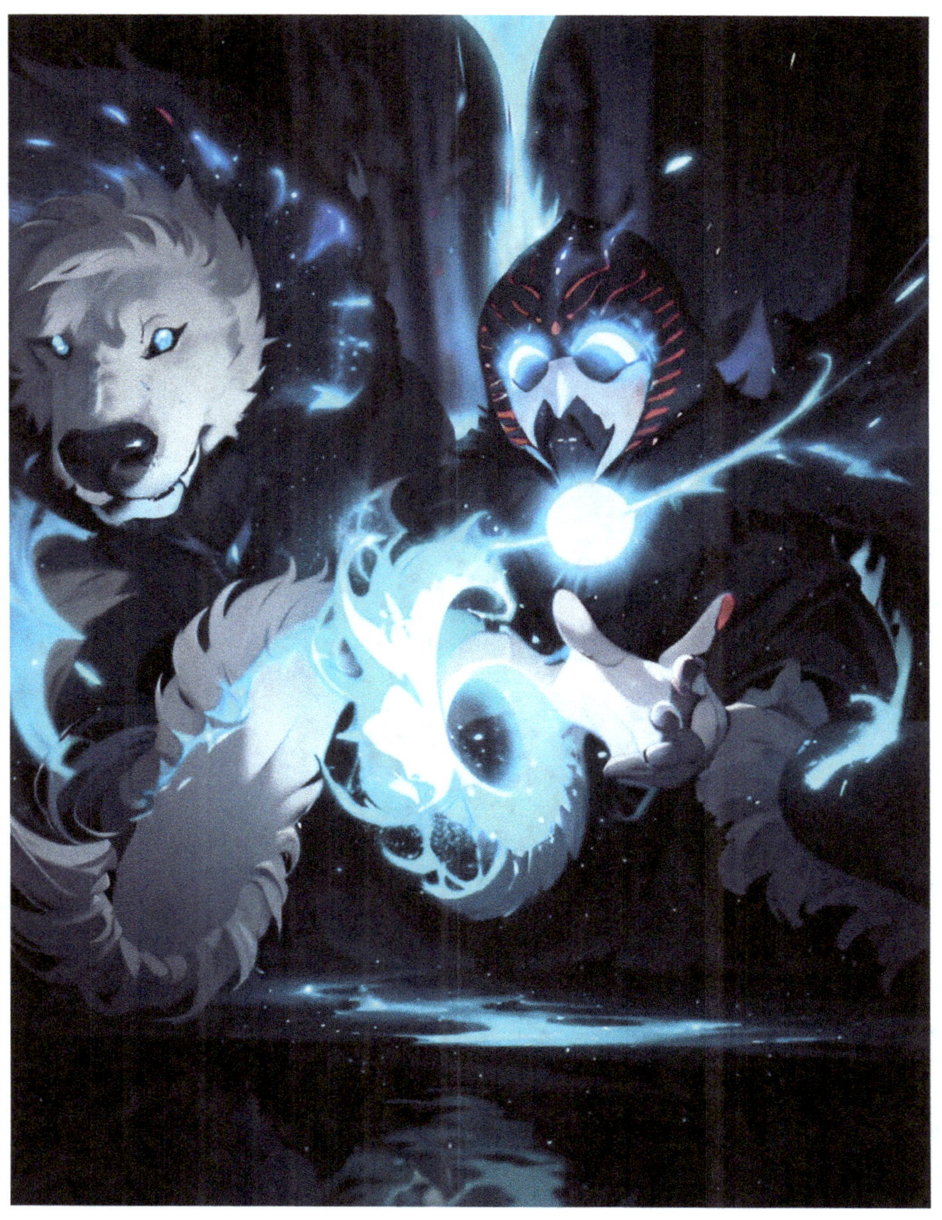

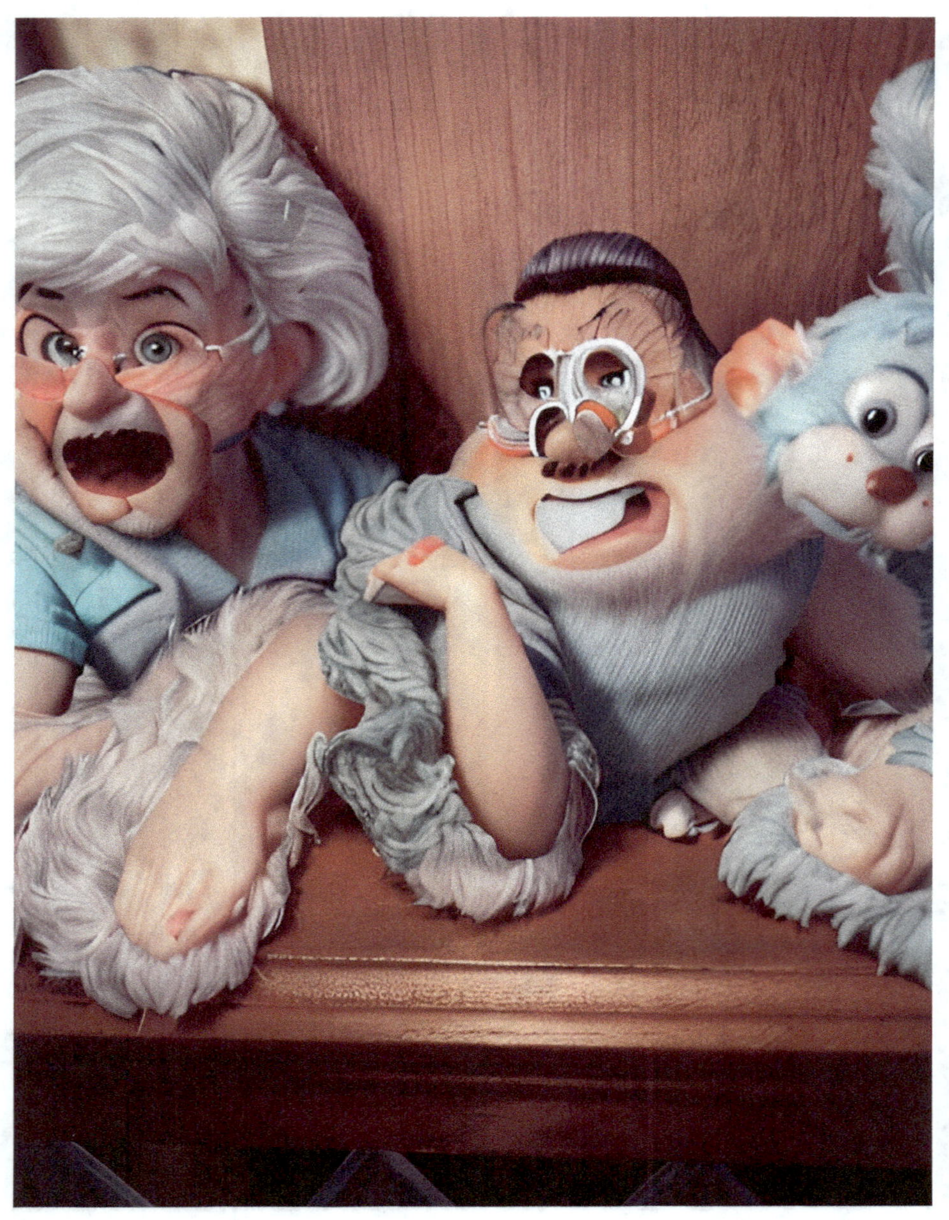

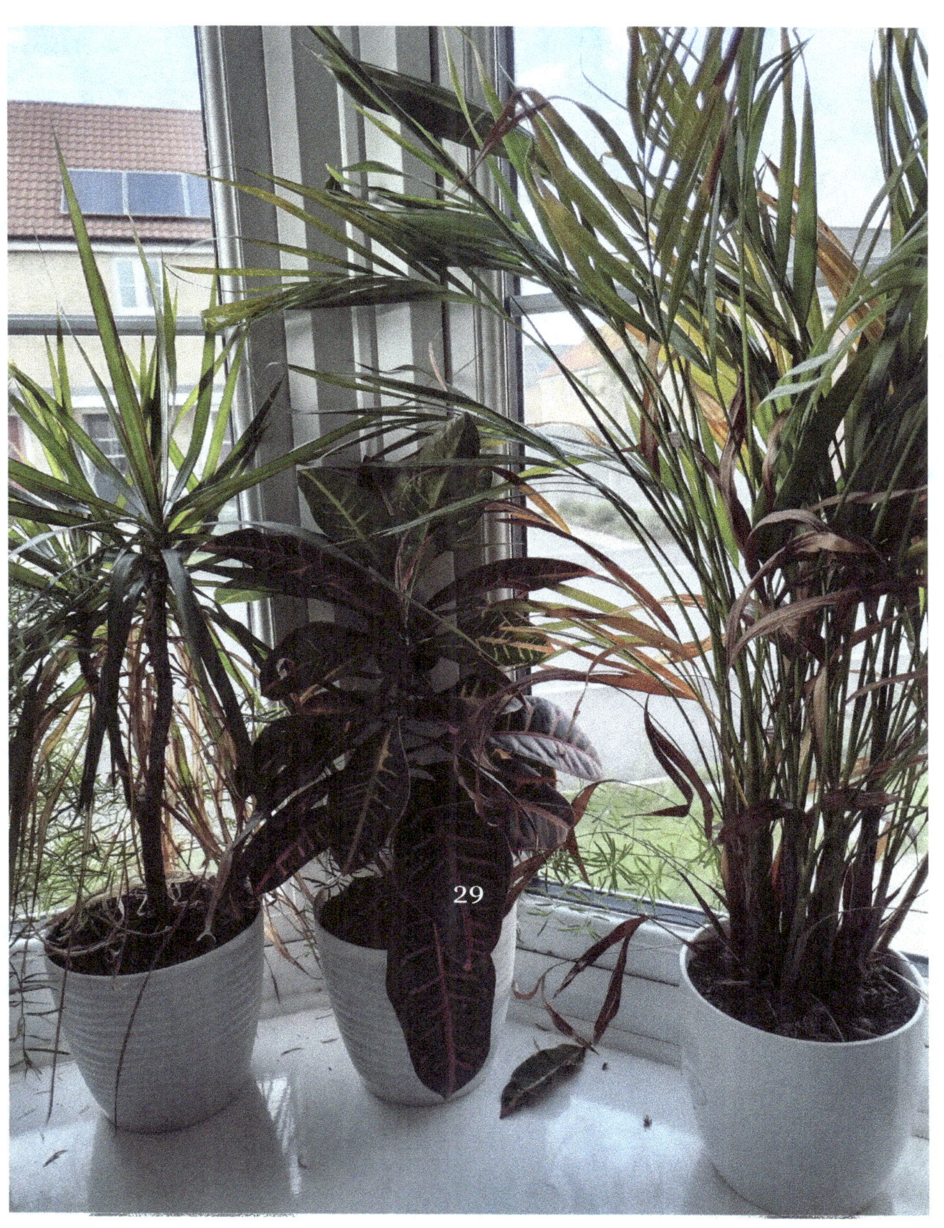

Window plants

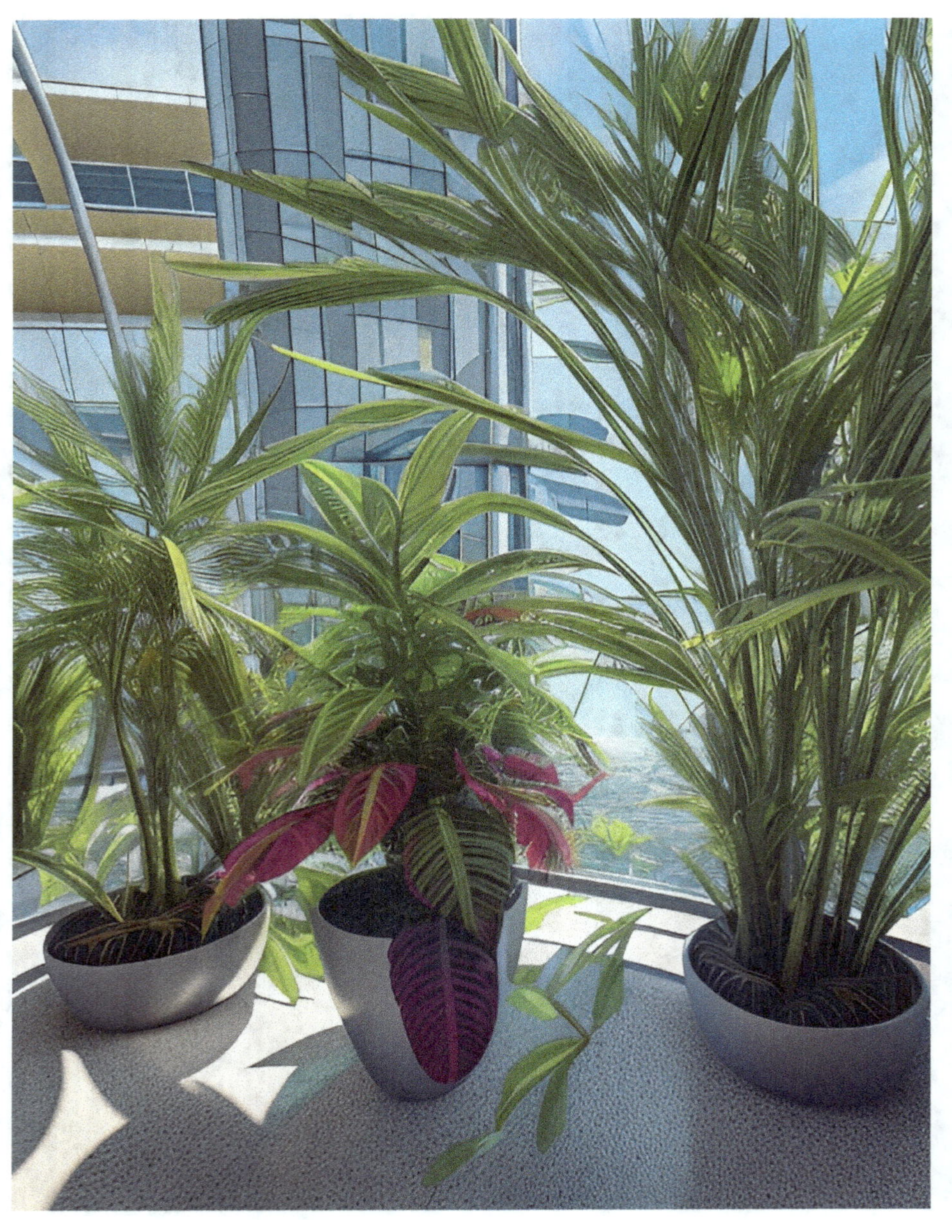

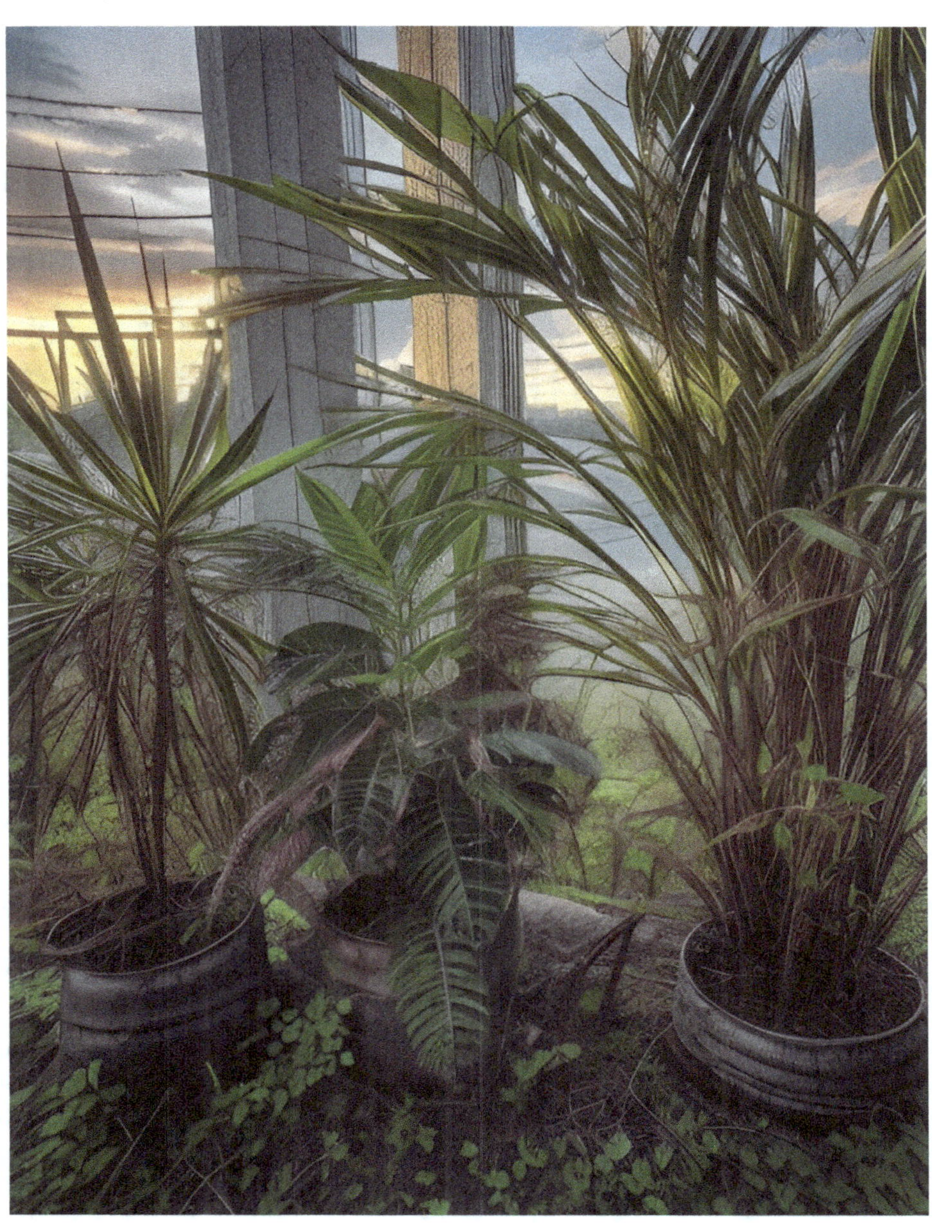

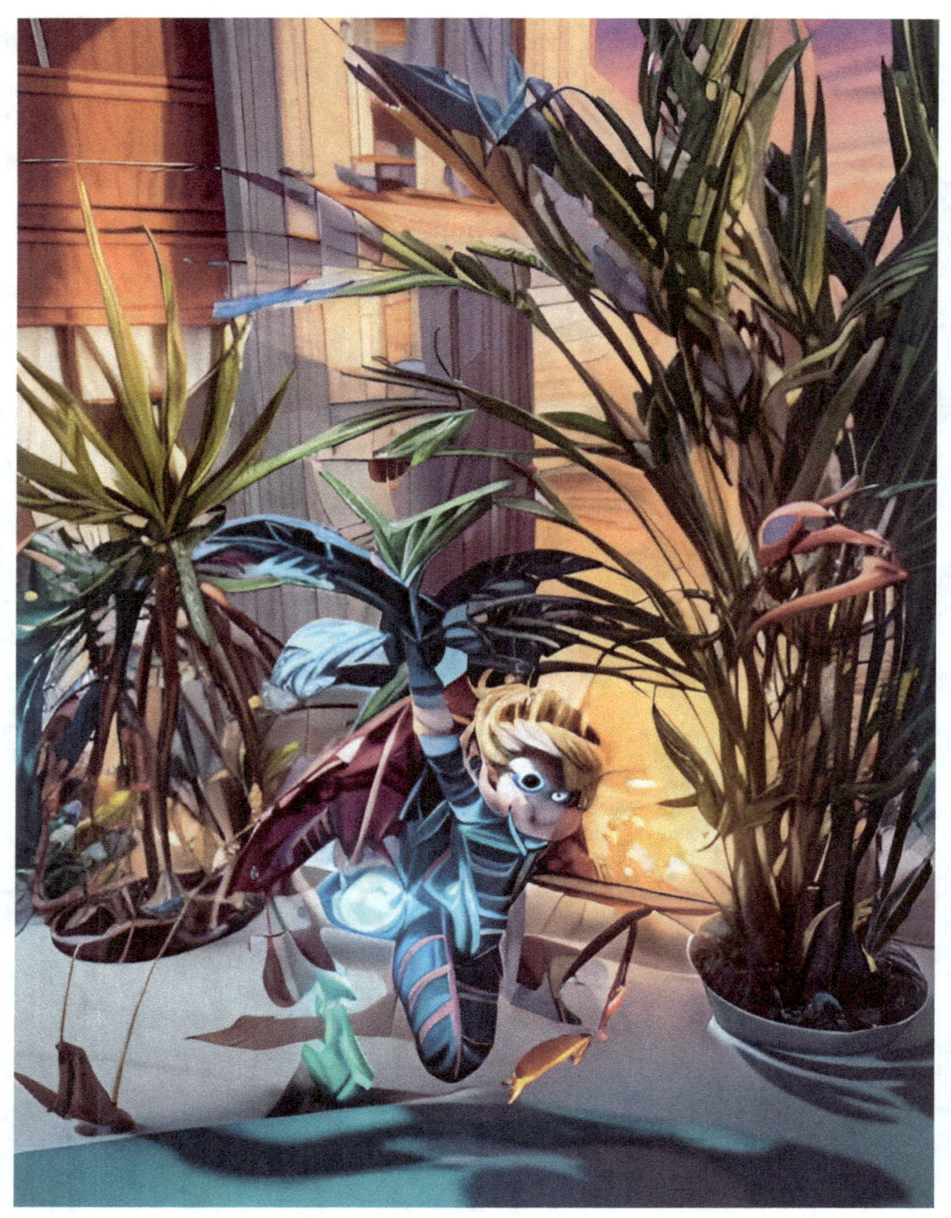

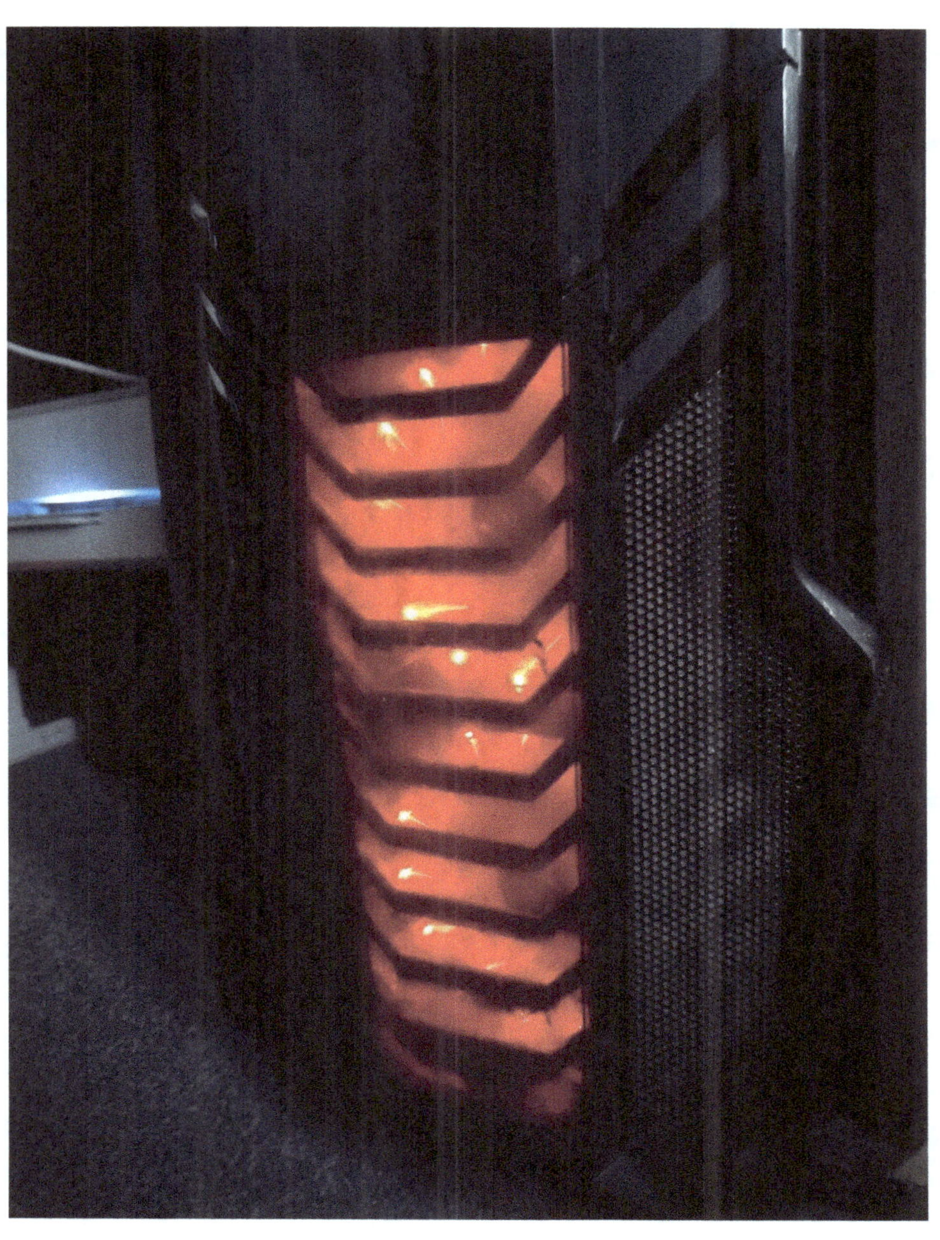

Computer glow

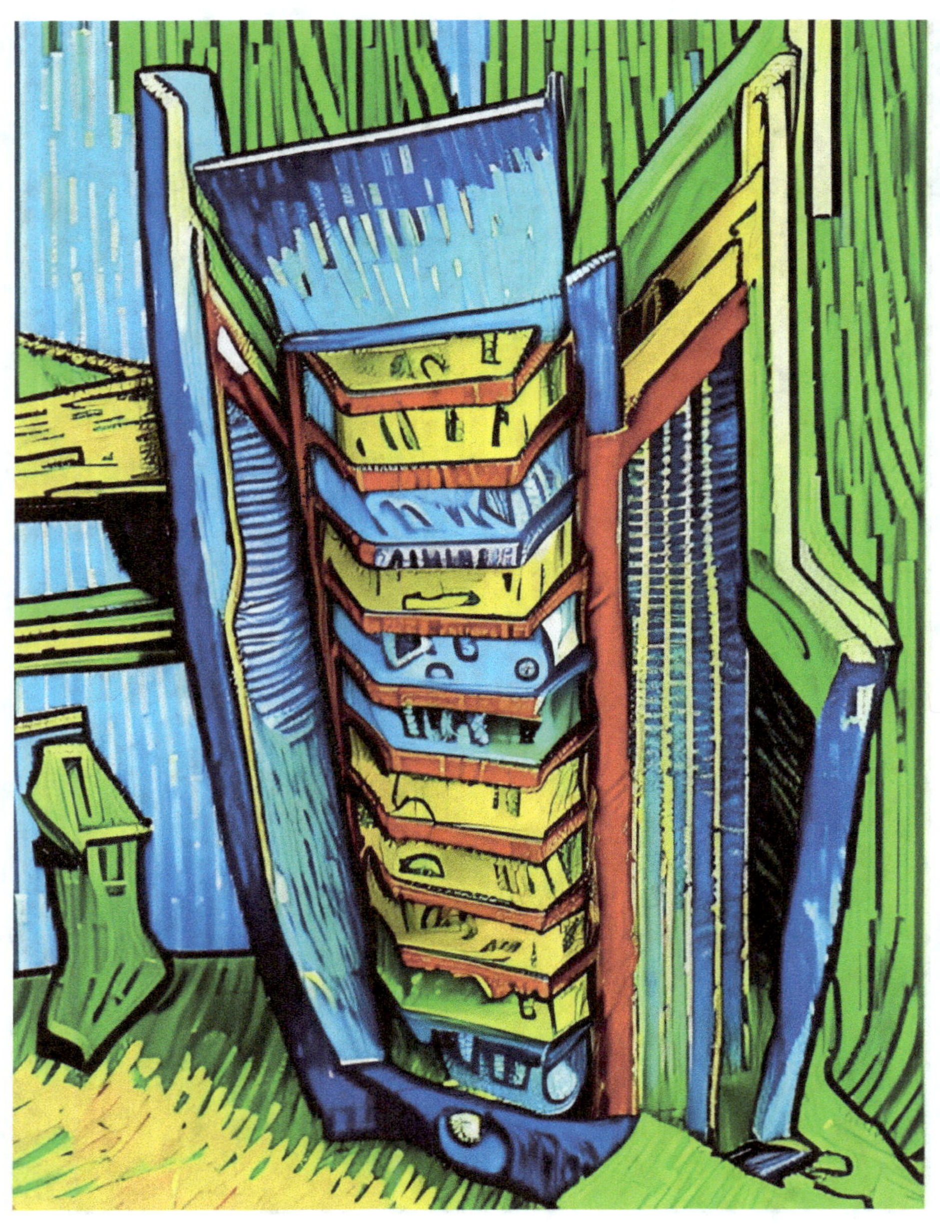

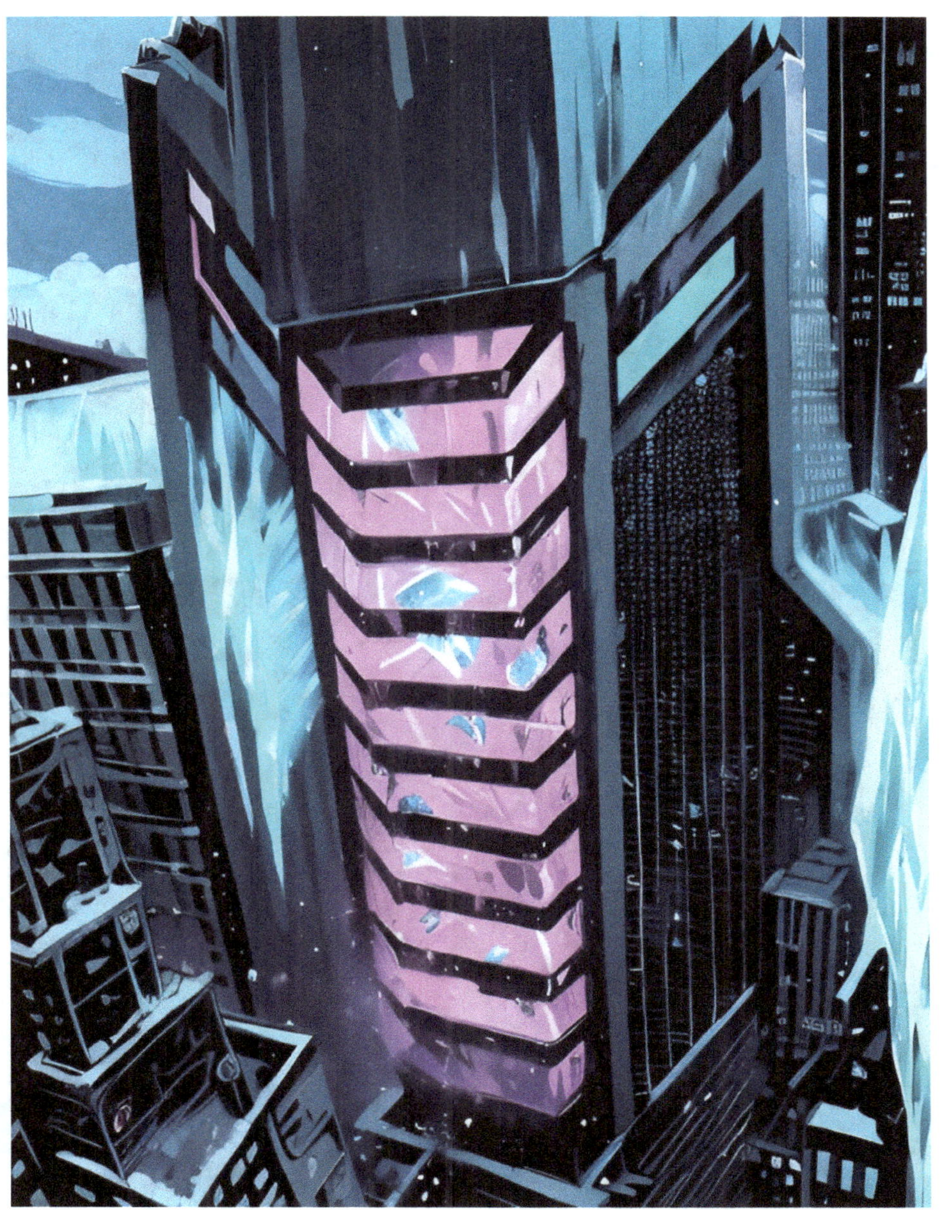

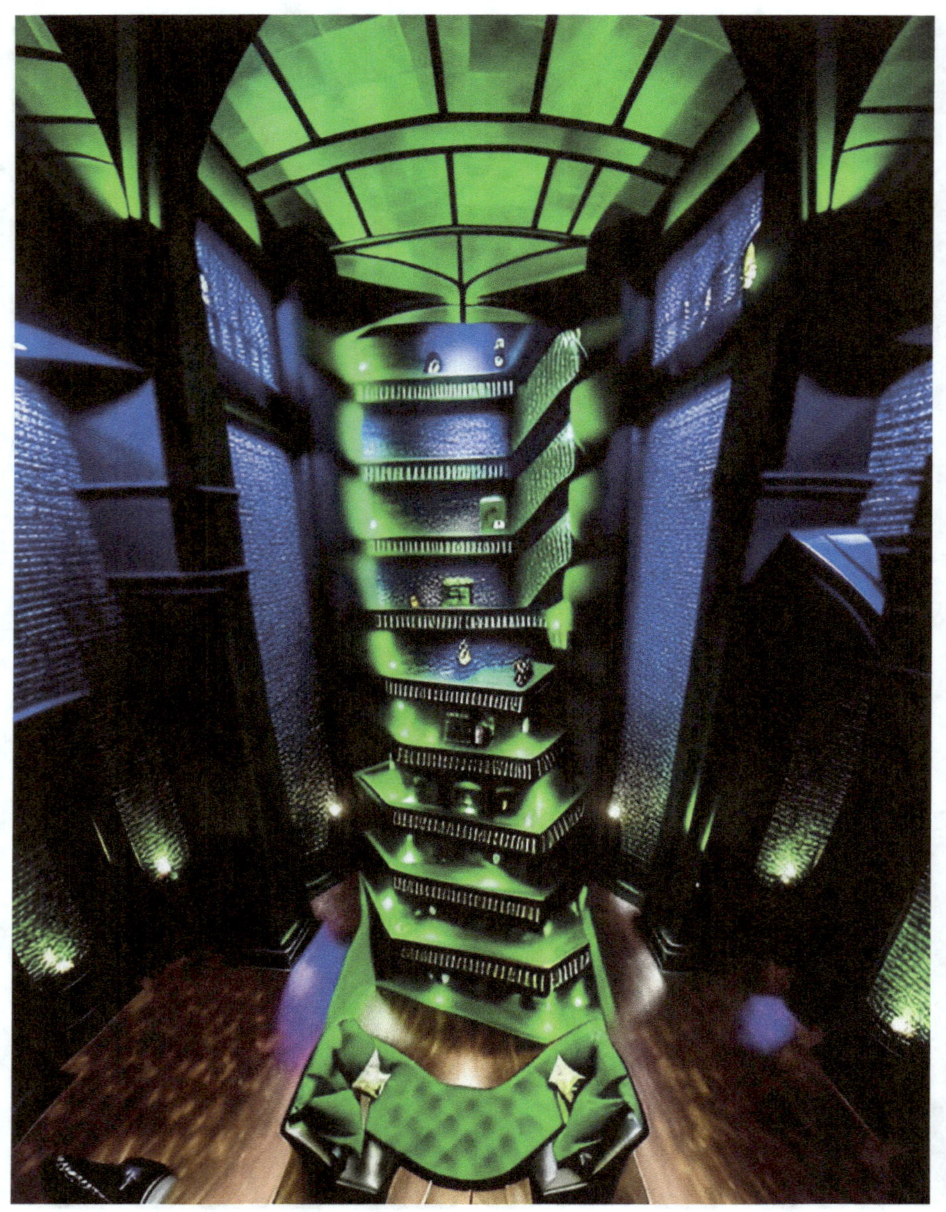

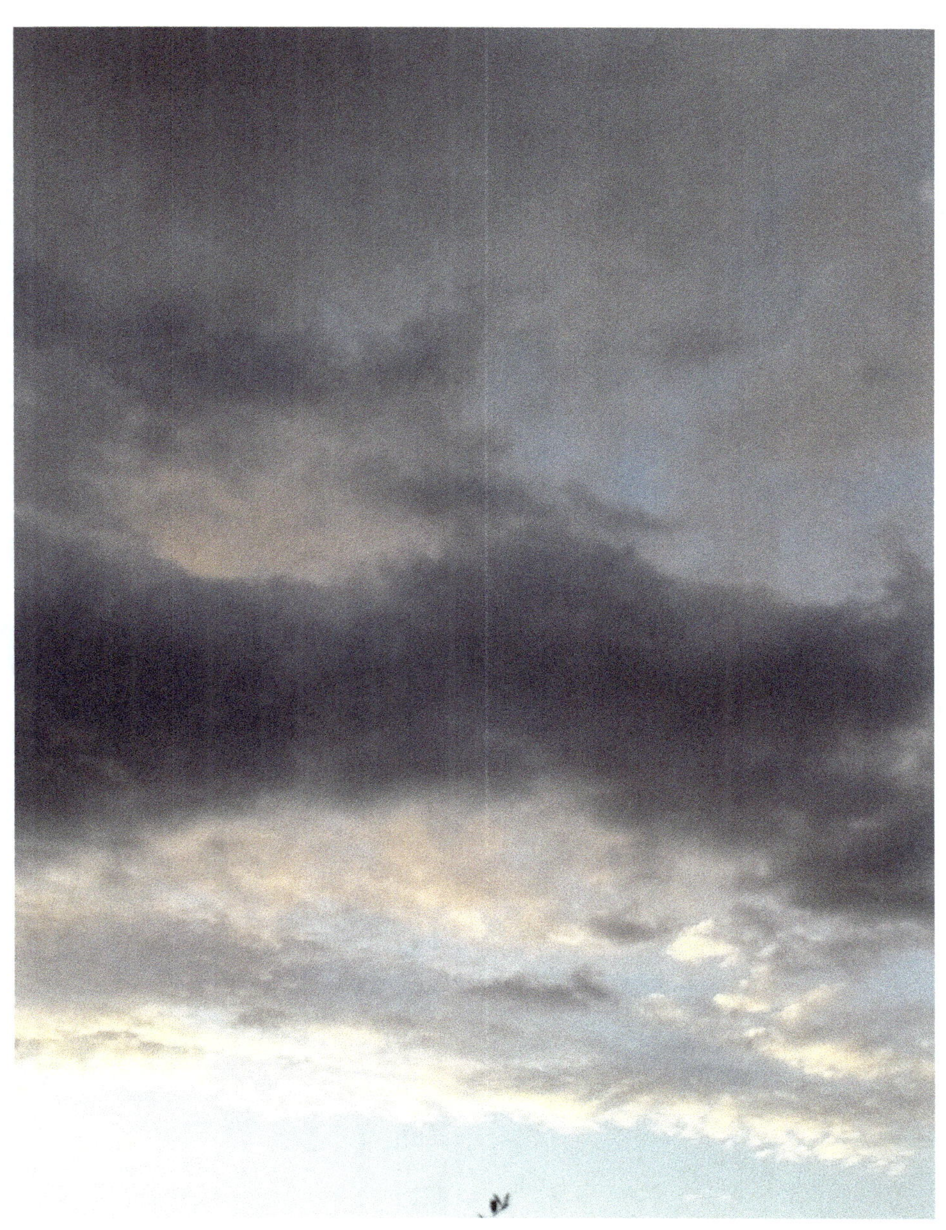

Sky

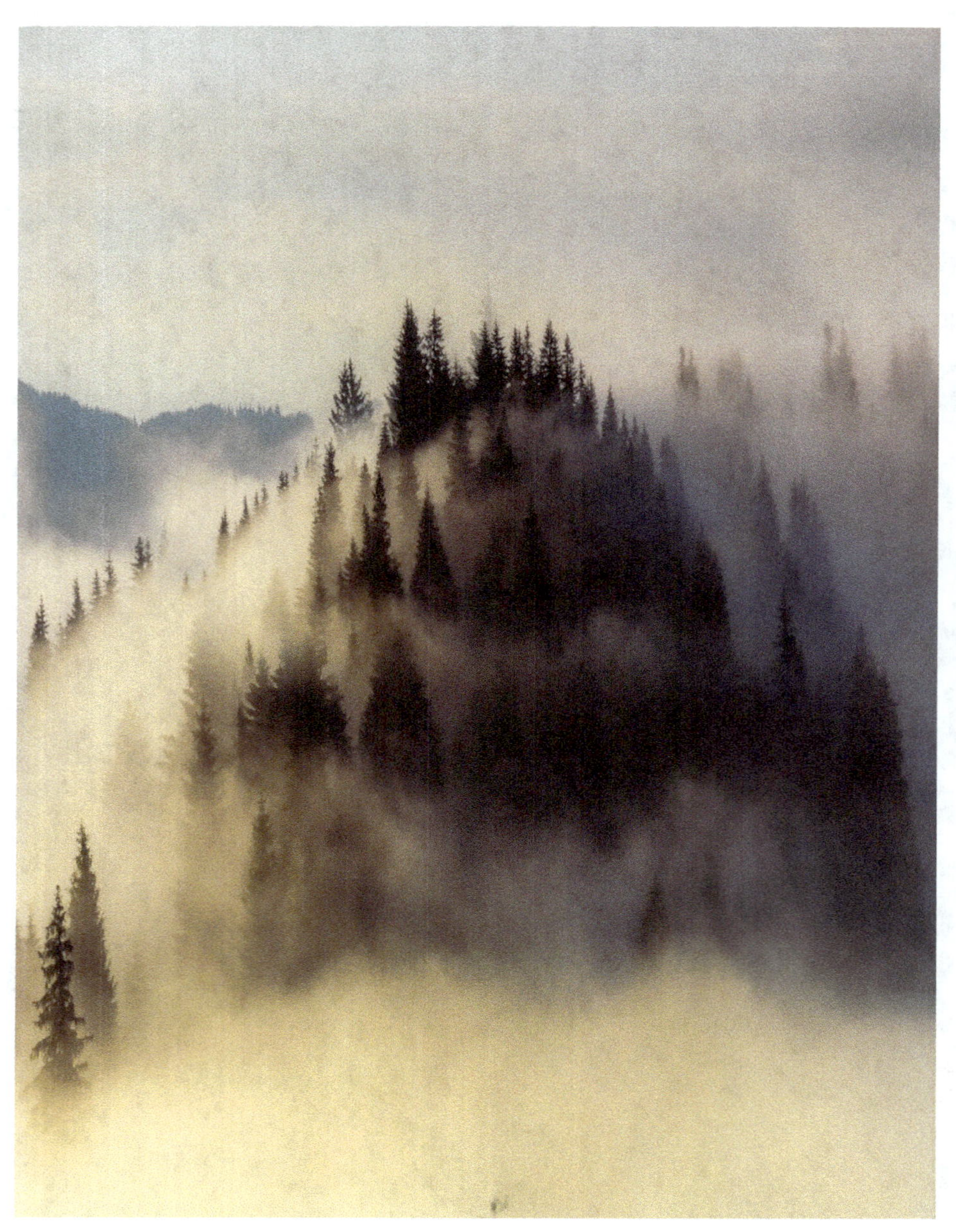

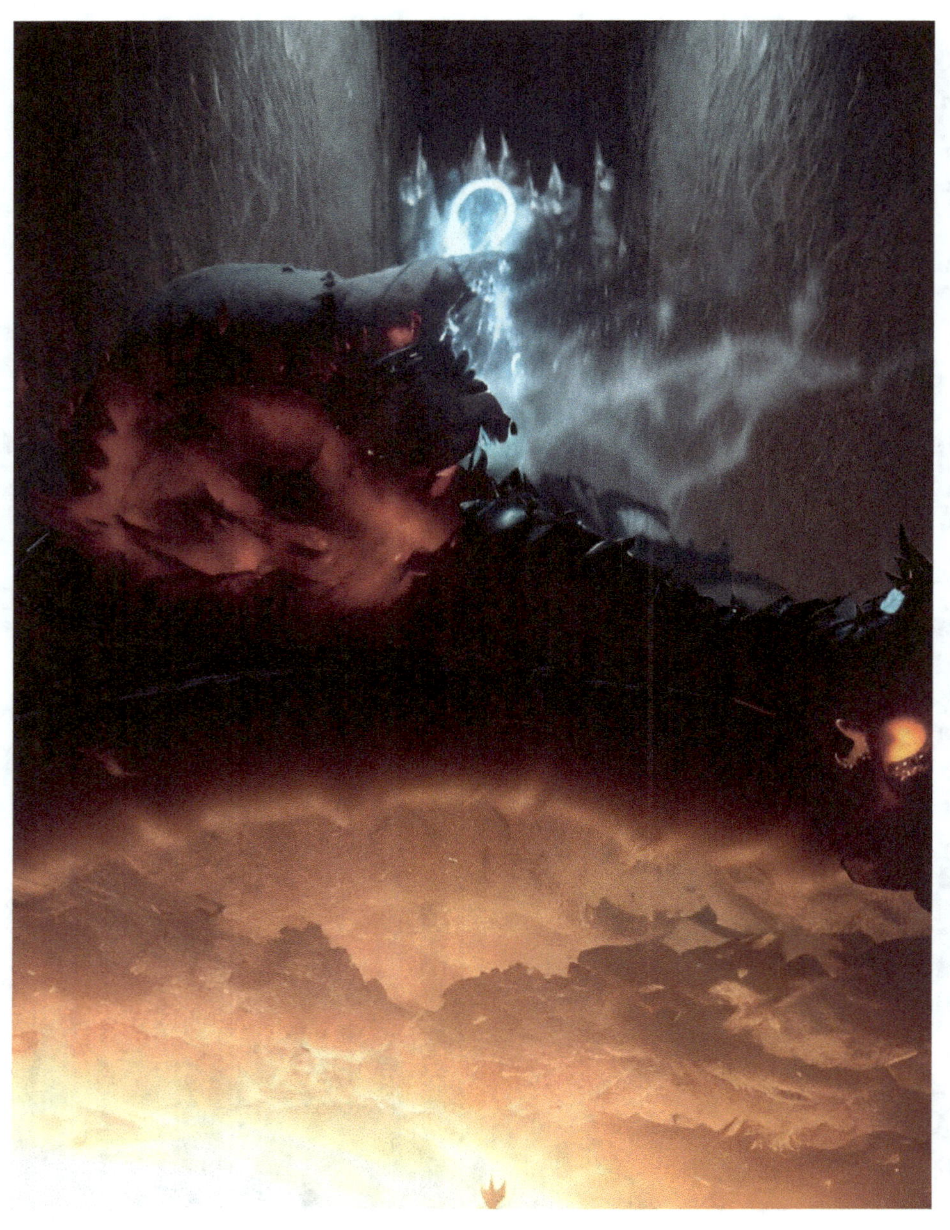

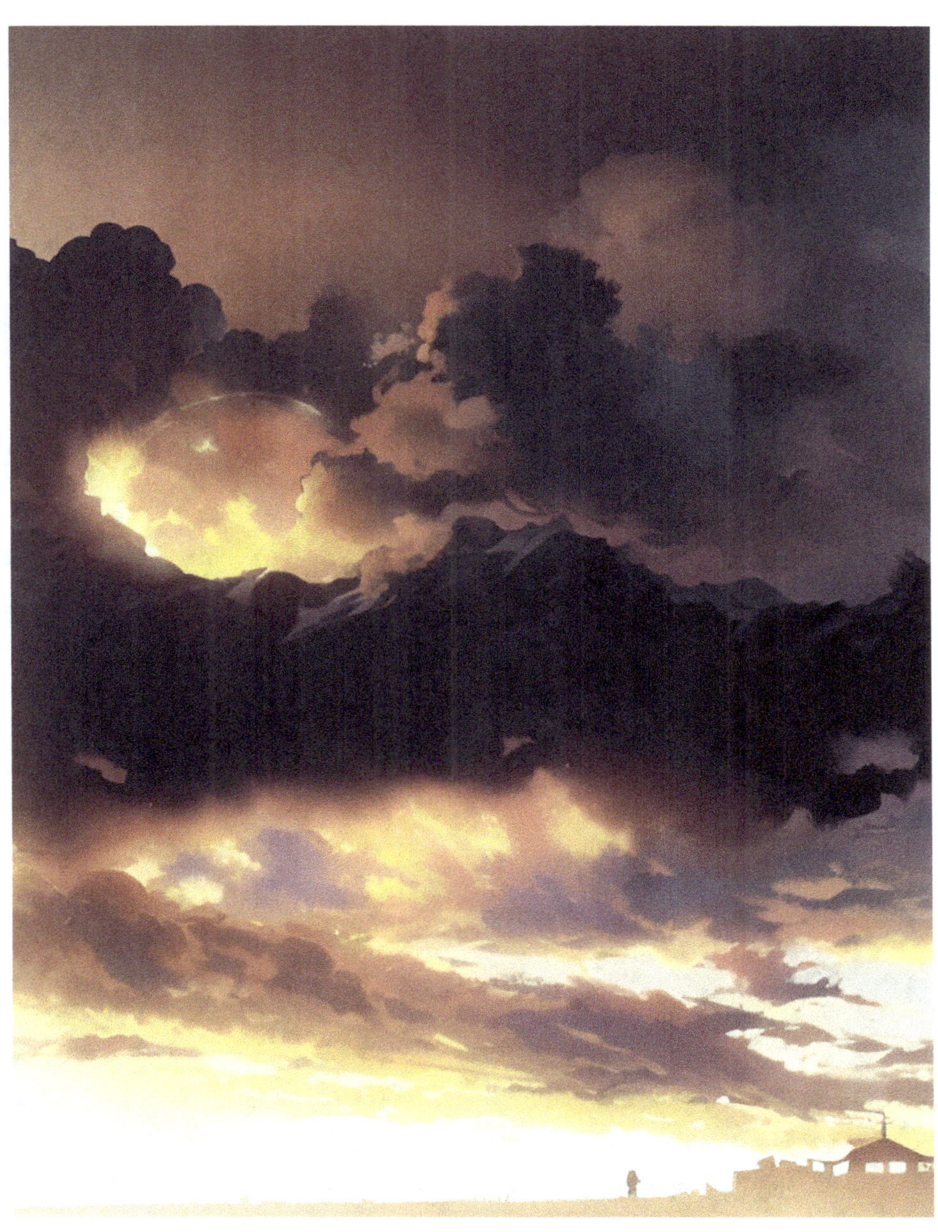

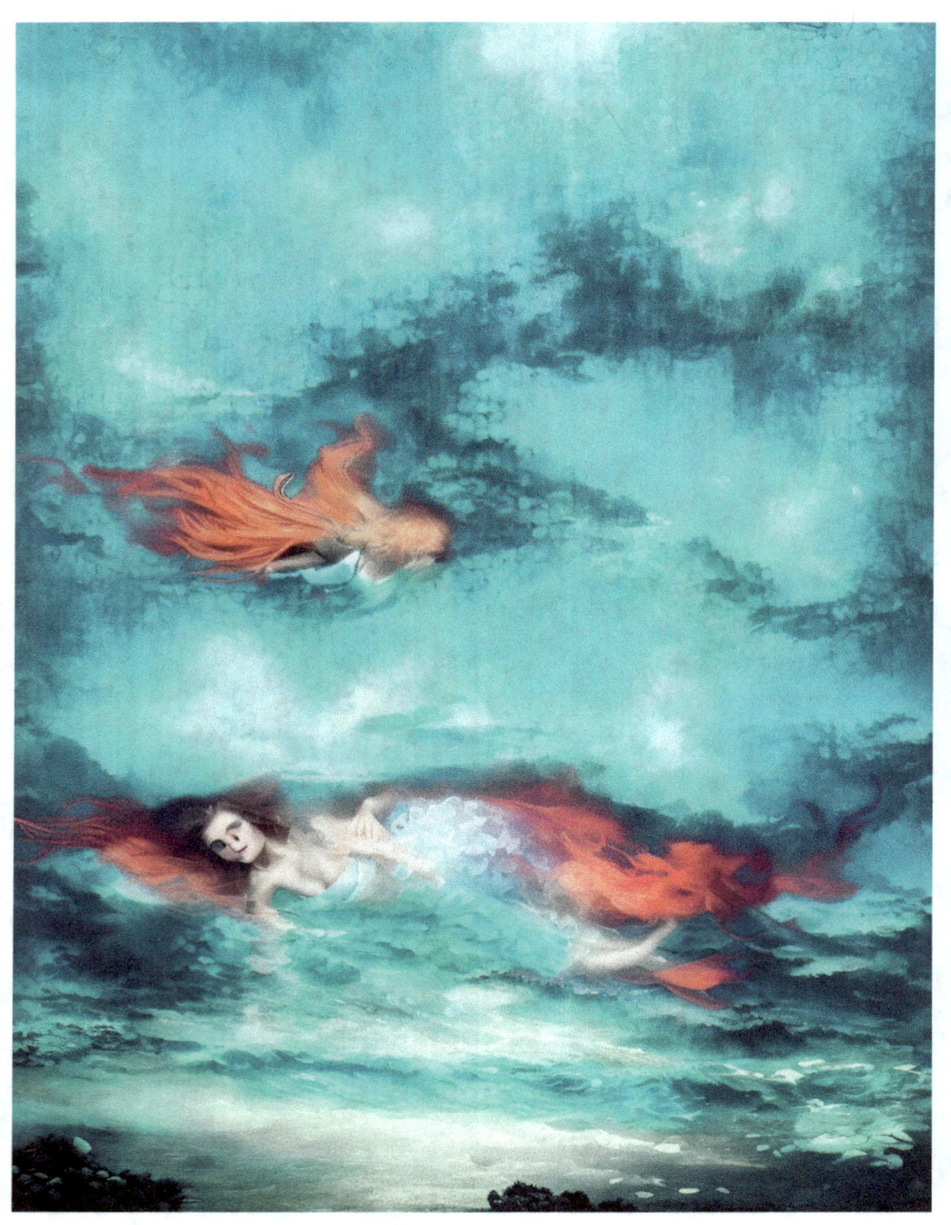

Remnant Door
Interface
LG
PART OF A MULTIPACK ONLY 75p
MAX
CHERRY
MAXIMUM TASTE
no sugar

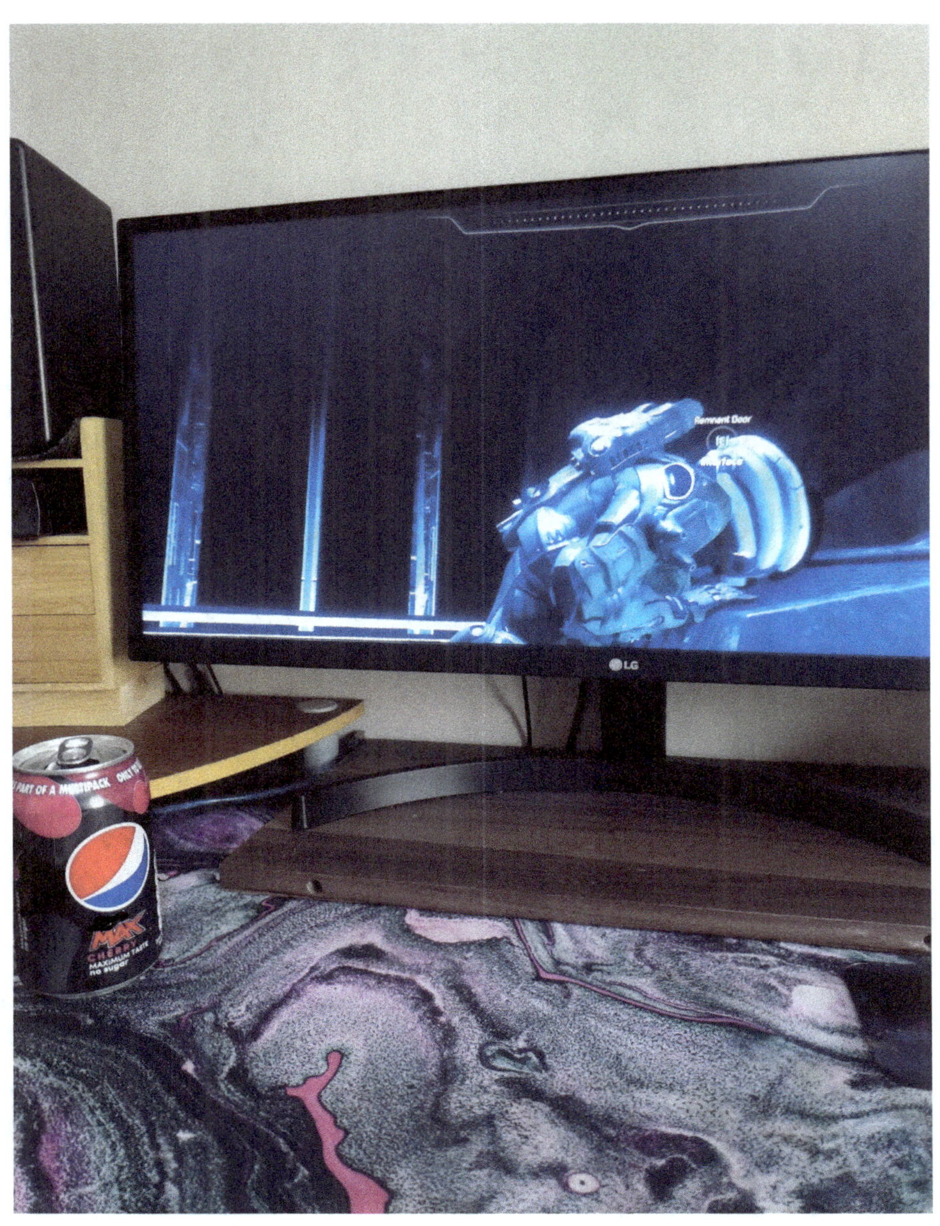

Game screen

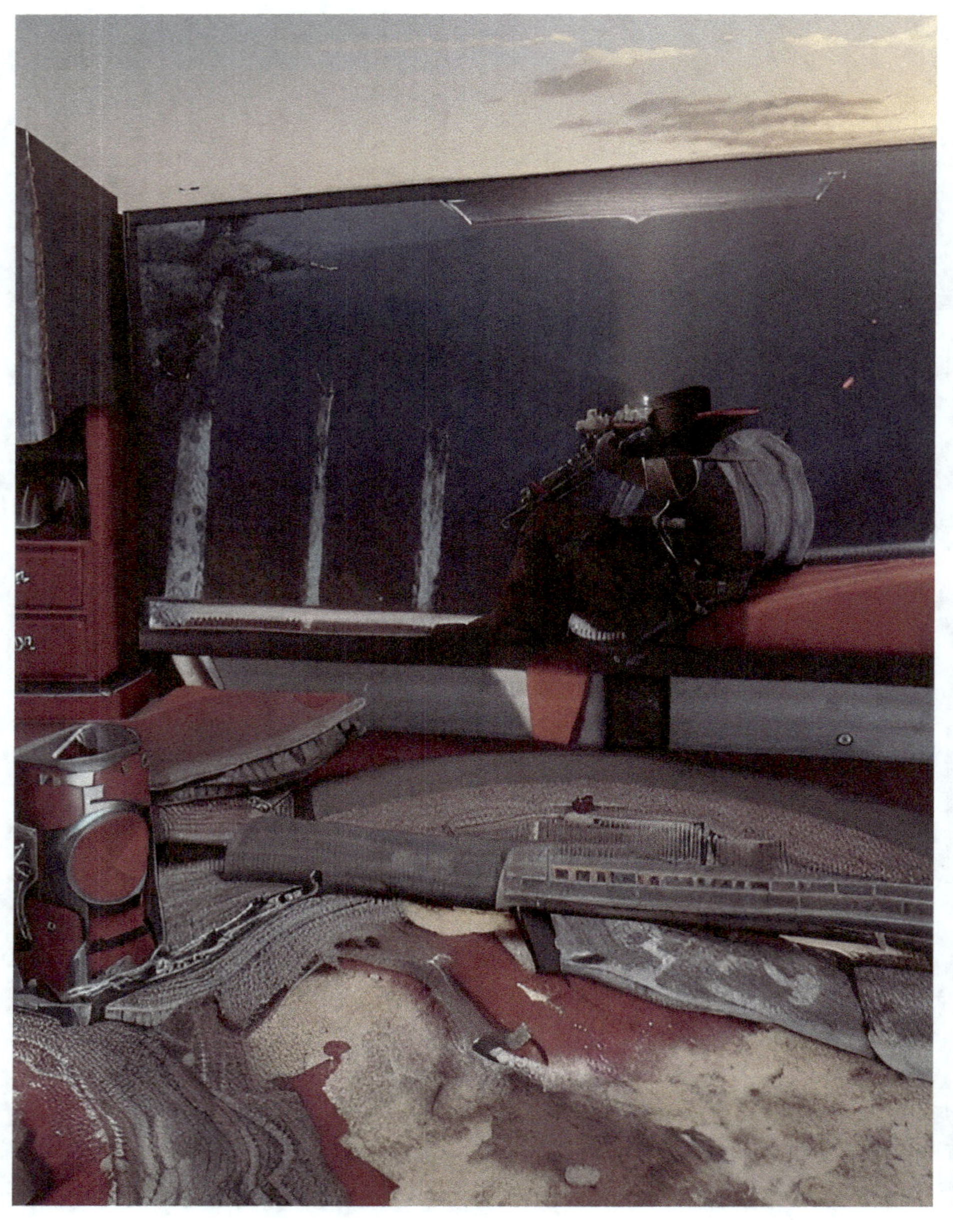

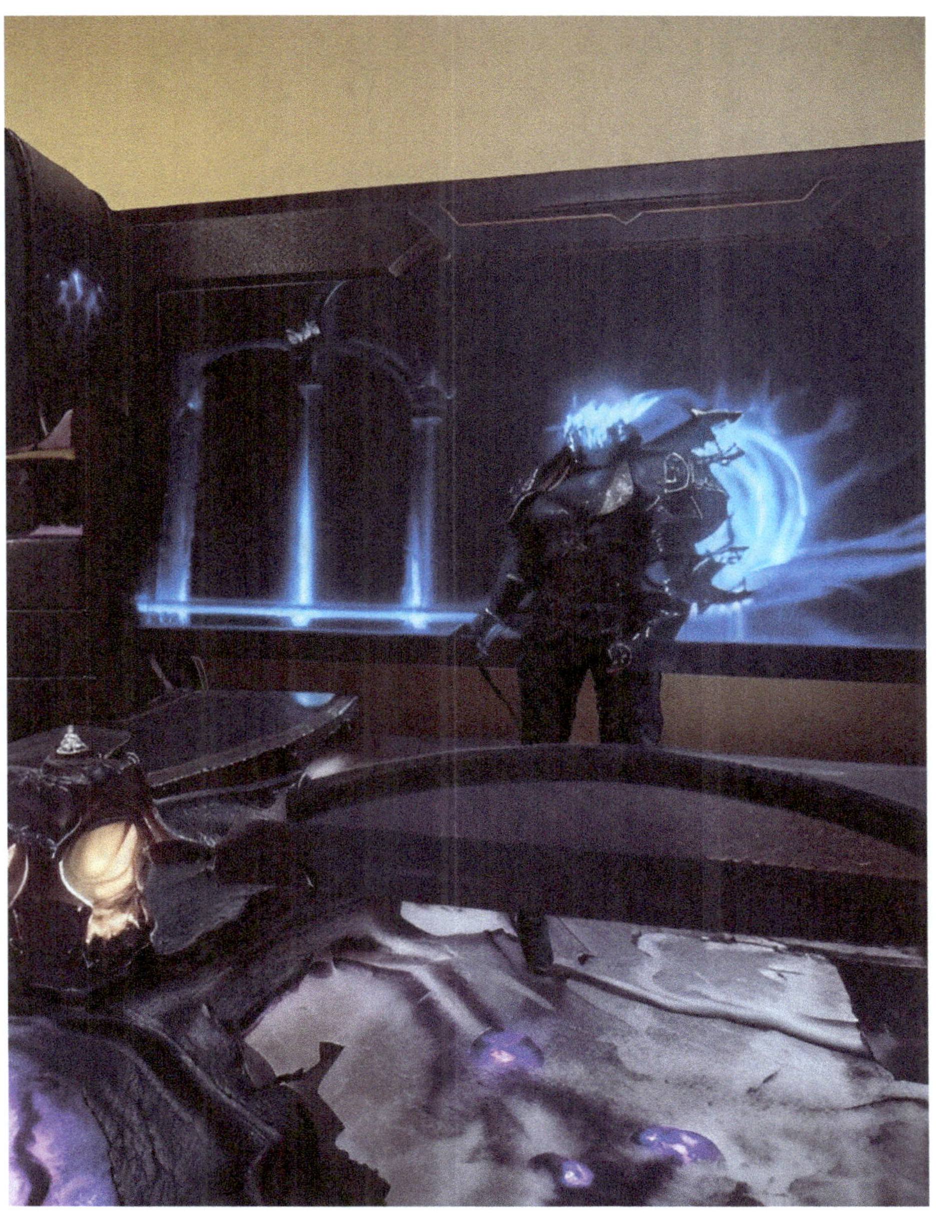

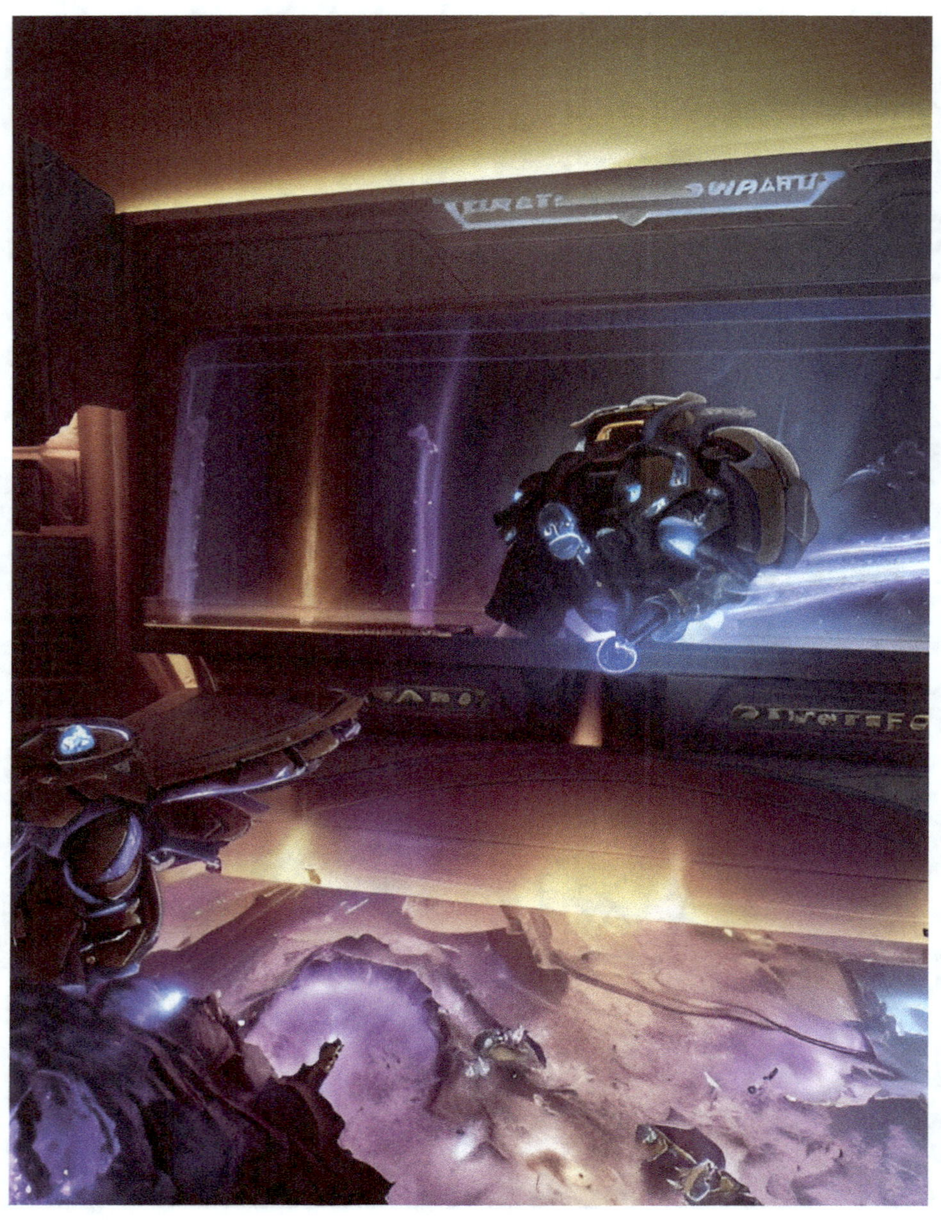
SWARM

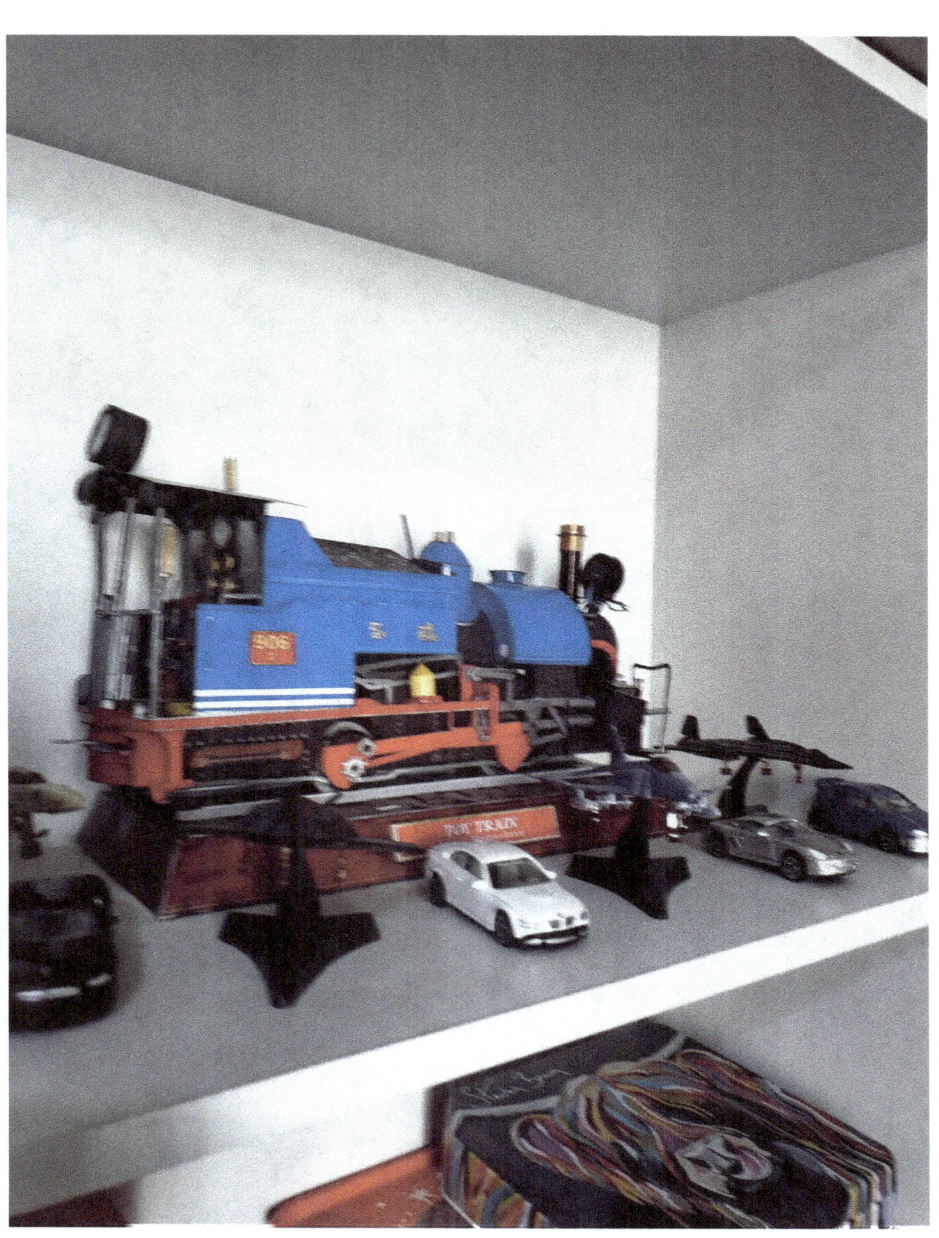

Card train model

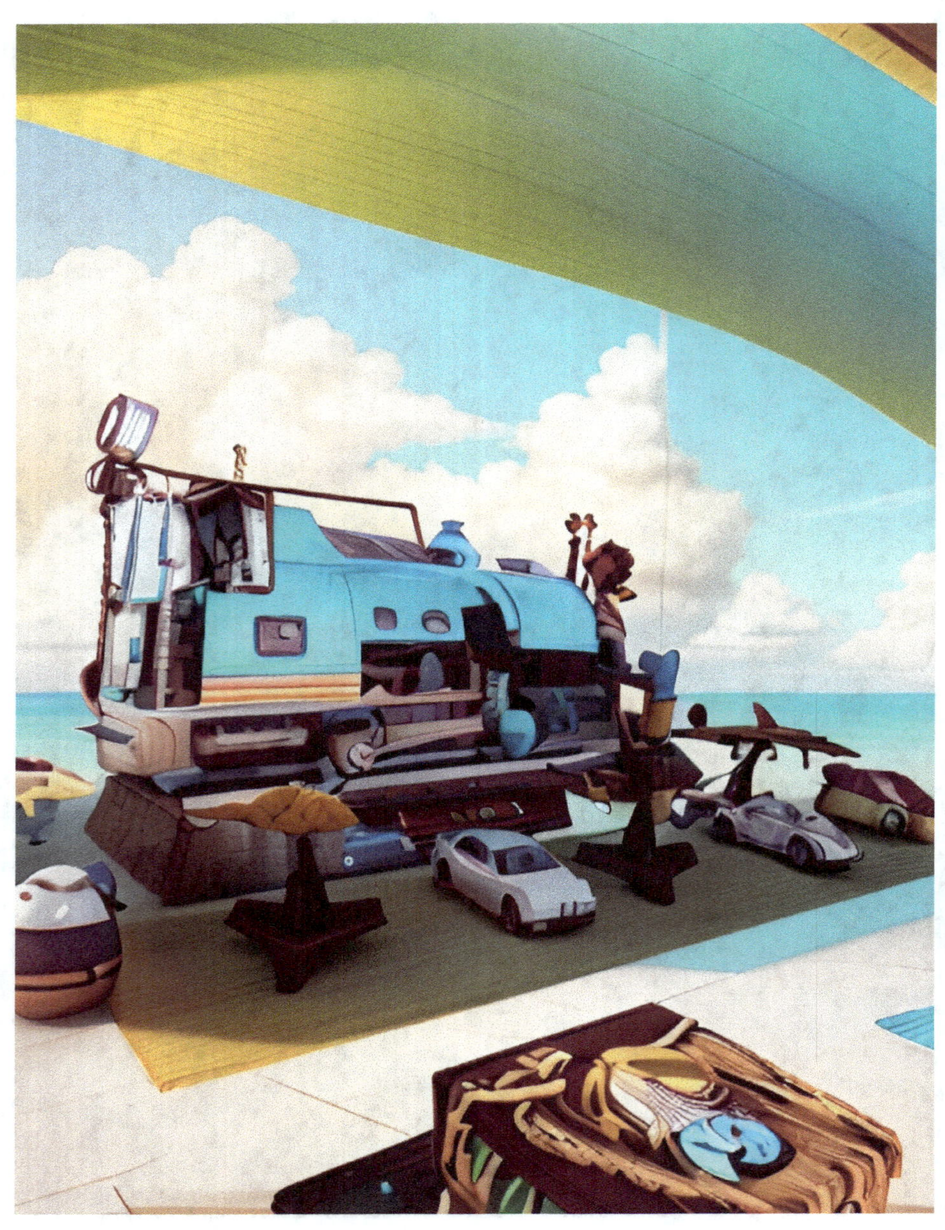

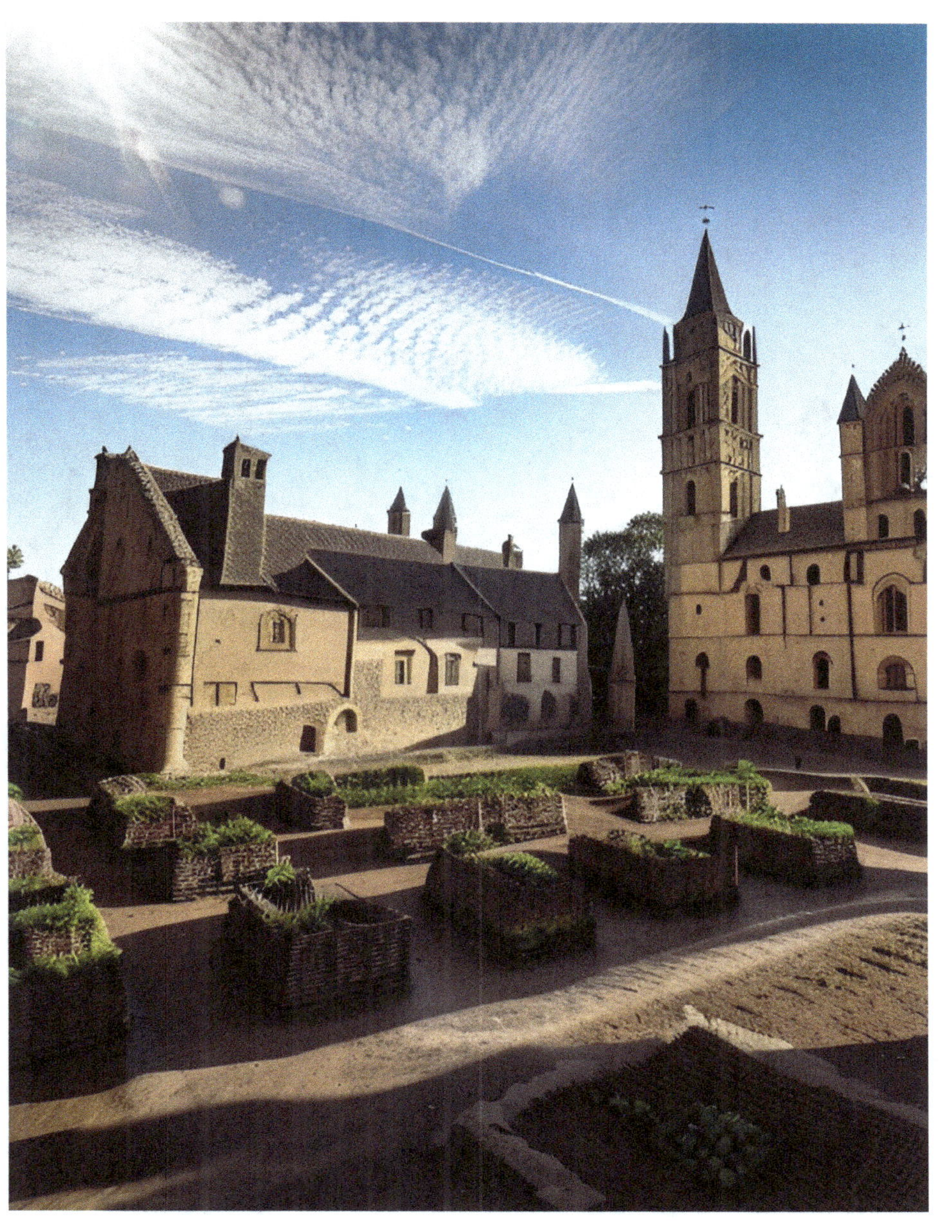

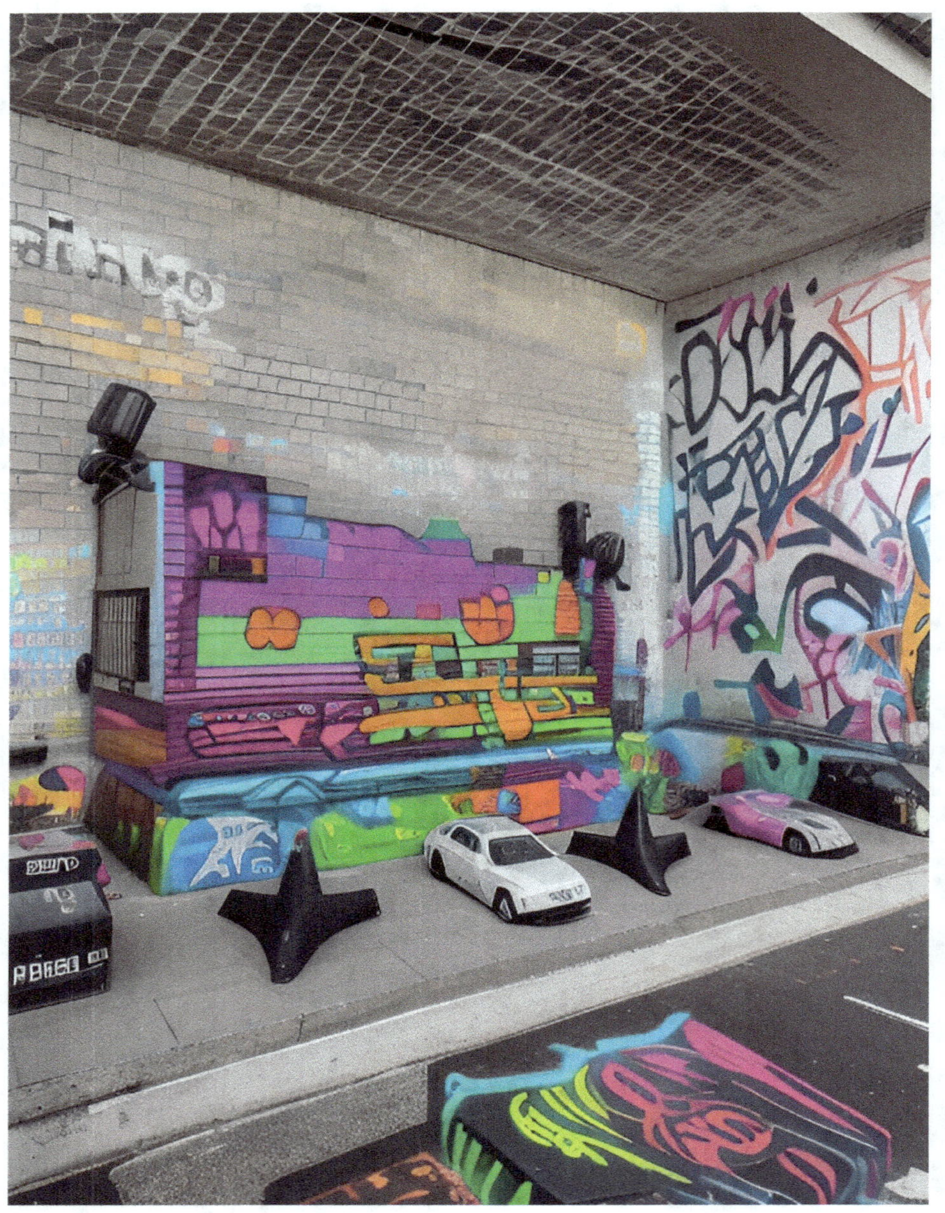

Wittner taktell
METRONOM PICCOLO
Largo 40-60
Larghet. 60-66
Adagio 66-76
Andante 76-108
Moderato 108-120
Allegro 120-168
Presto 168-200
Prestissimo 200-208

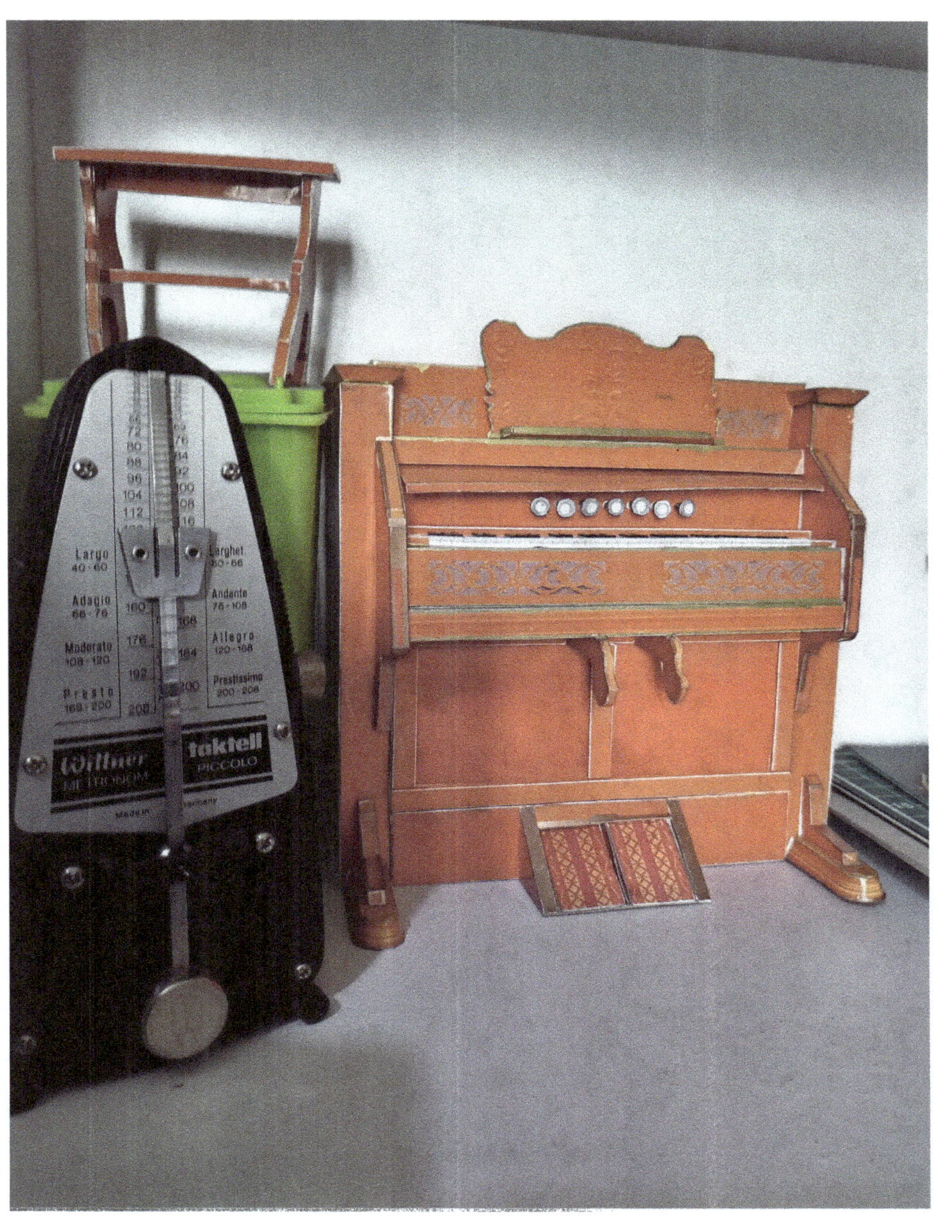

Piano

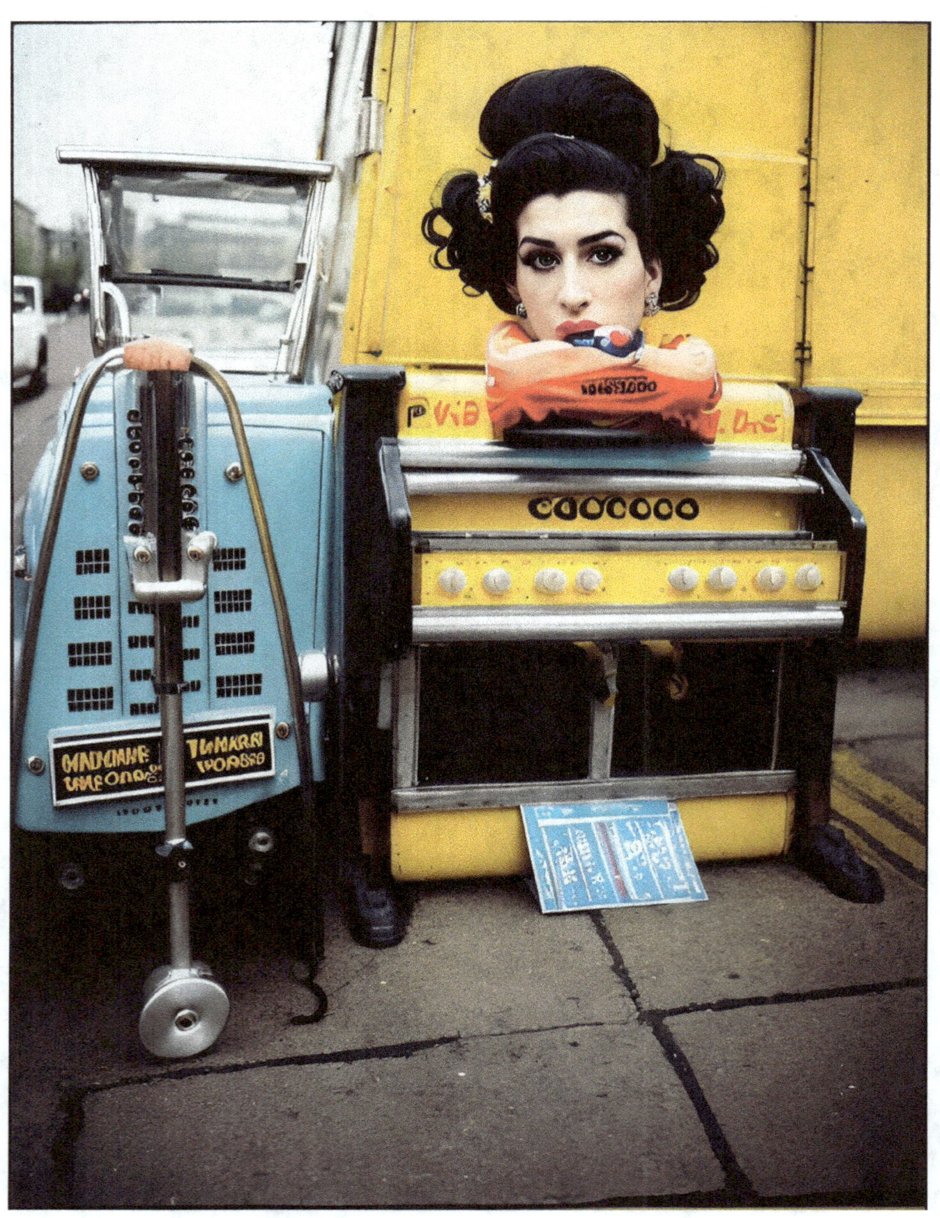

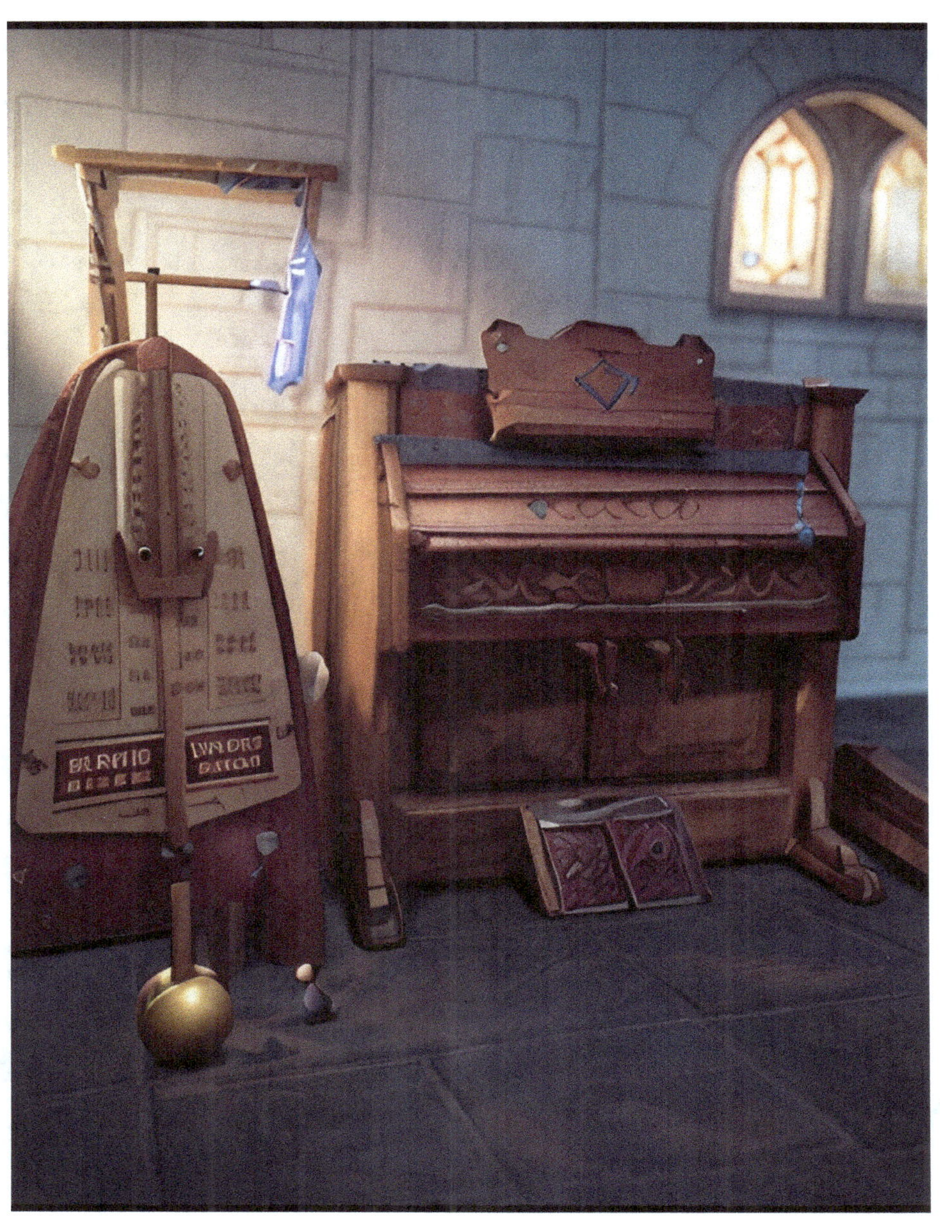

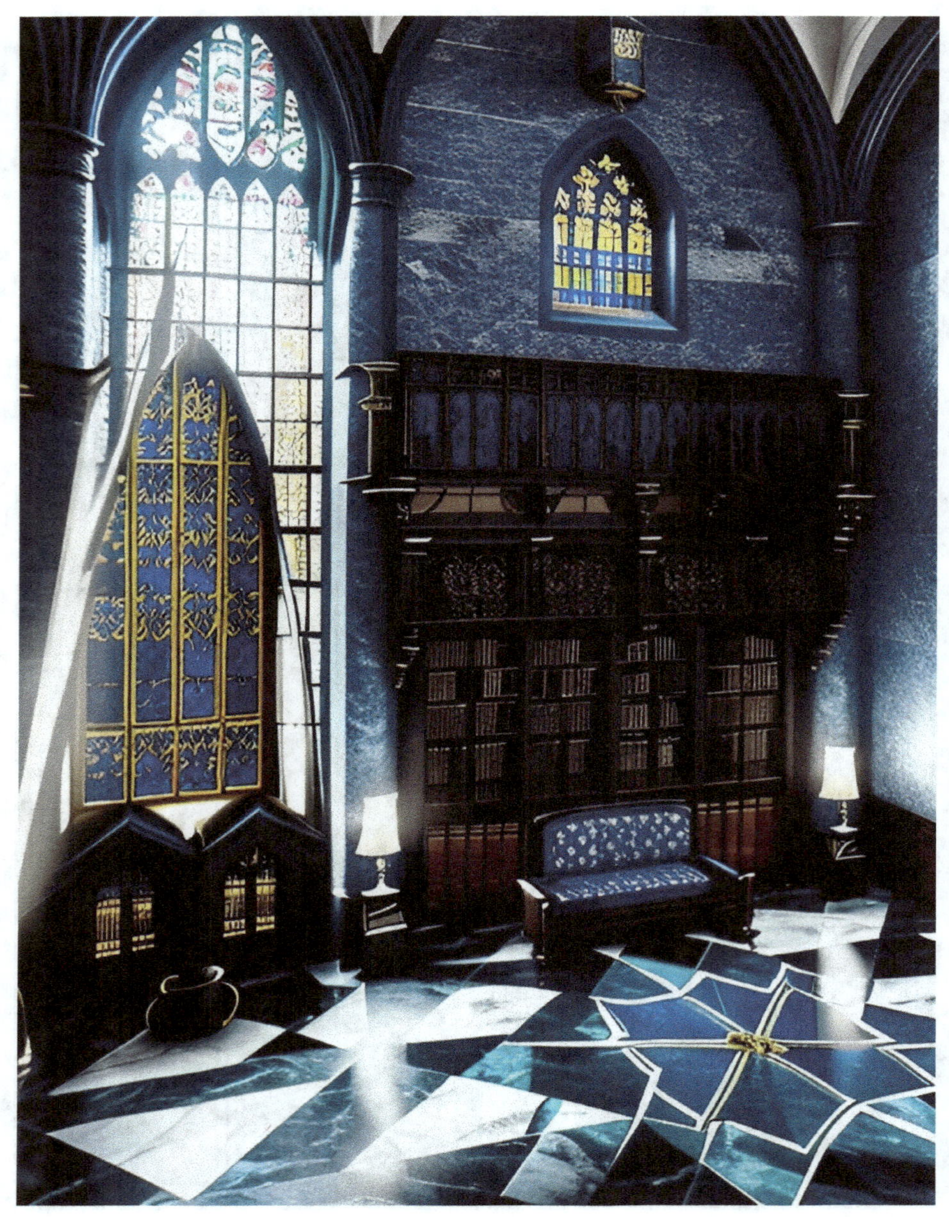

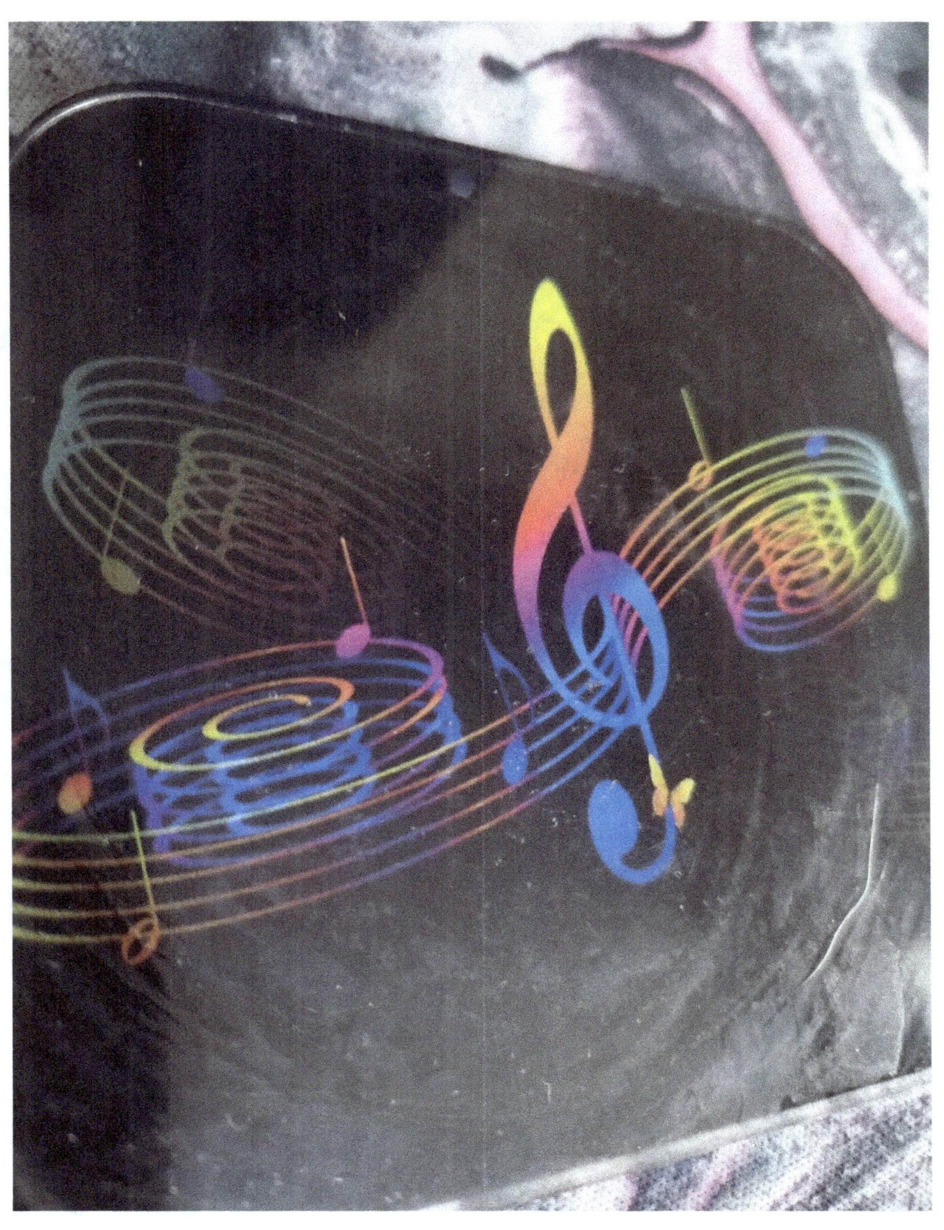

Music coaster

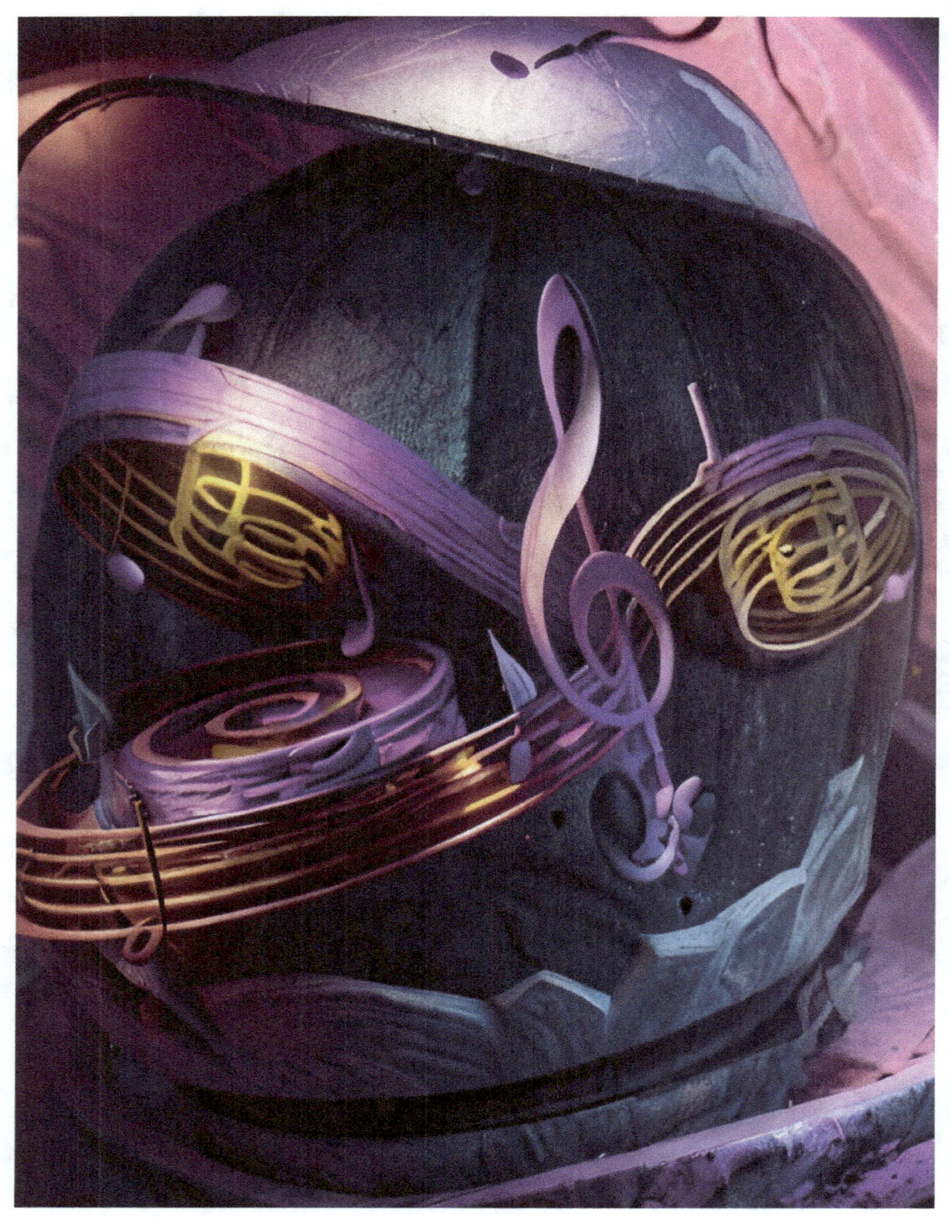

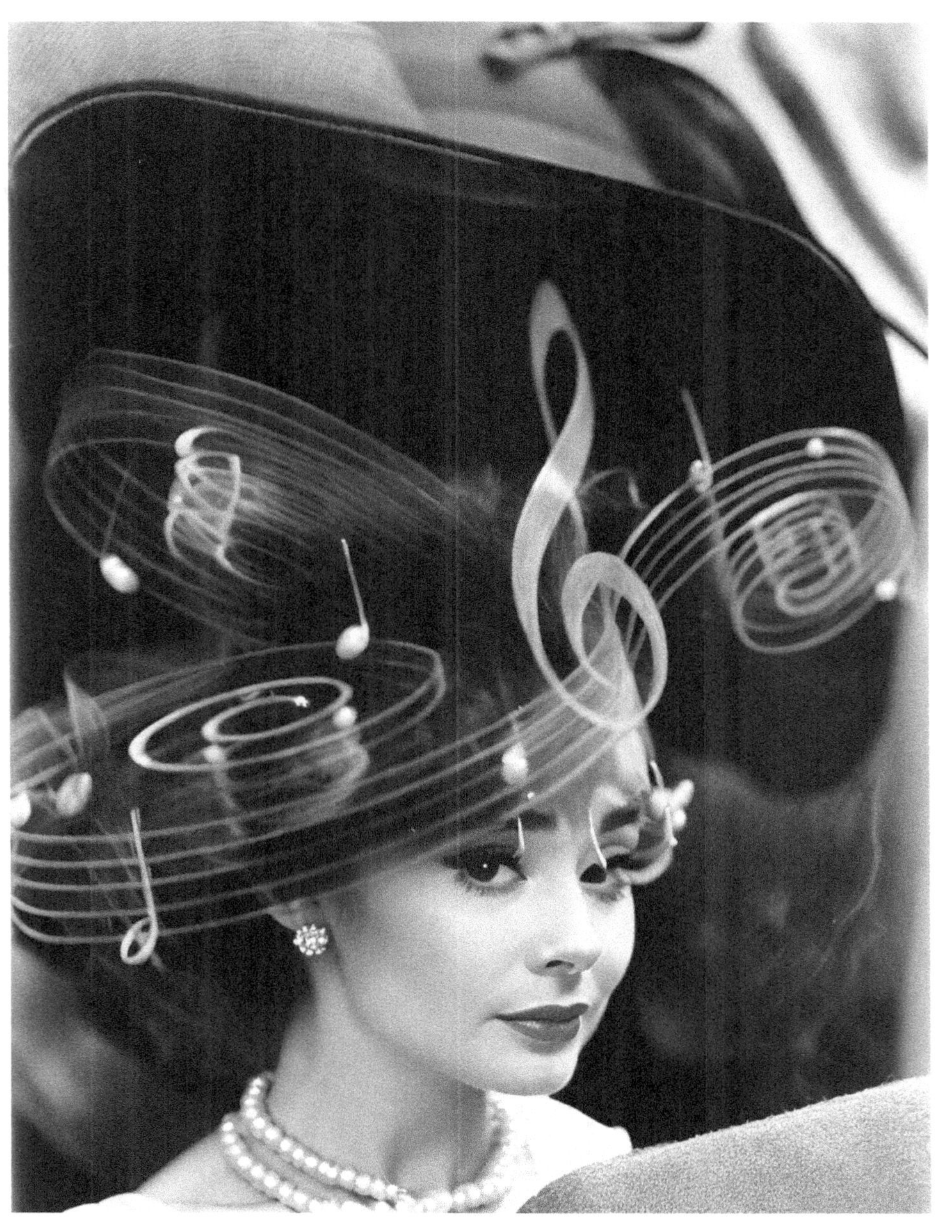

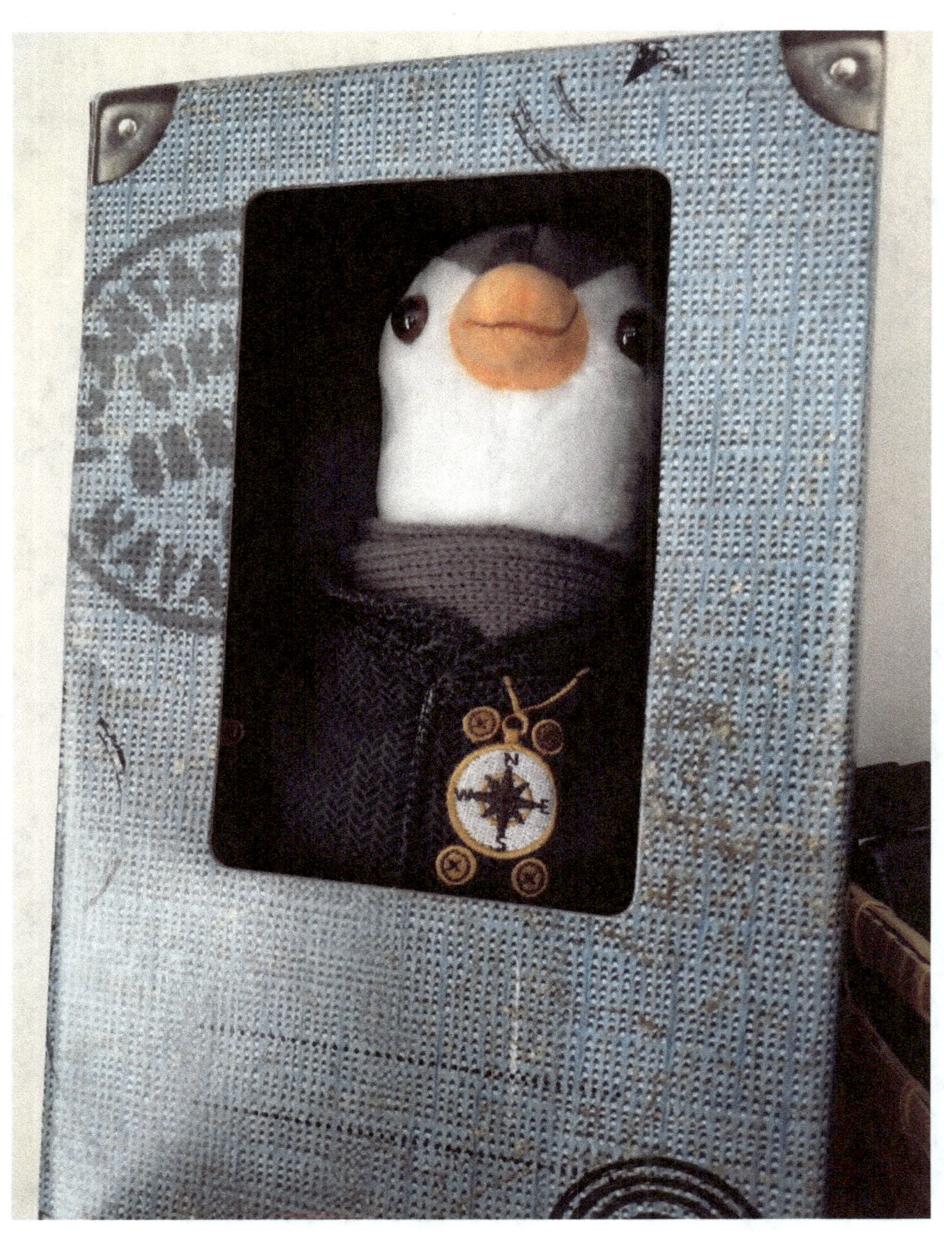

Penguin

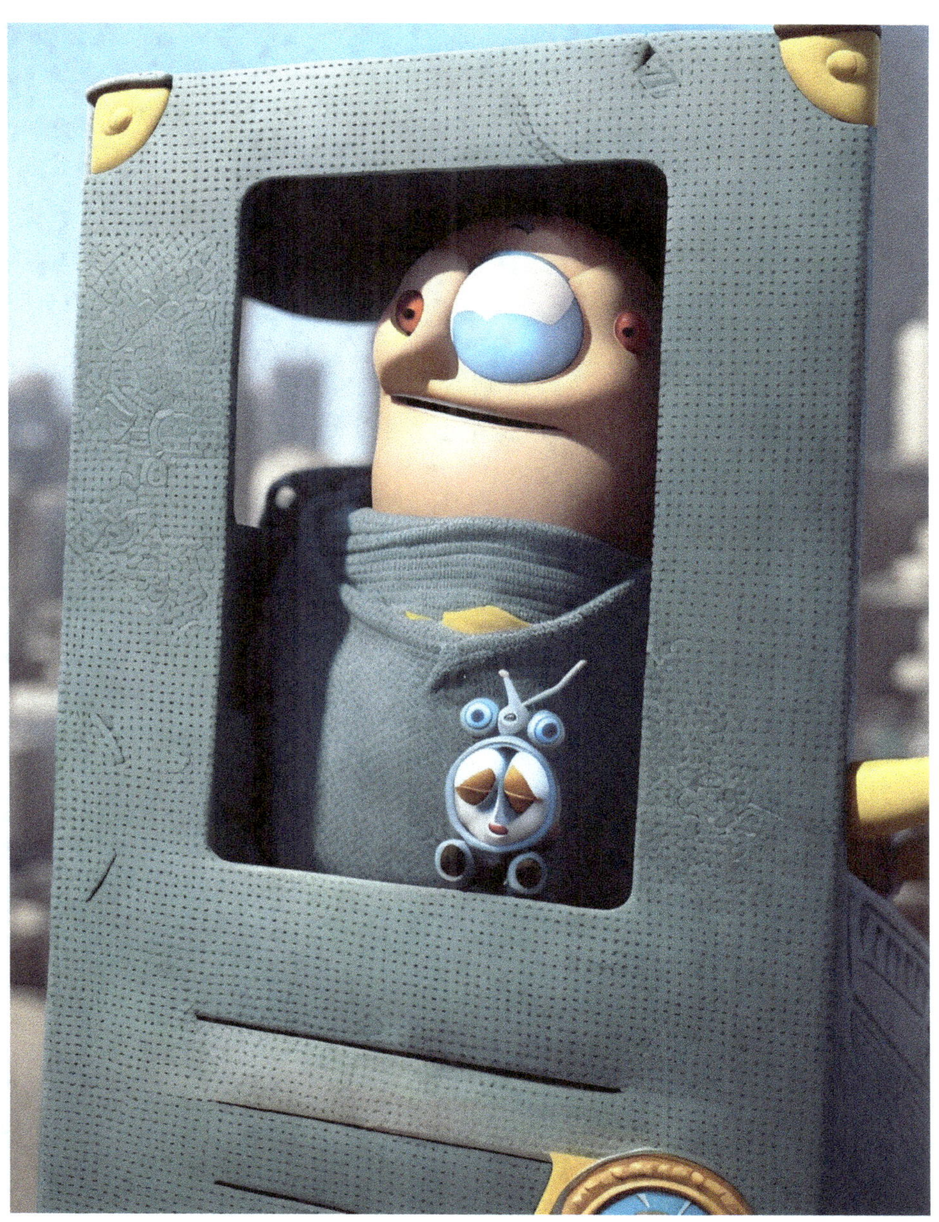

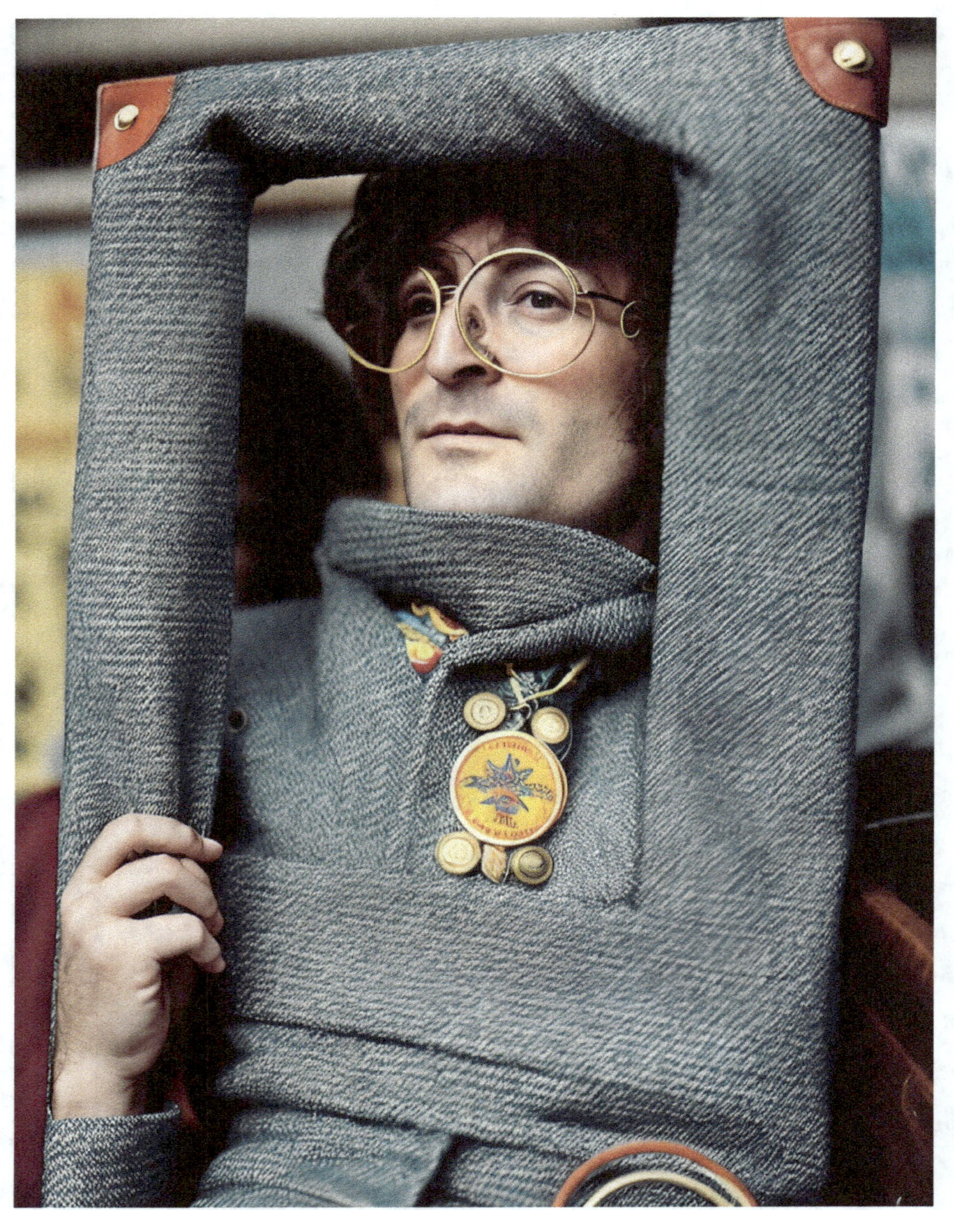

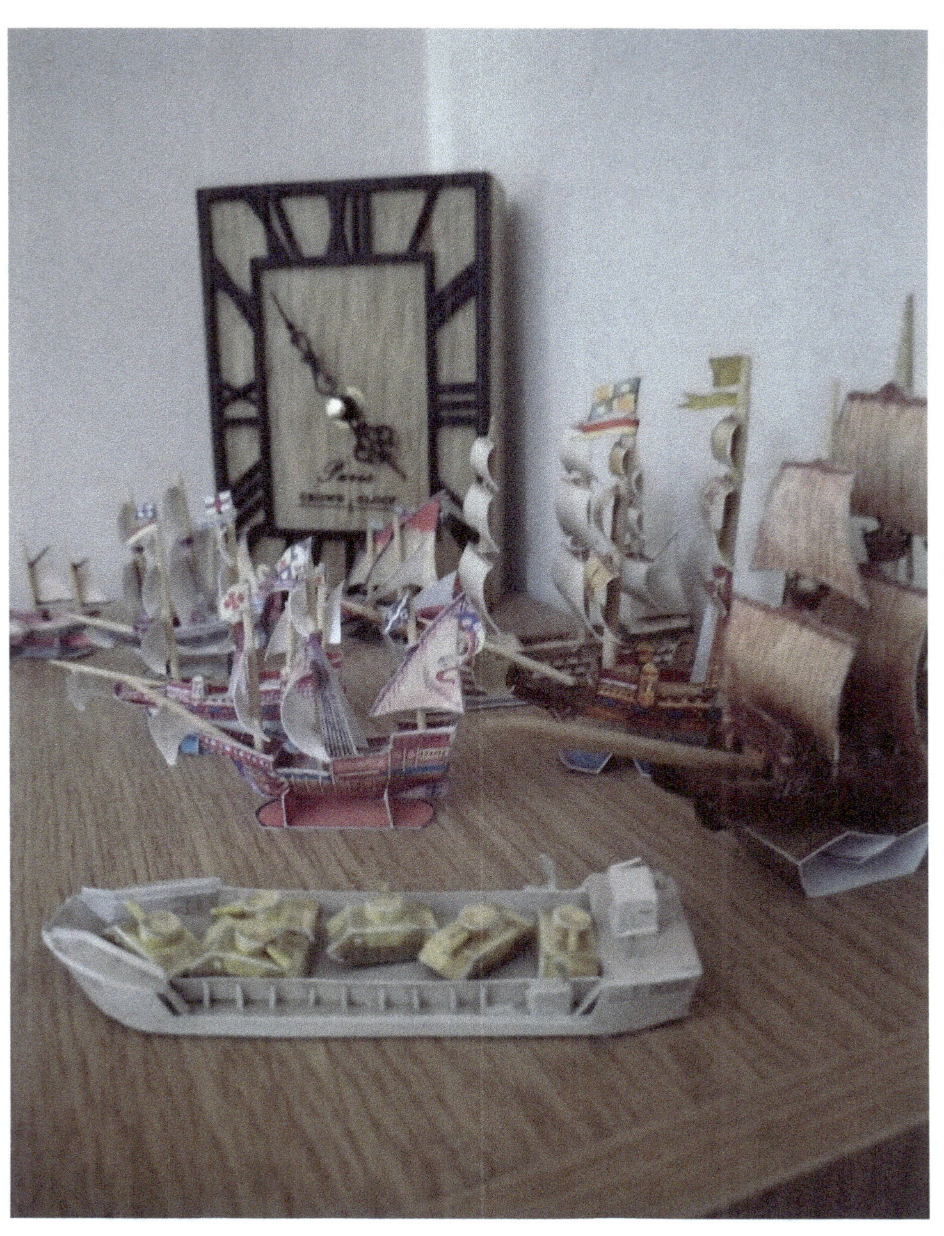

Clock and ships

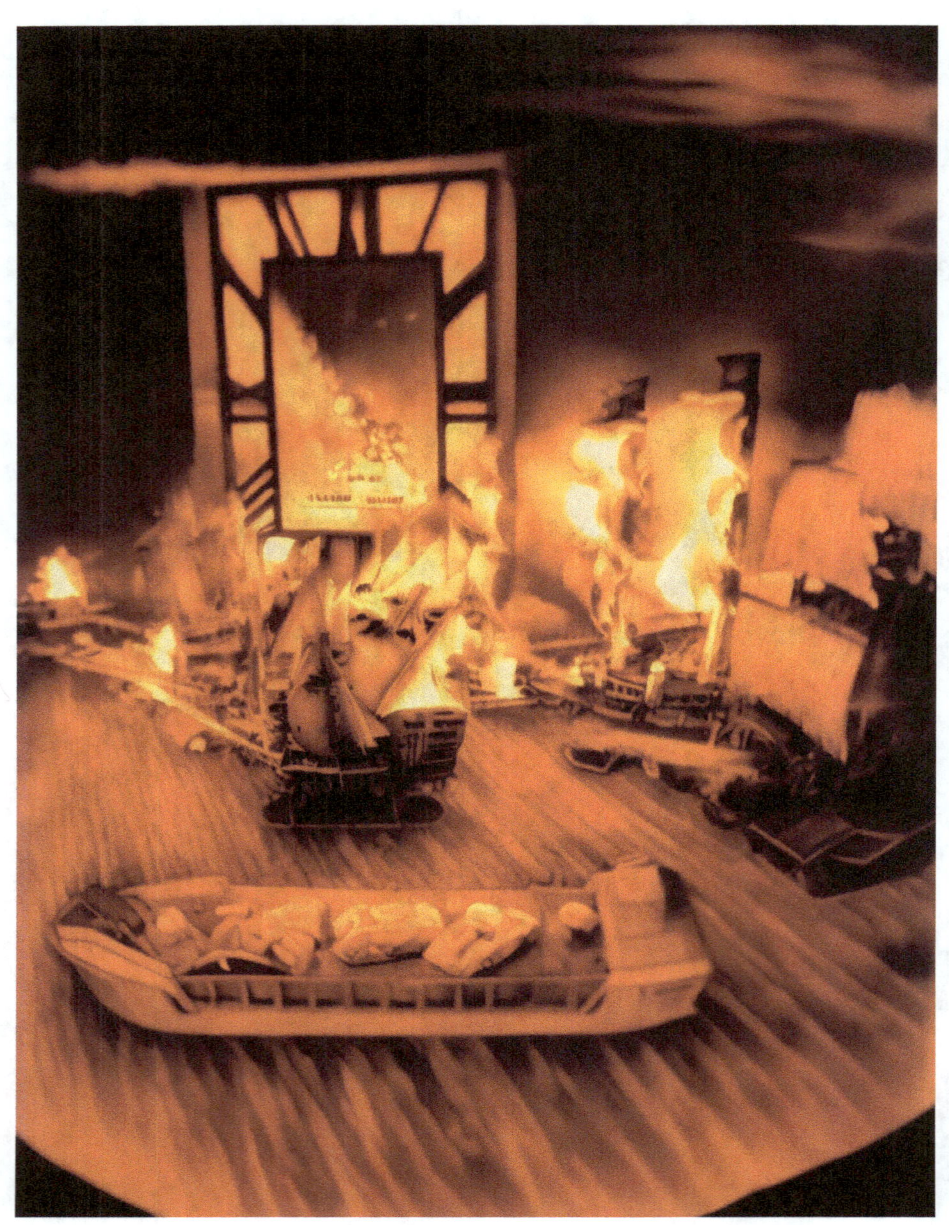

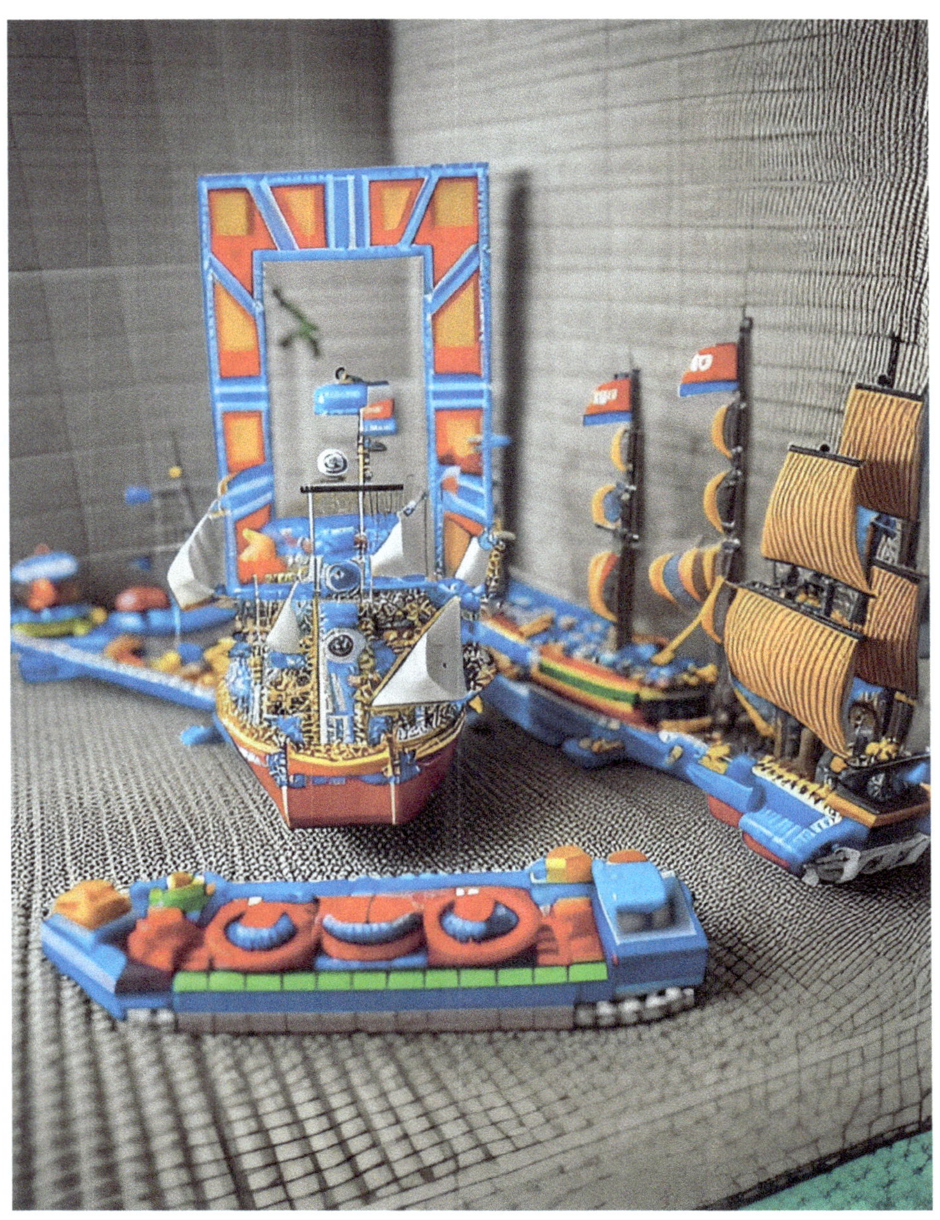

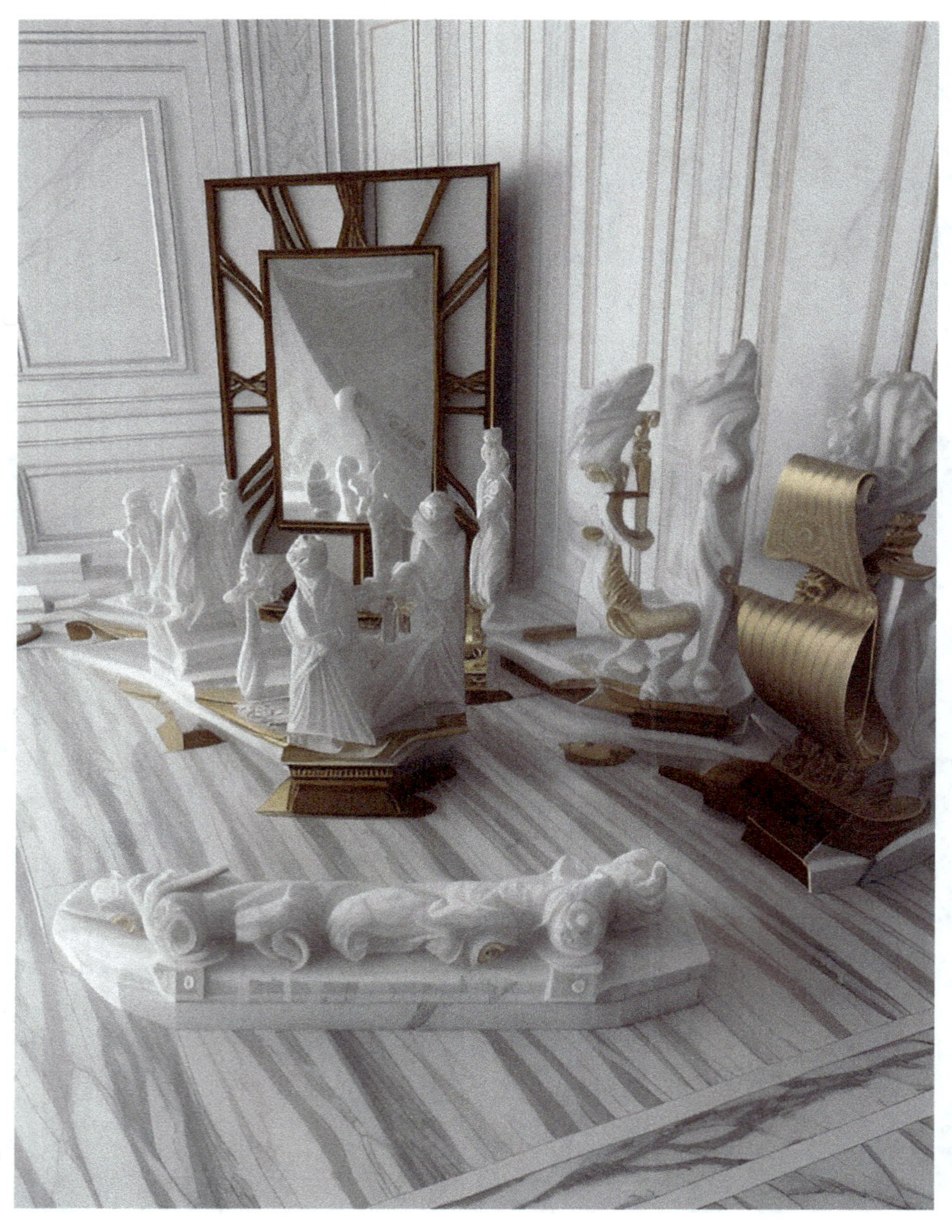

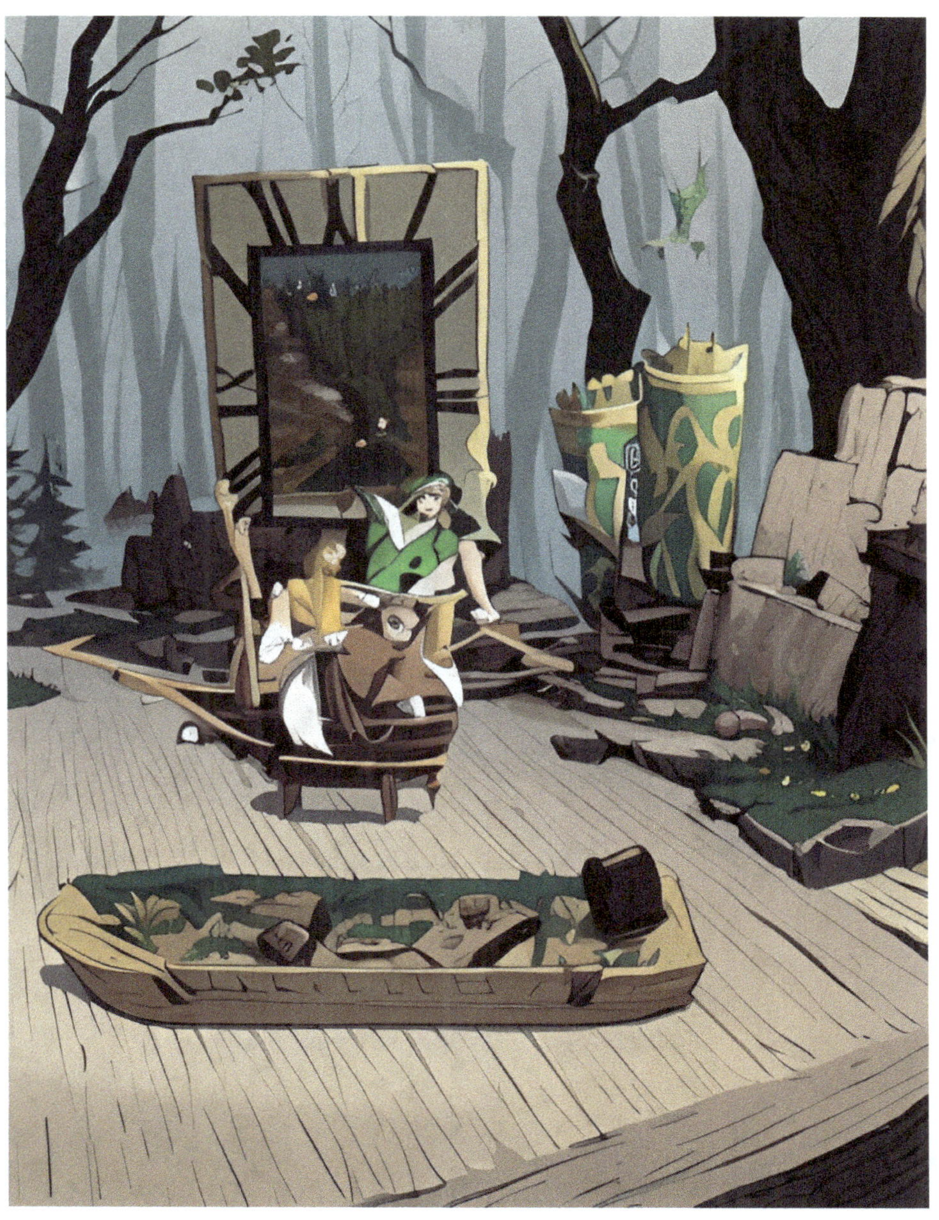

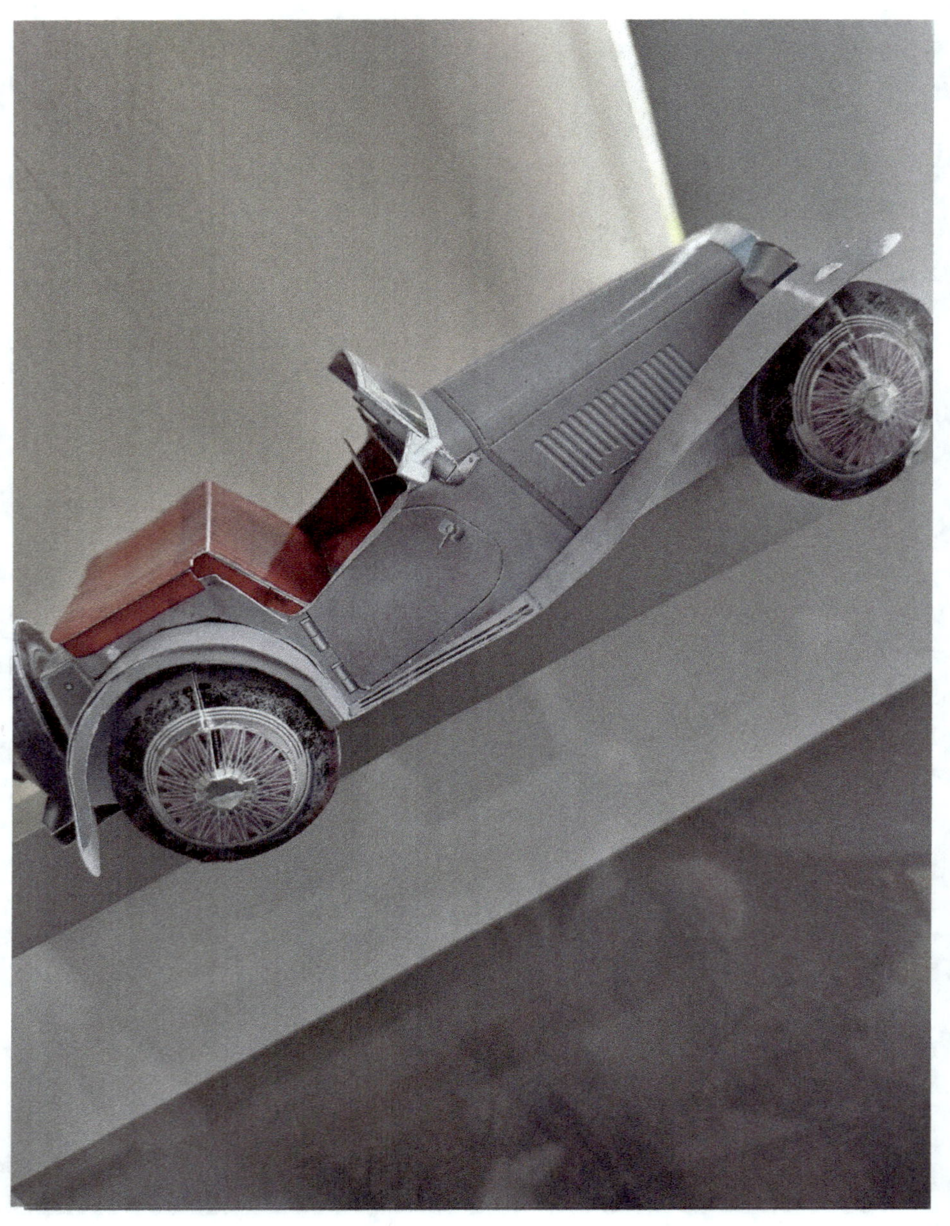

Car

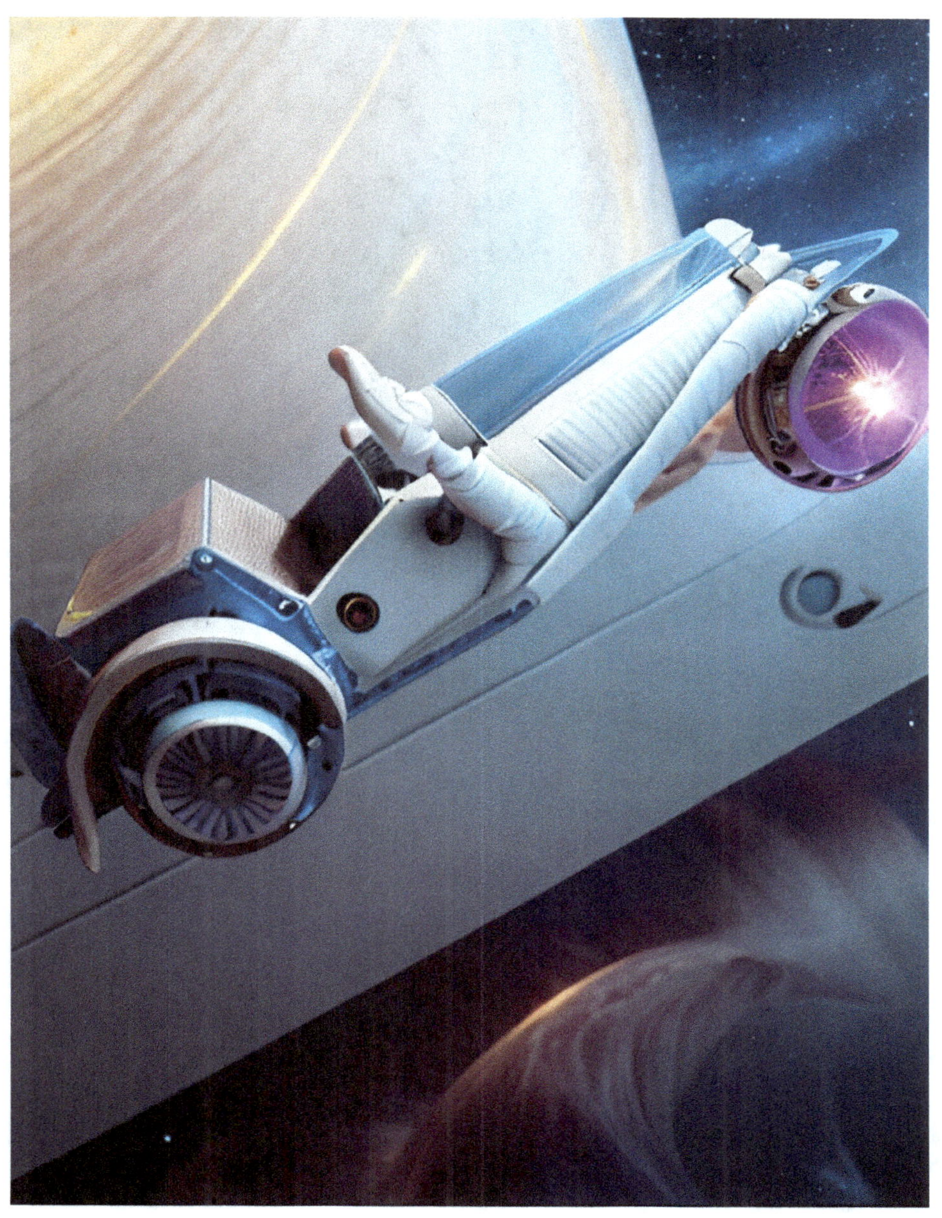

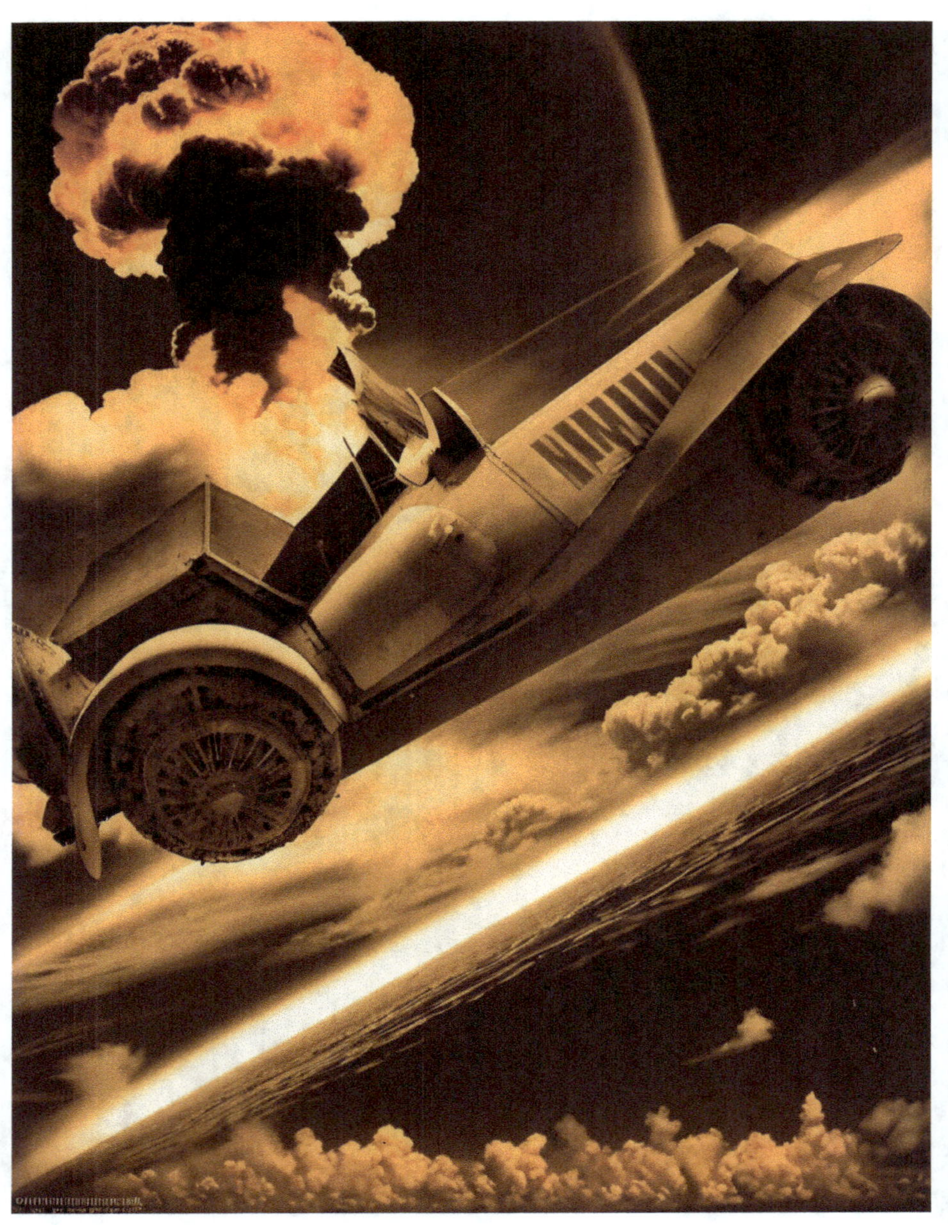

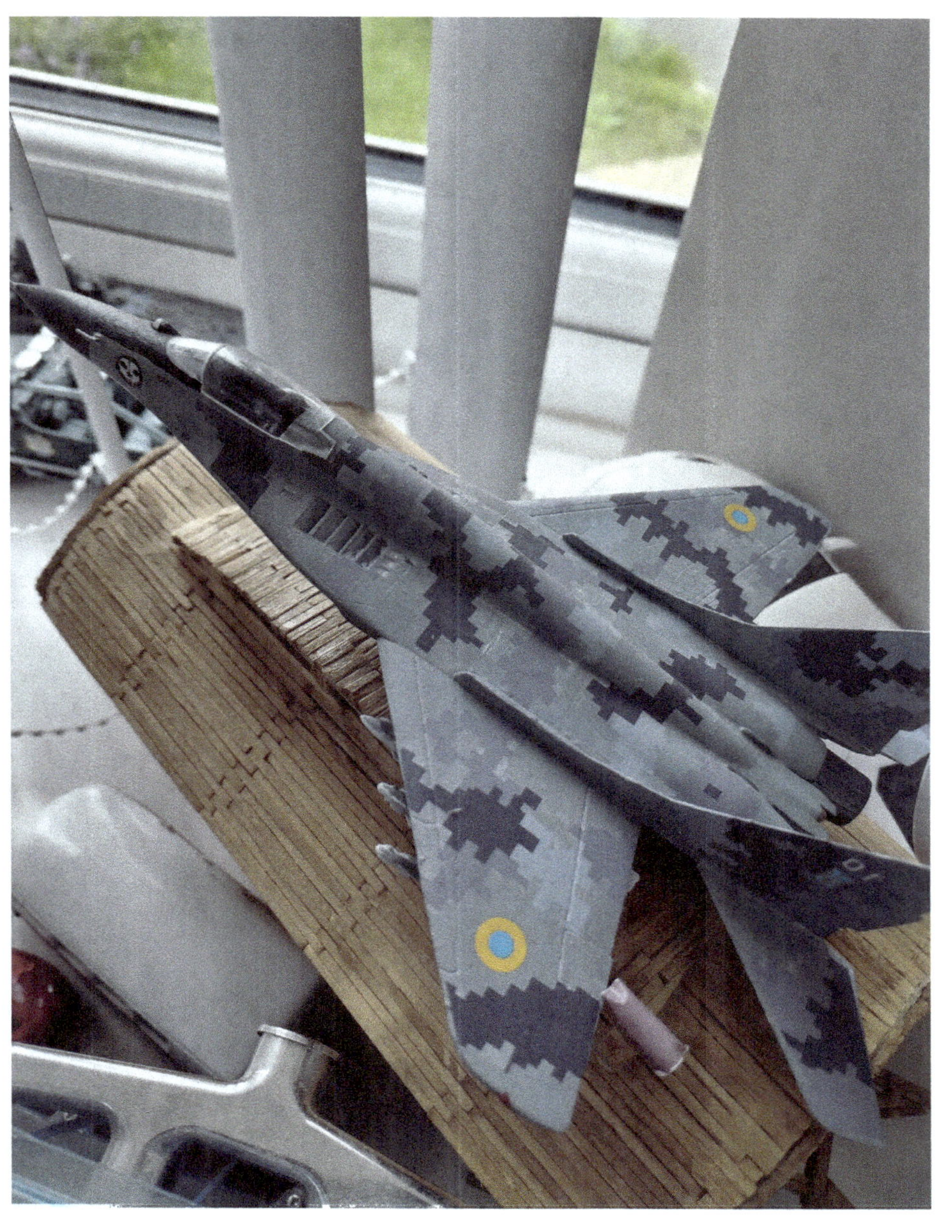

Jet

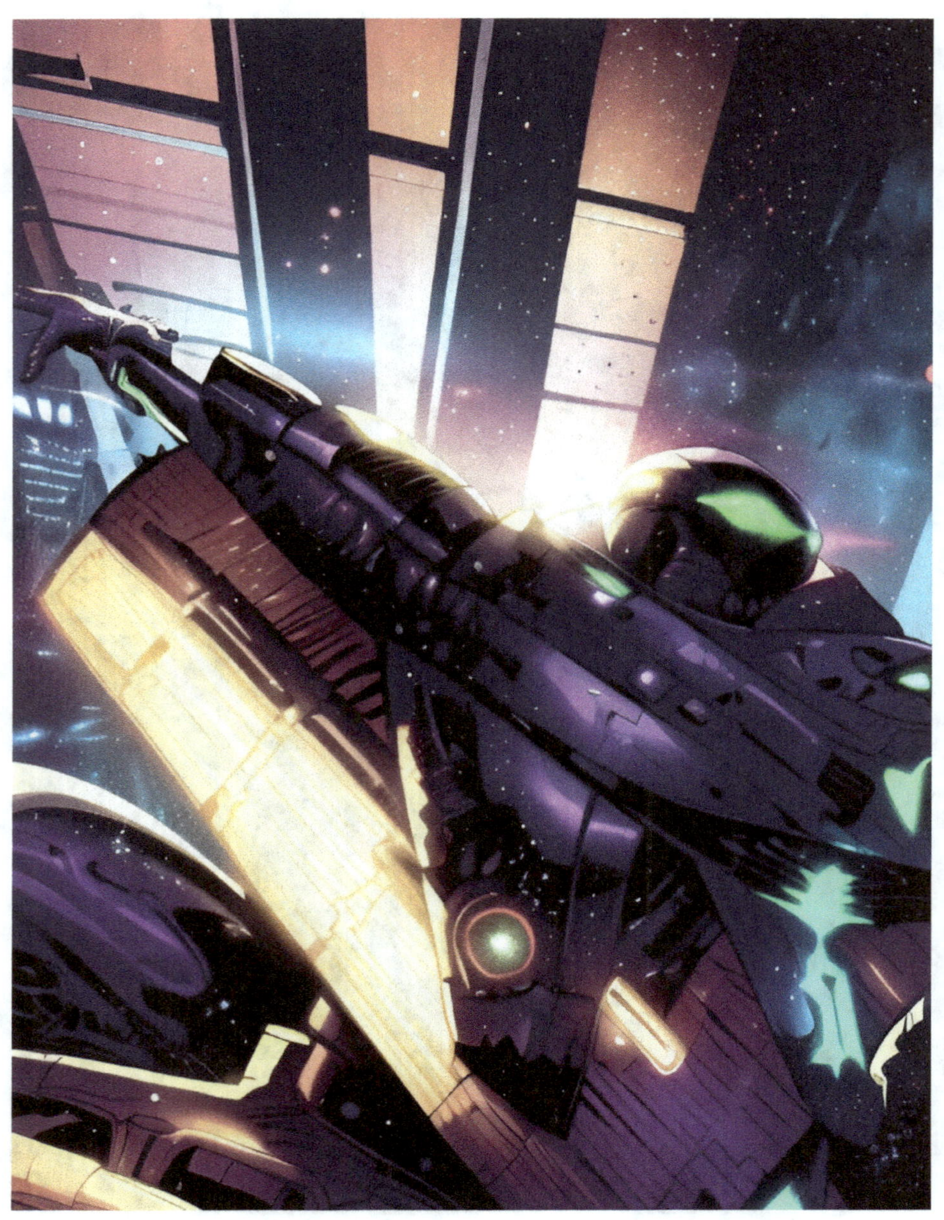

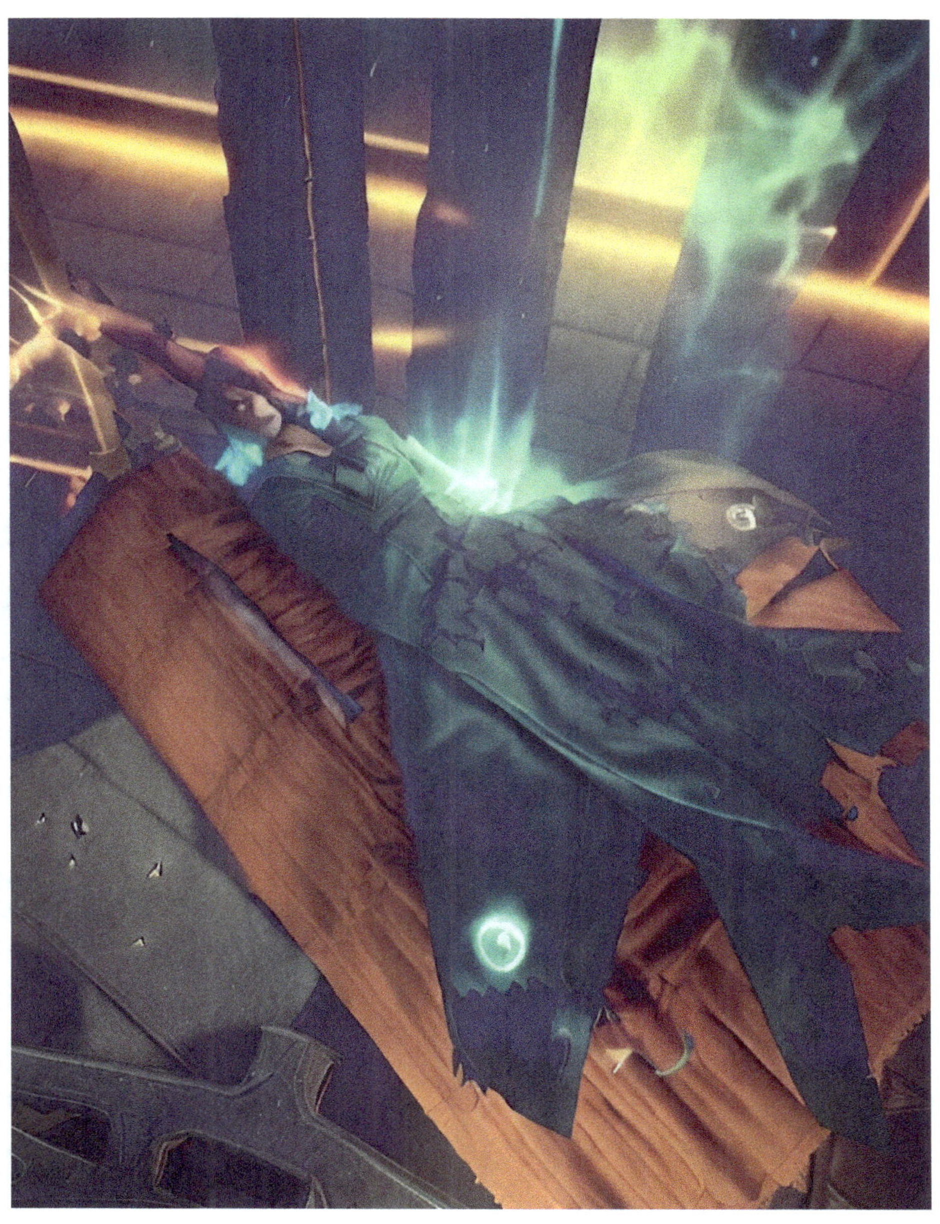

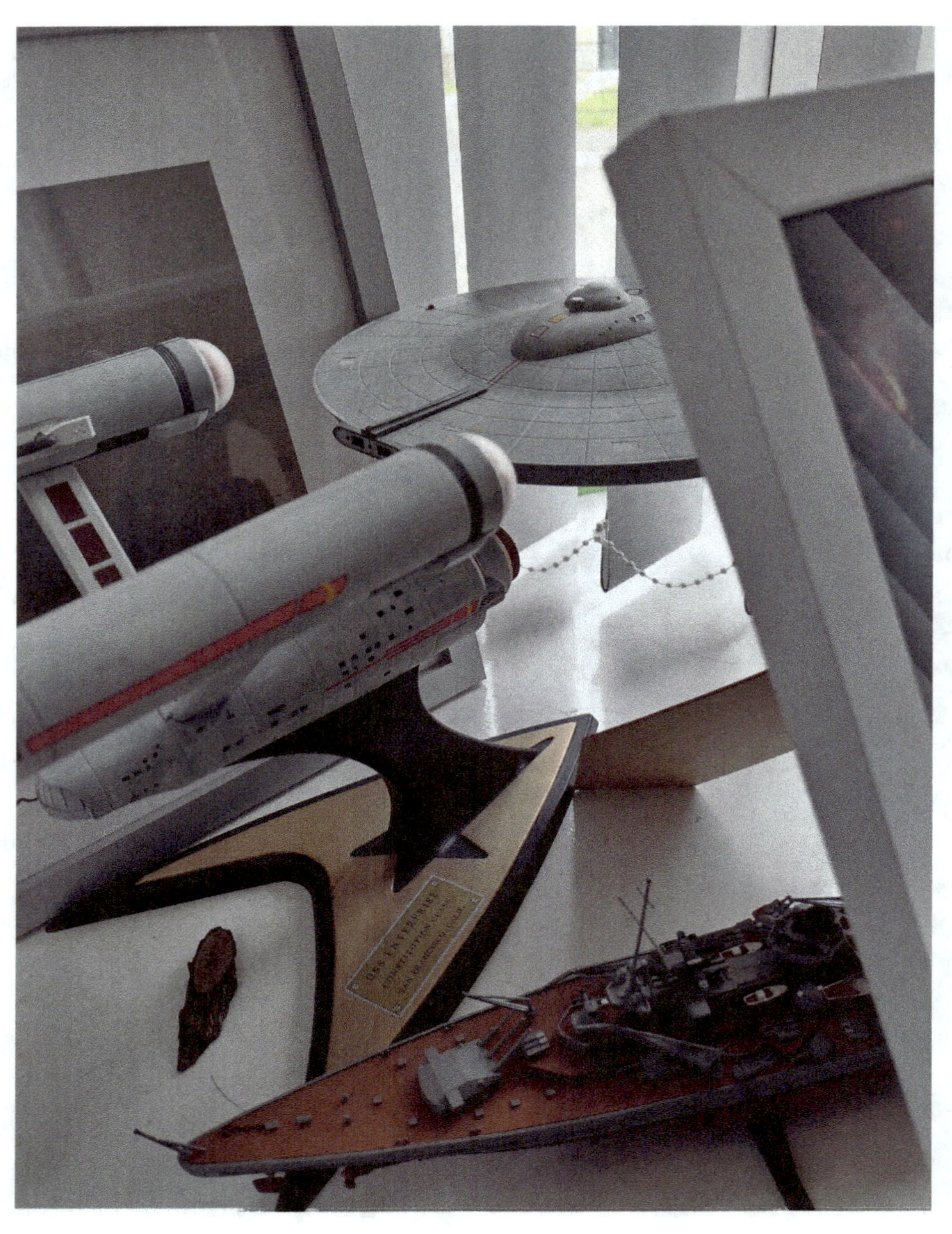

Spaceship

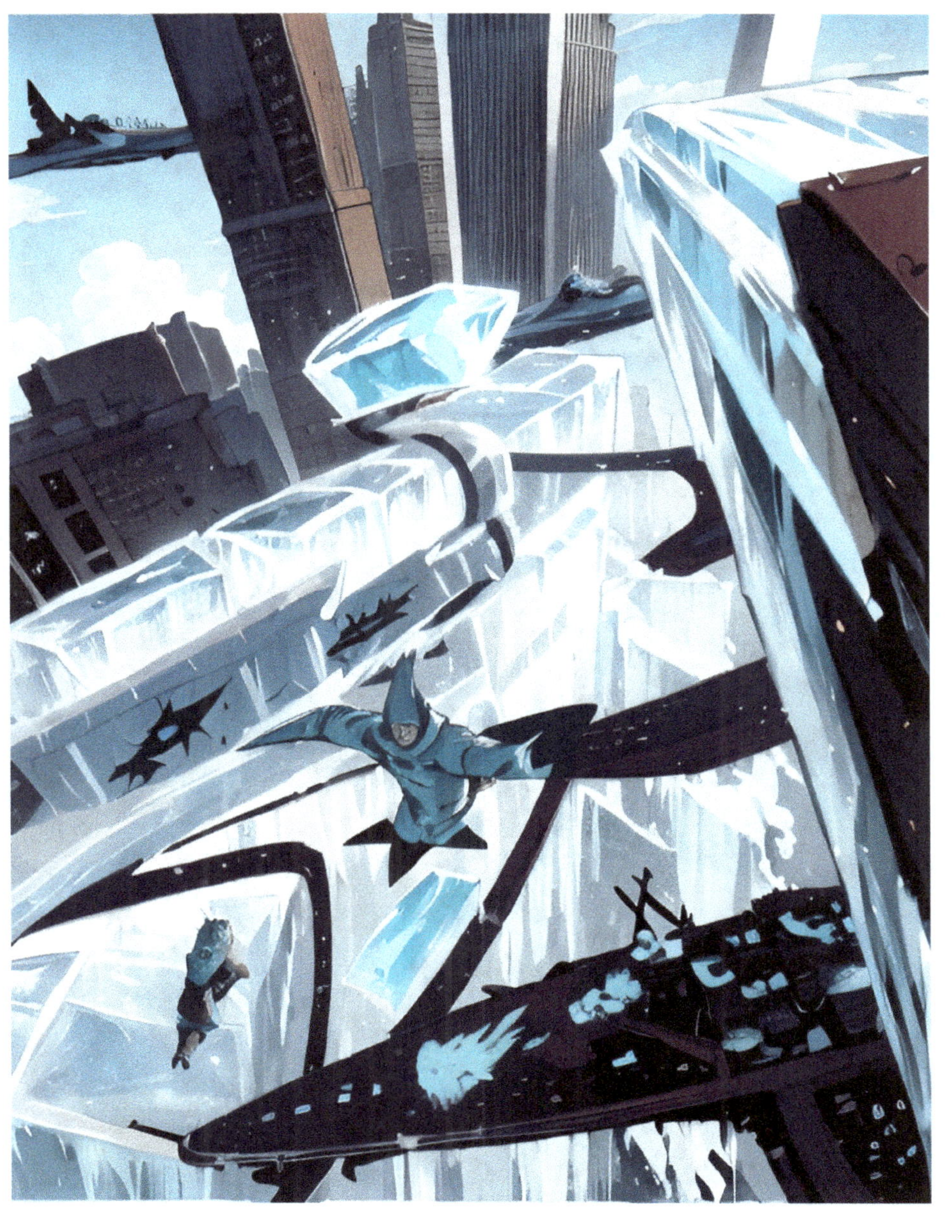

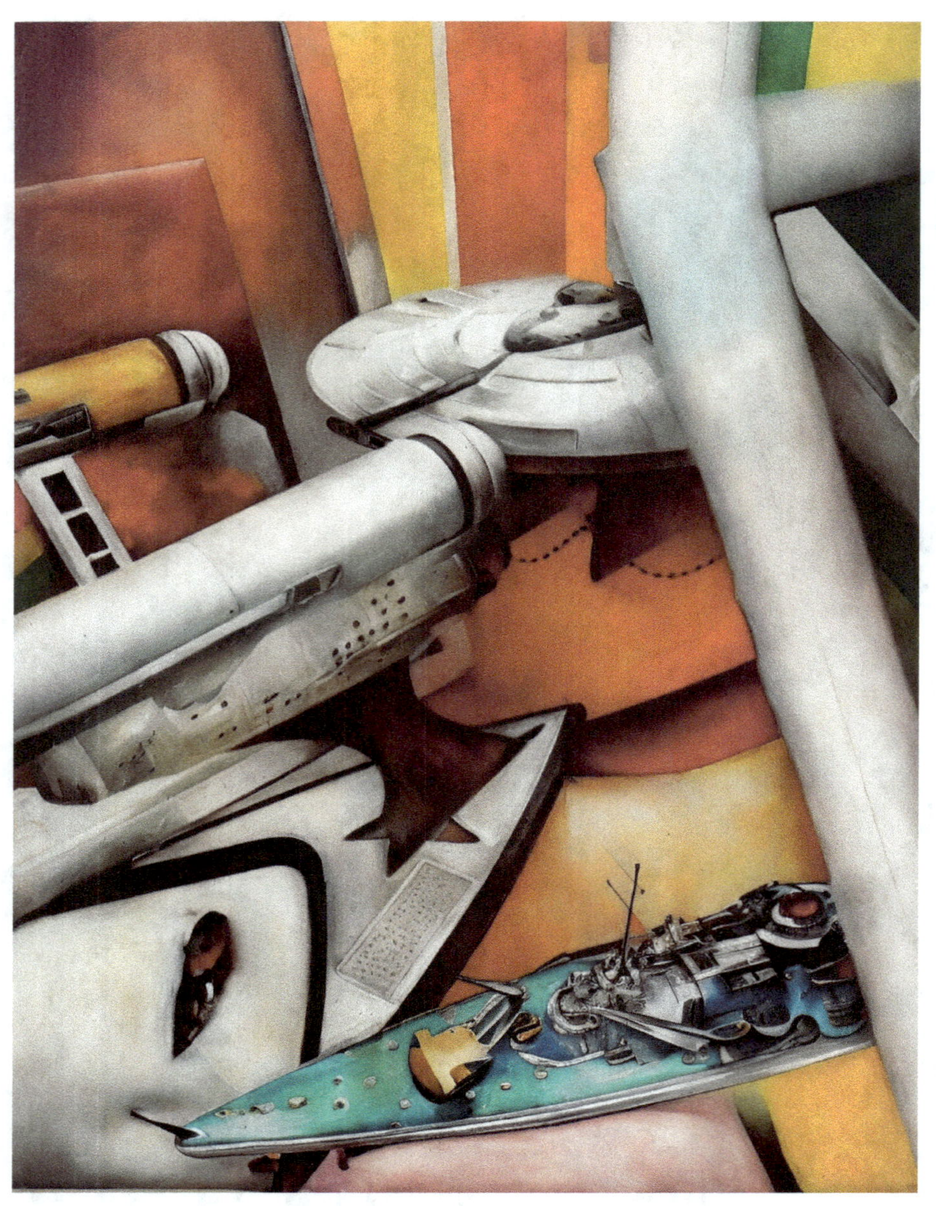

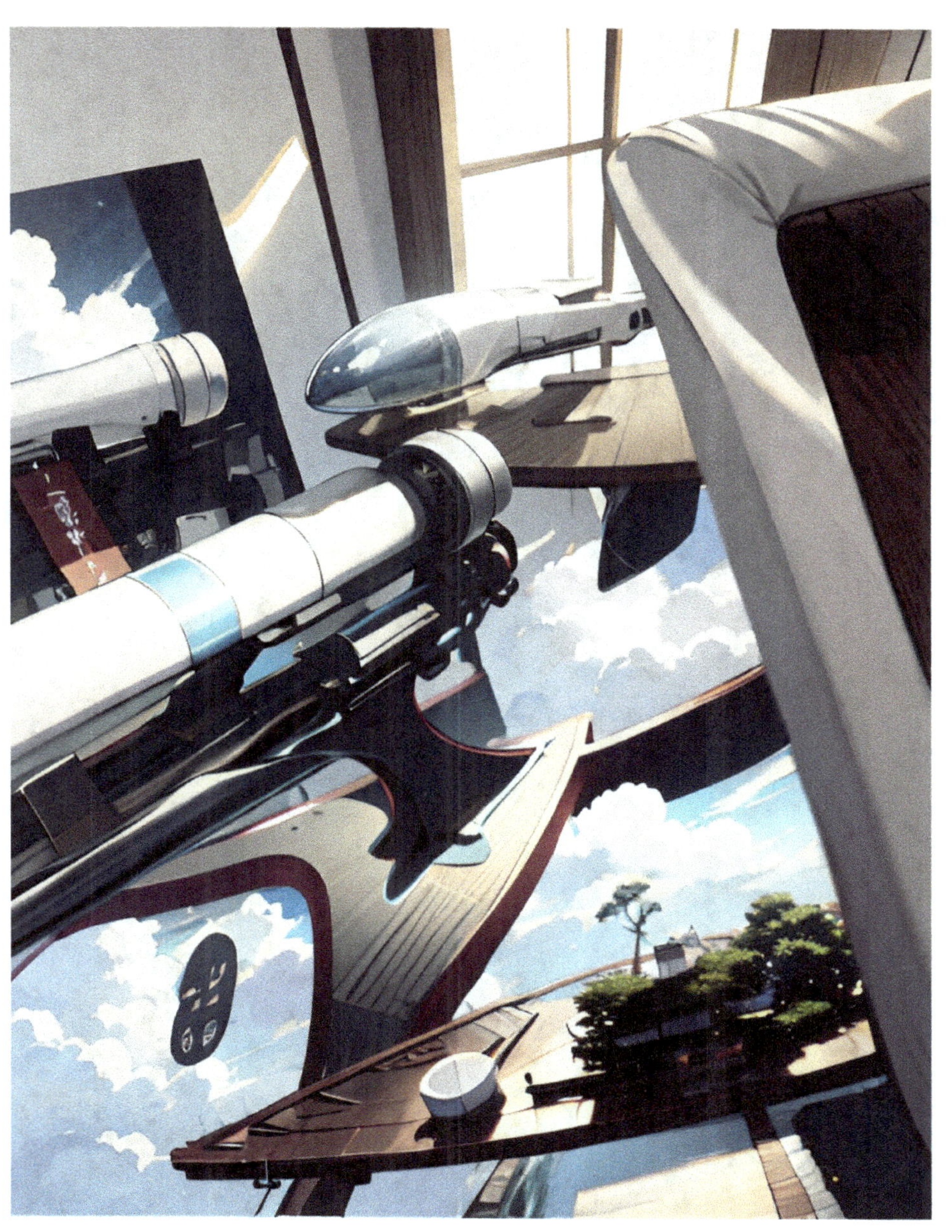

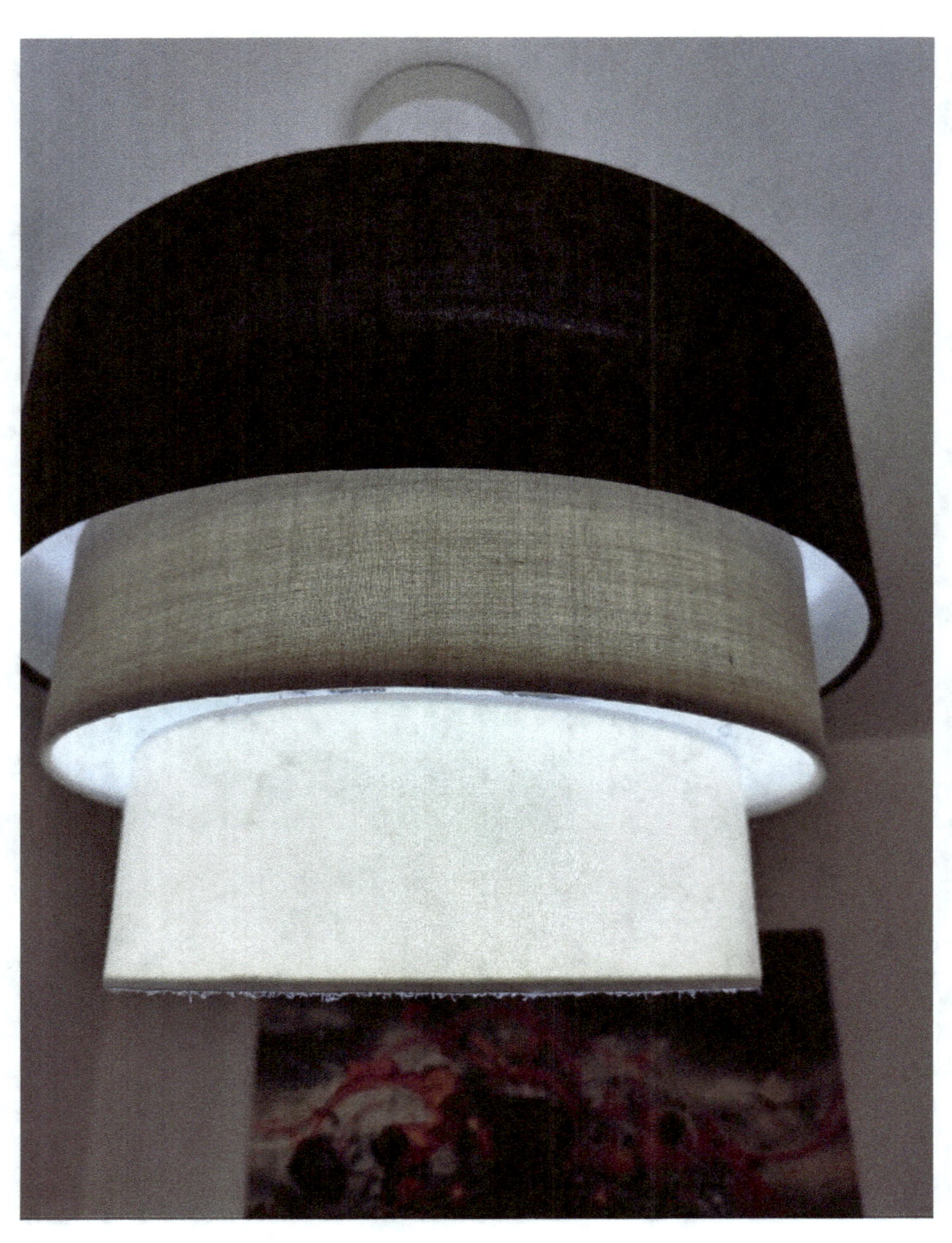

Lampshade

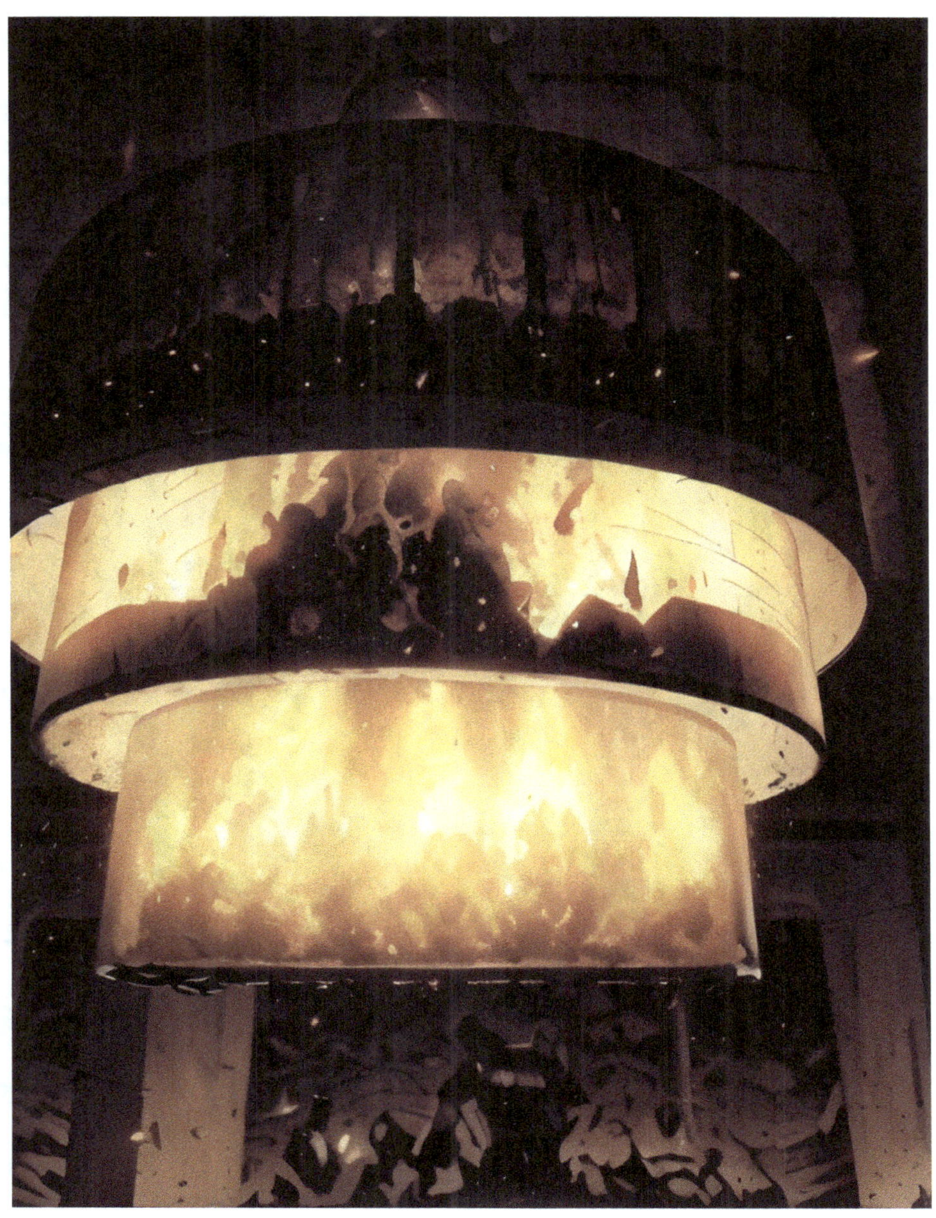

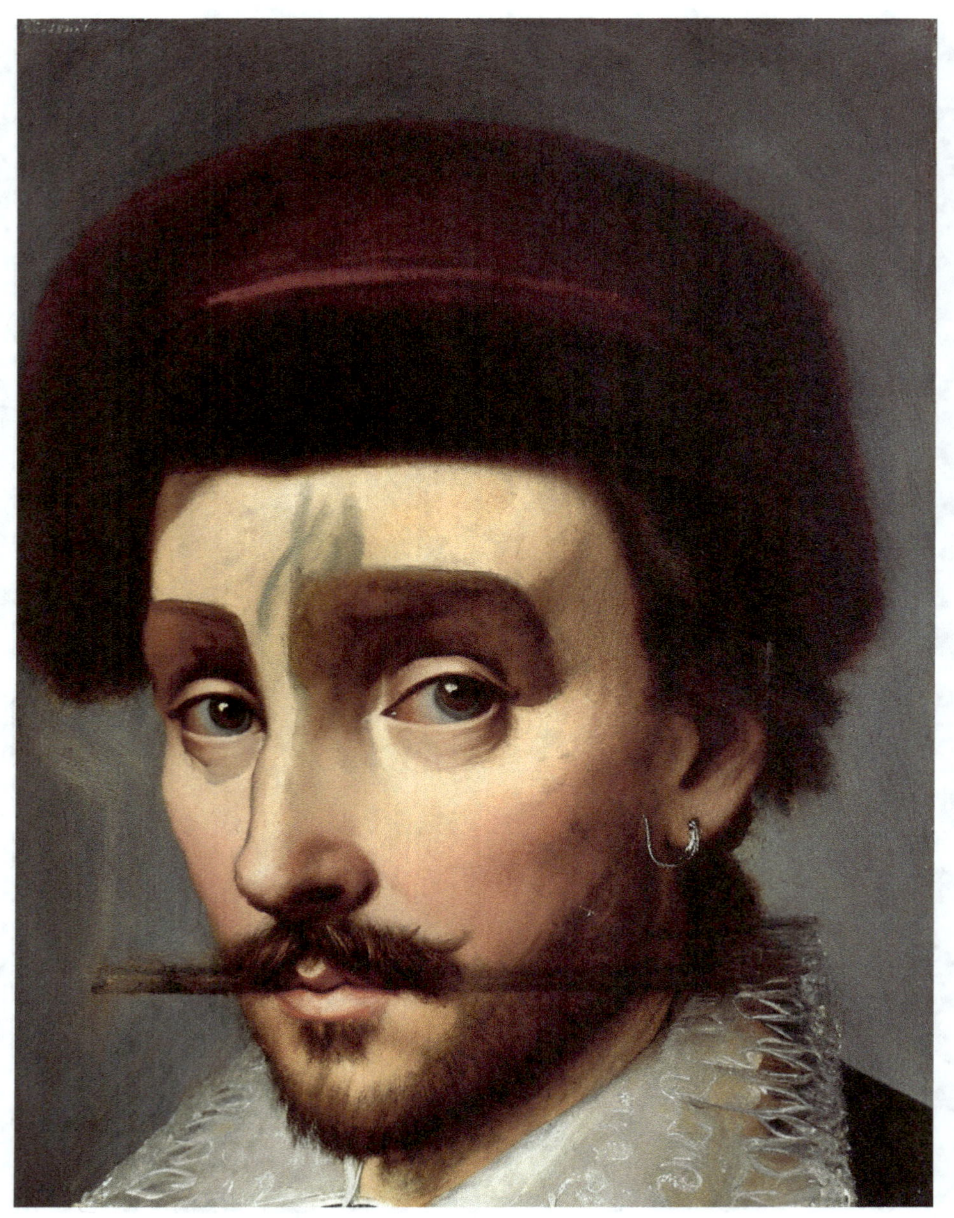

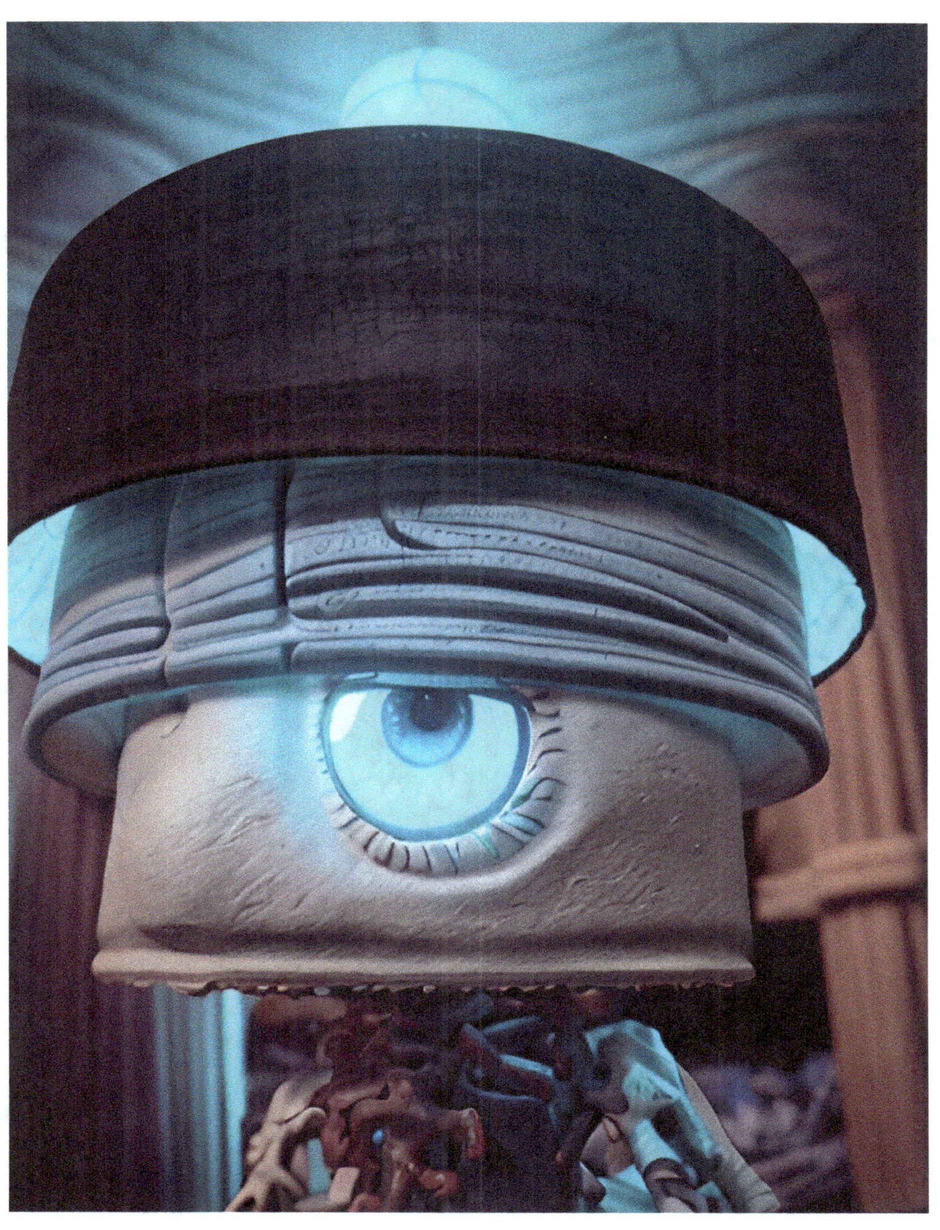

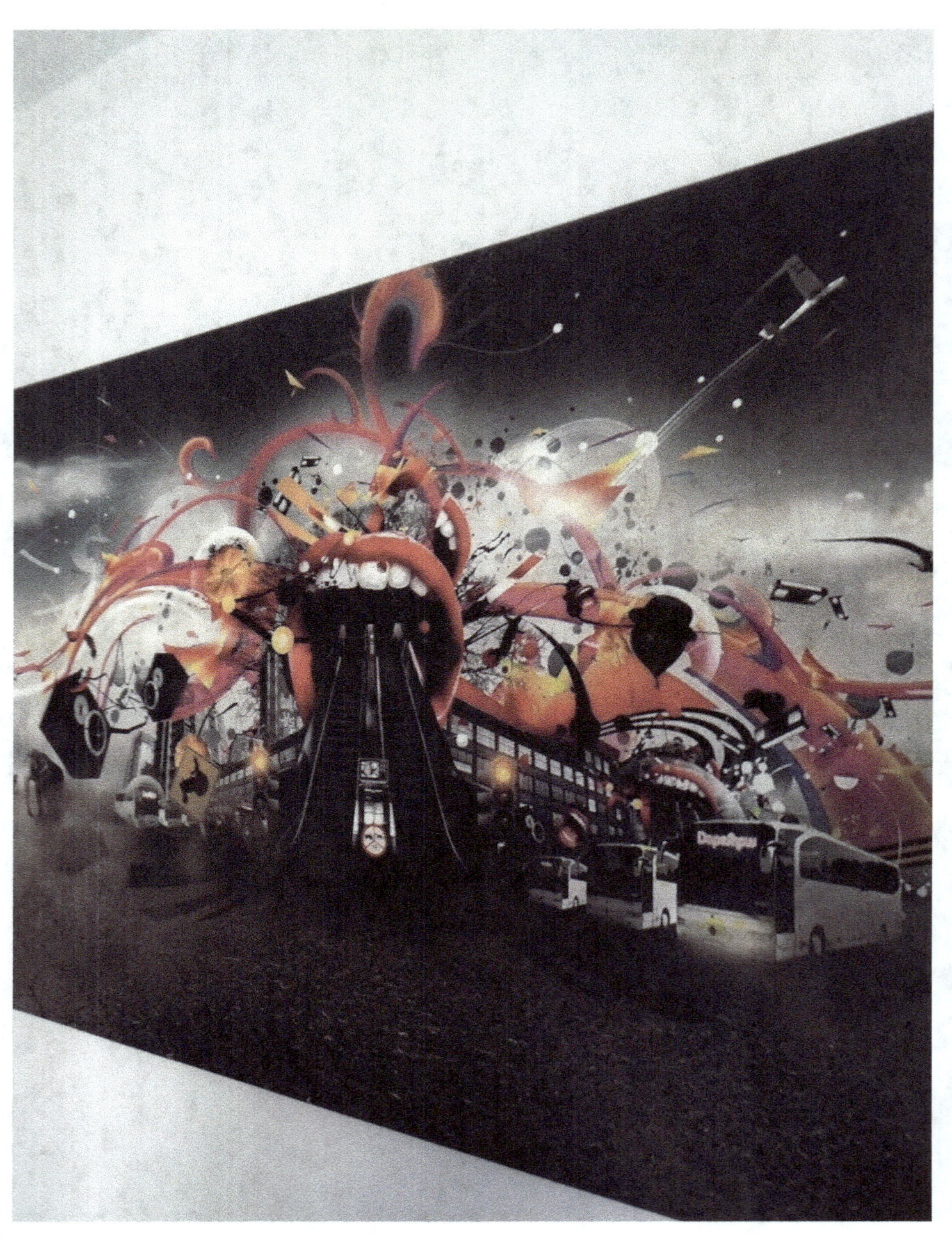

Wall art print

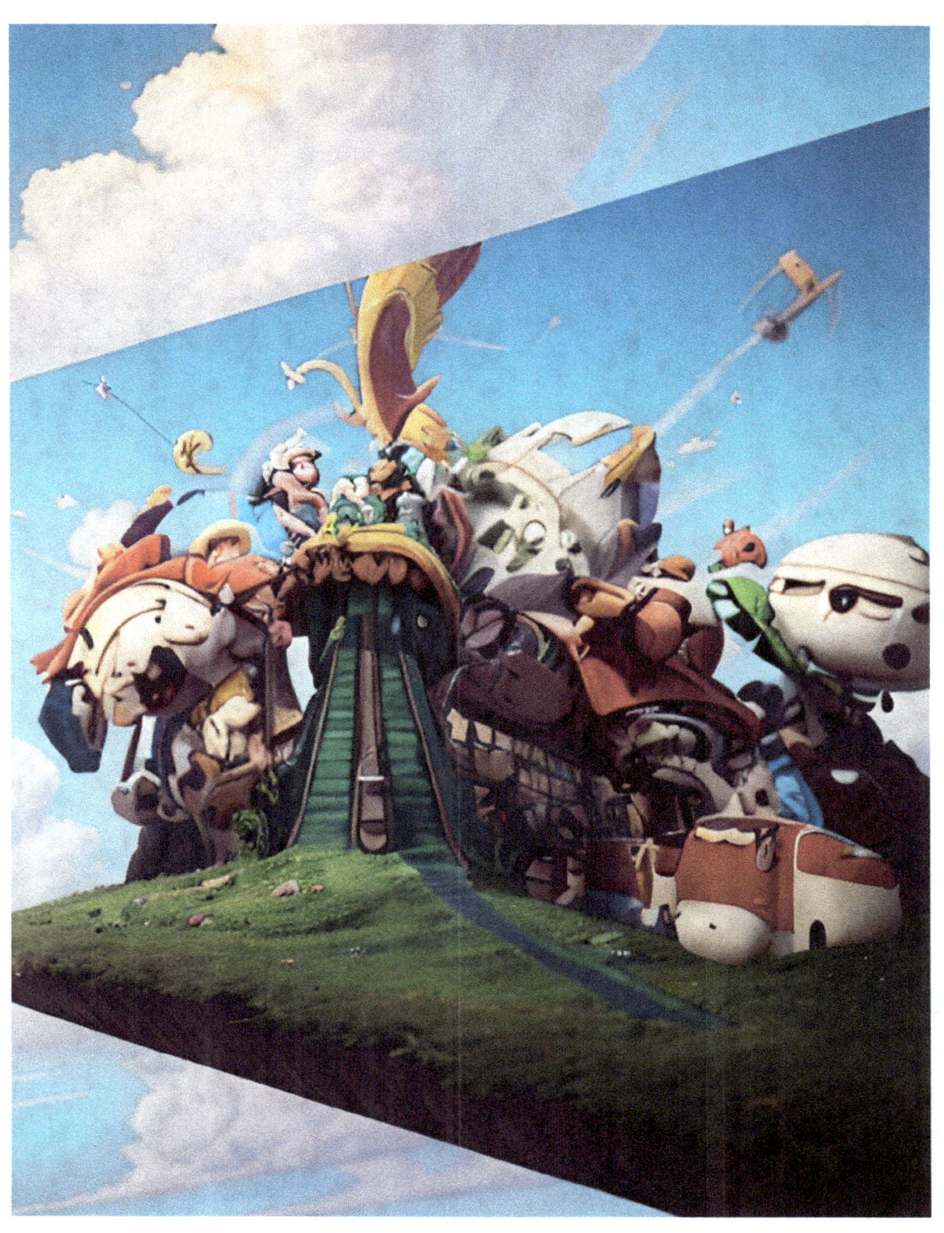

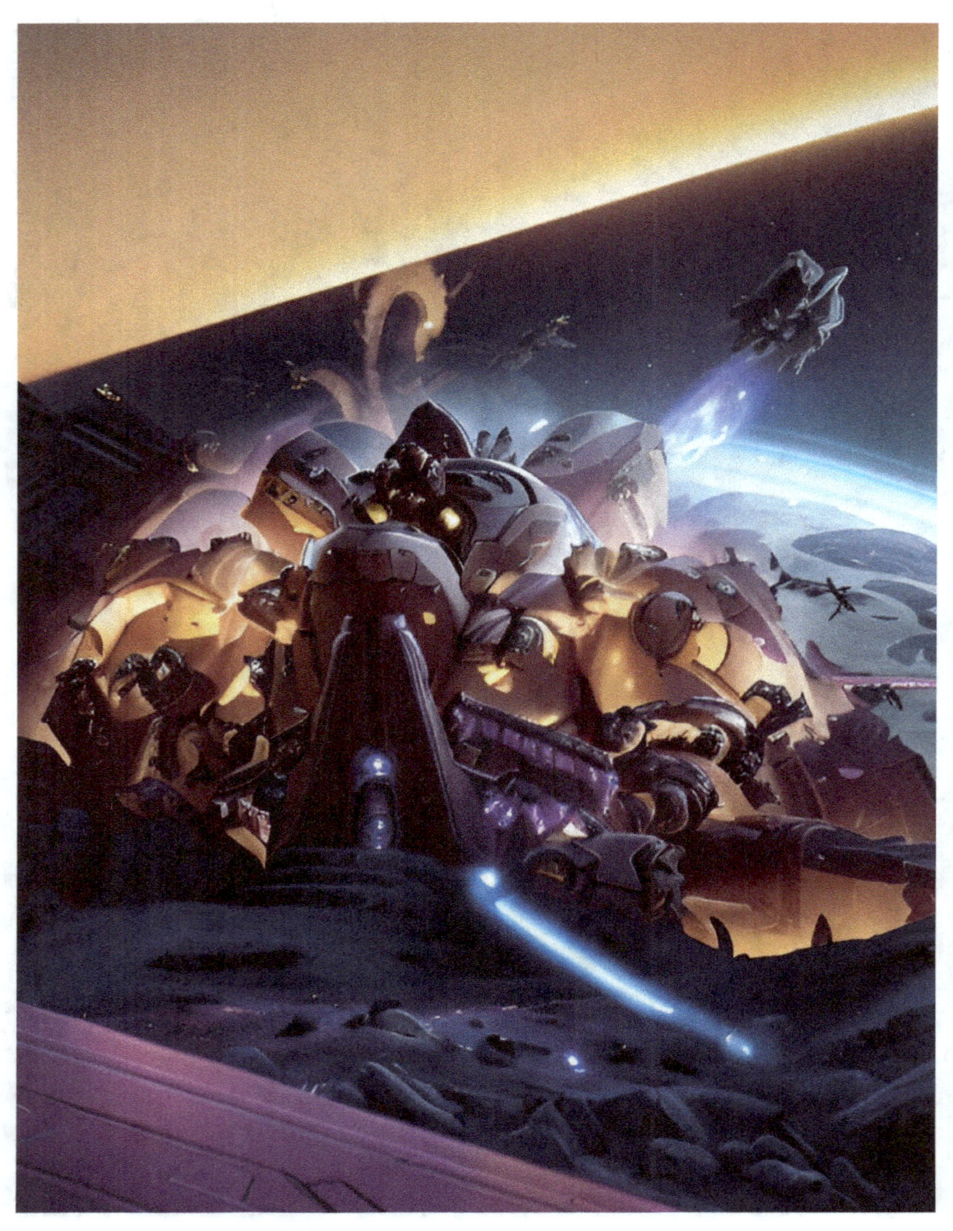

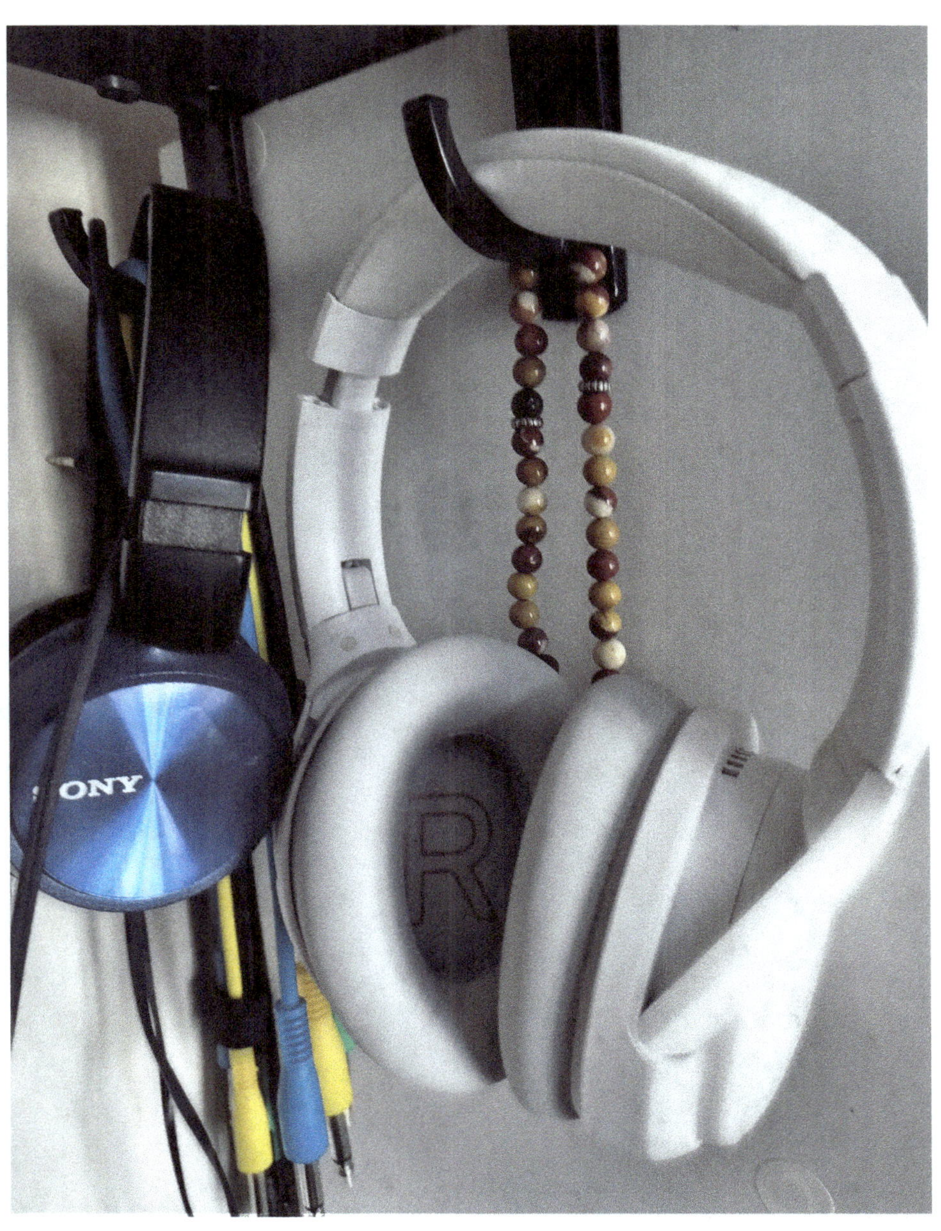

Headphones 83

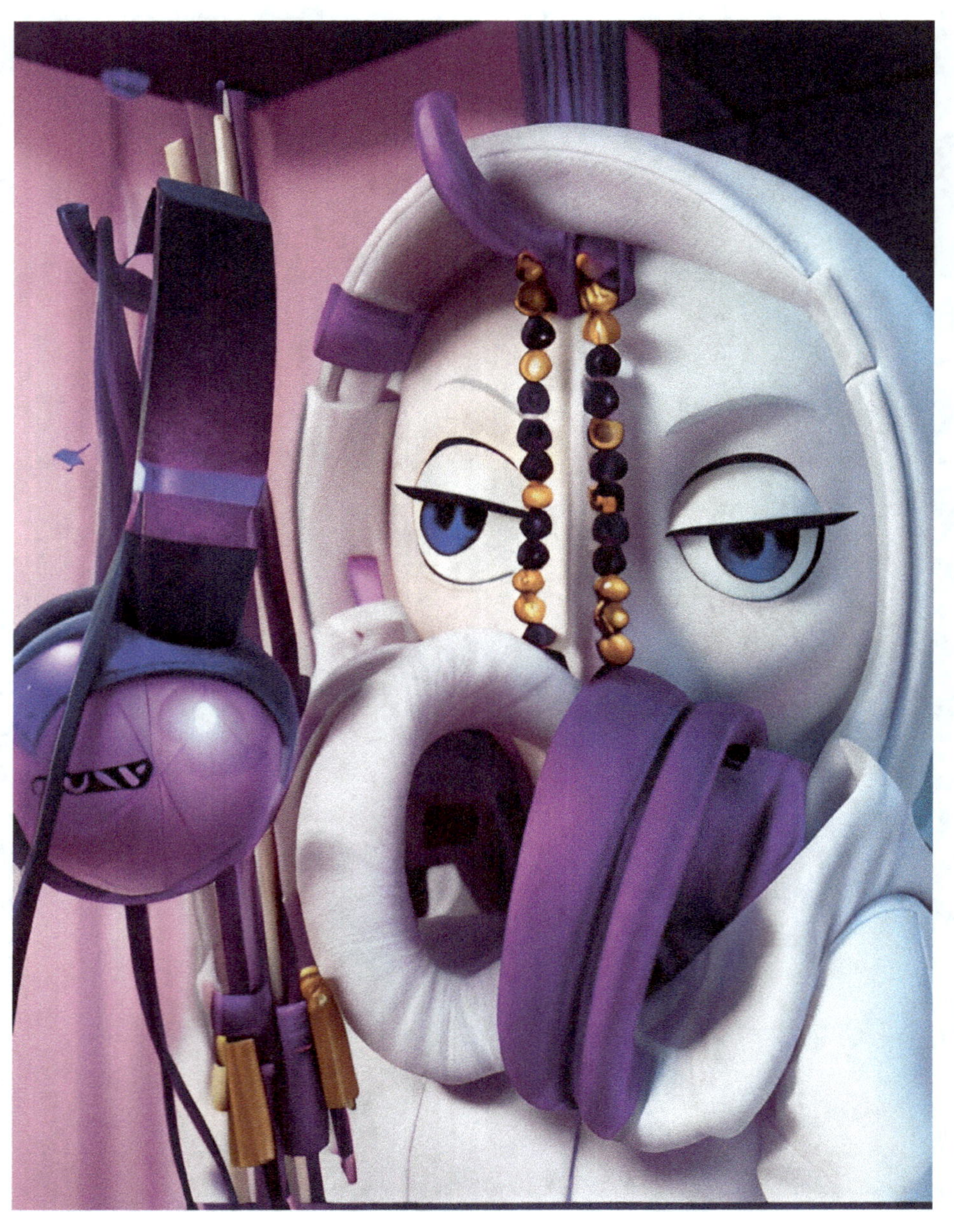

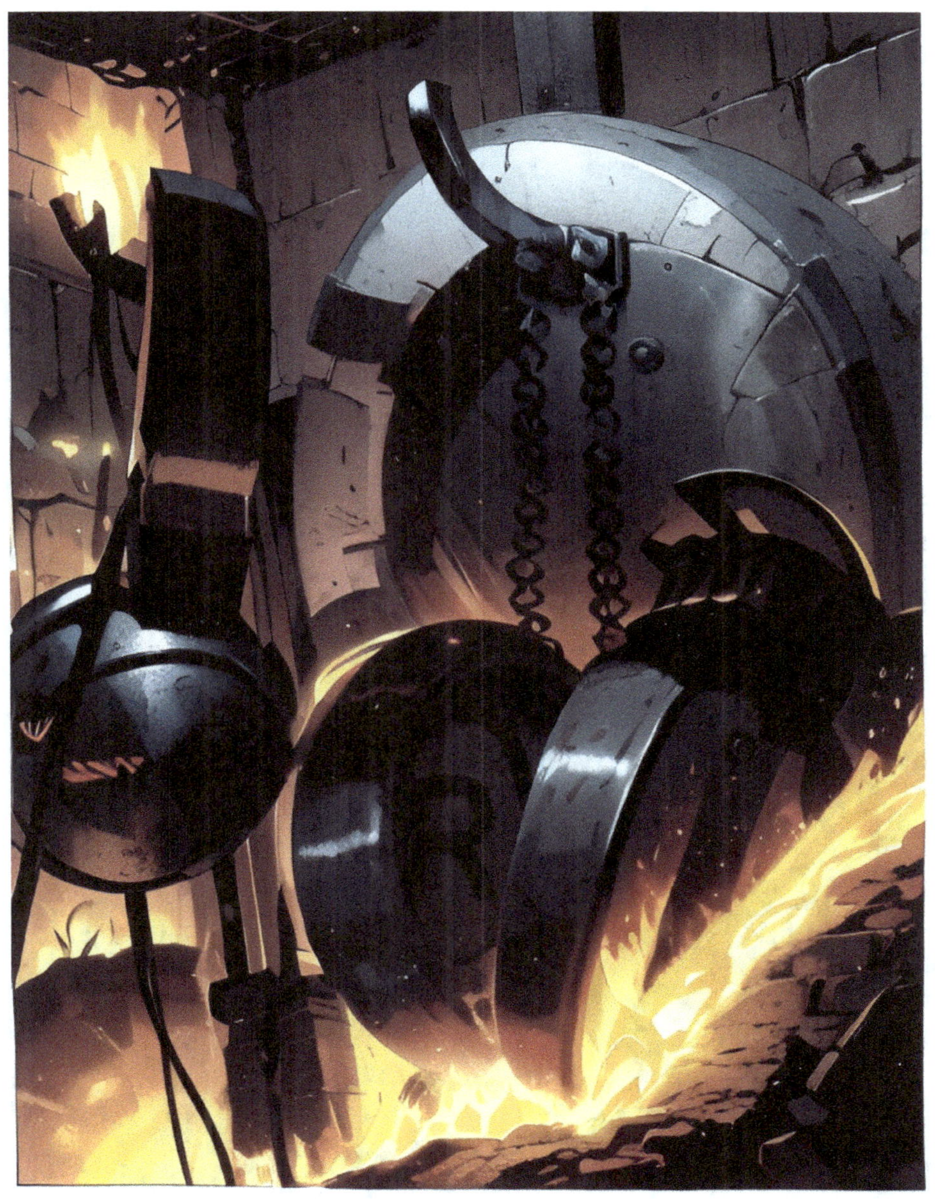

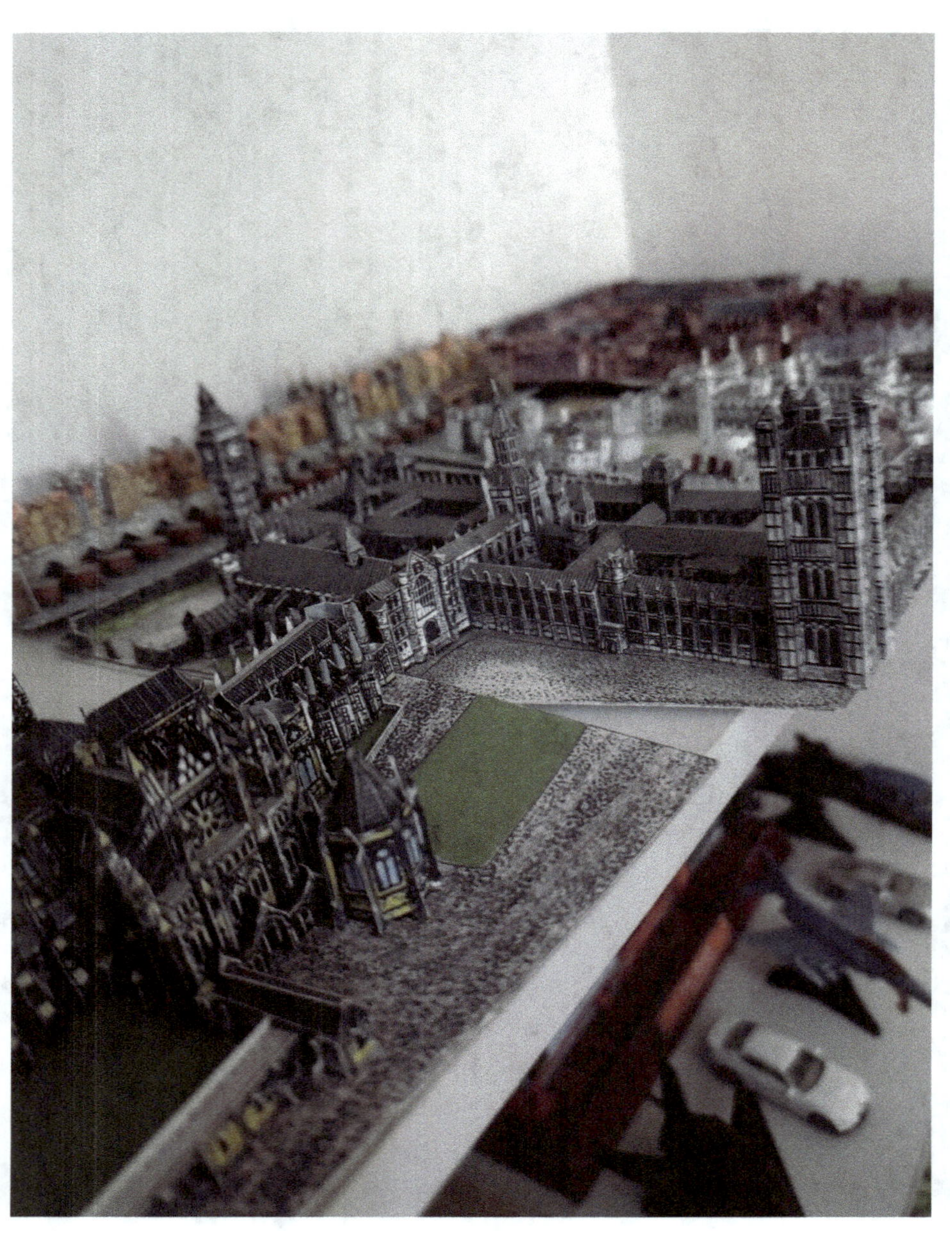

London card models

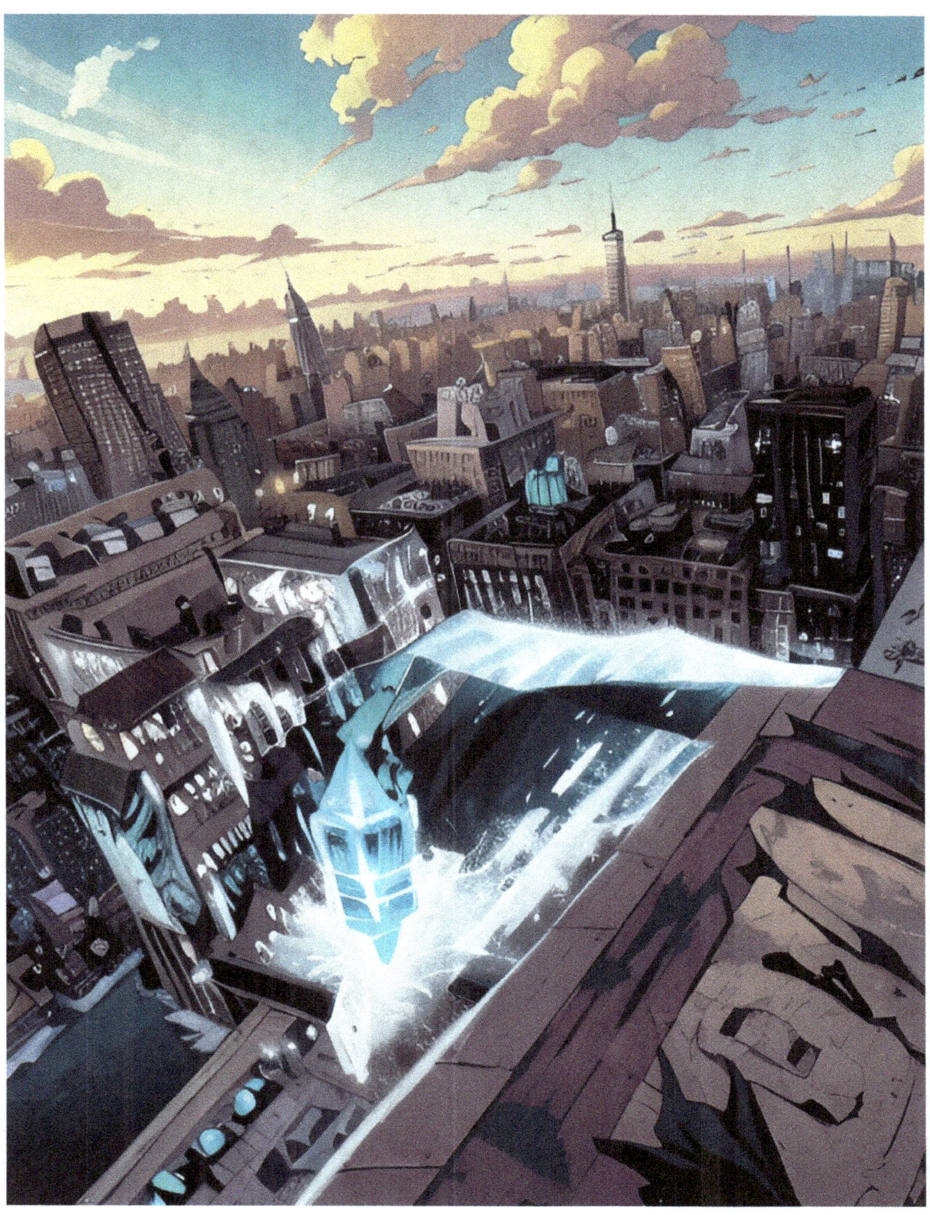

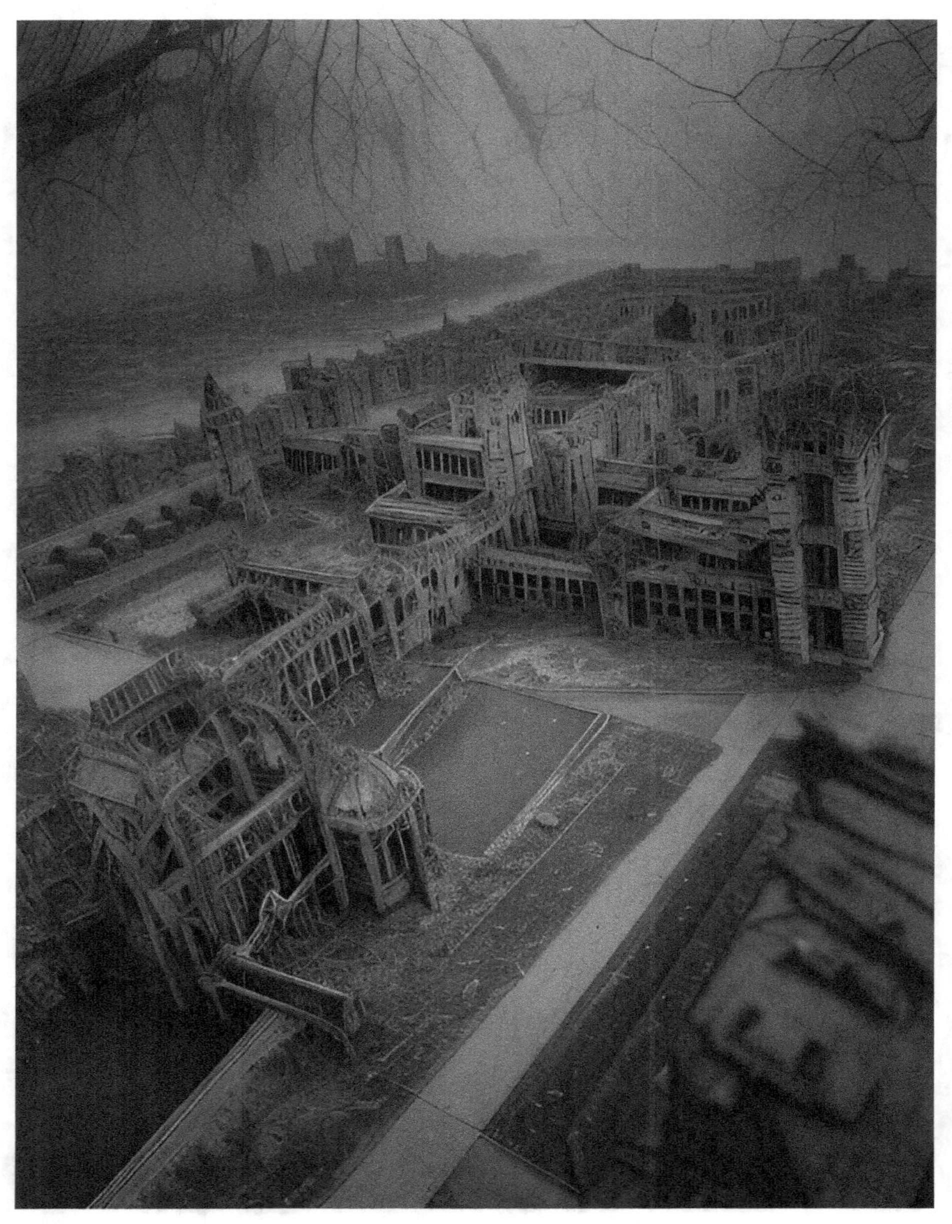

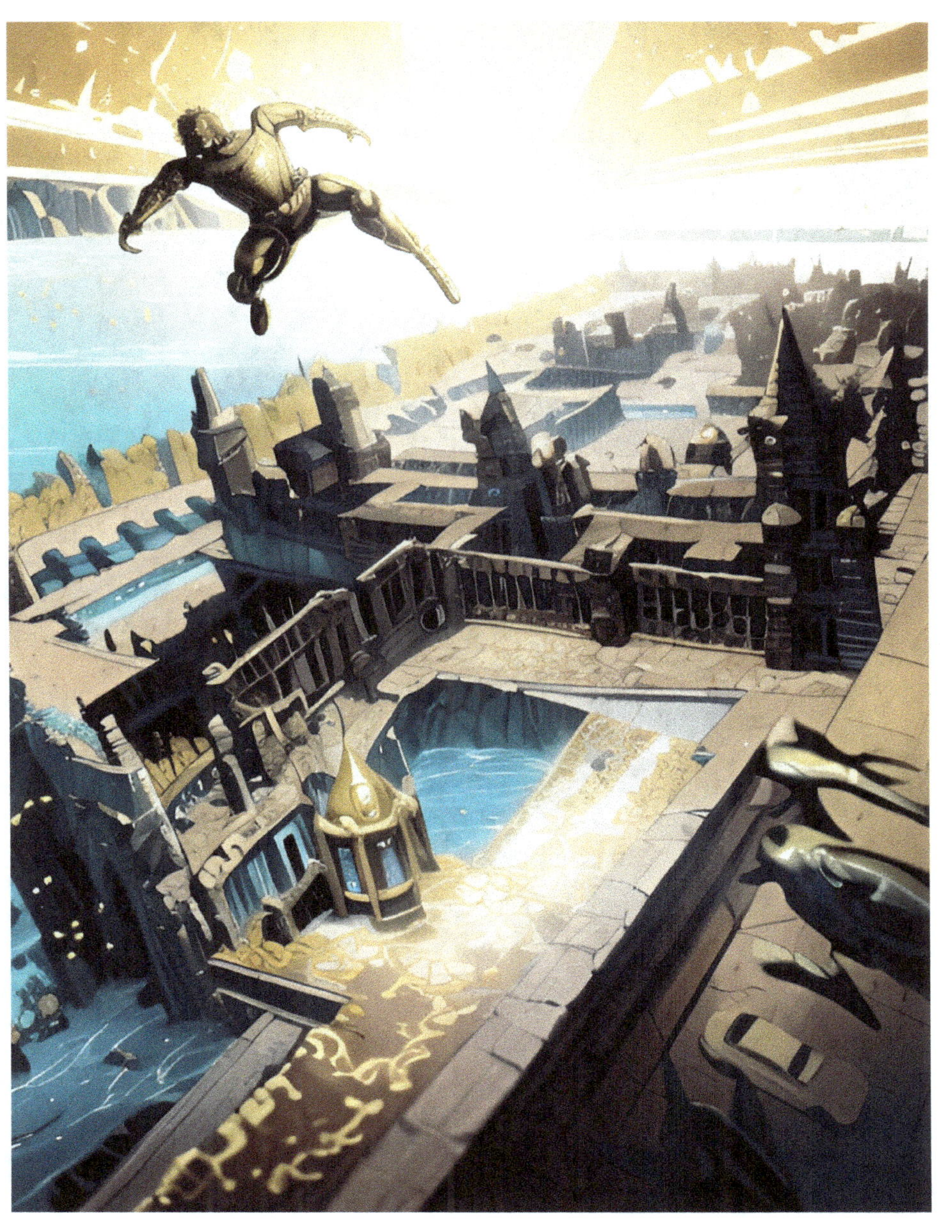

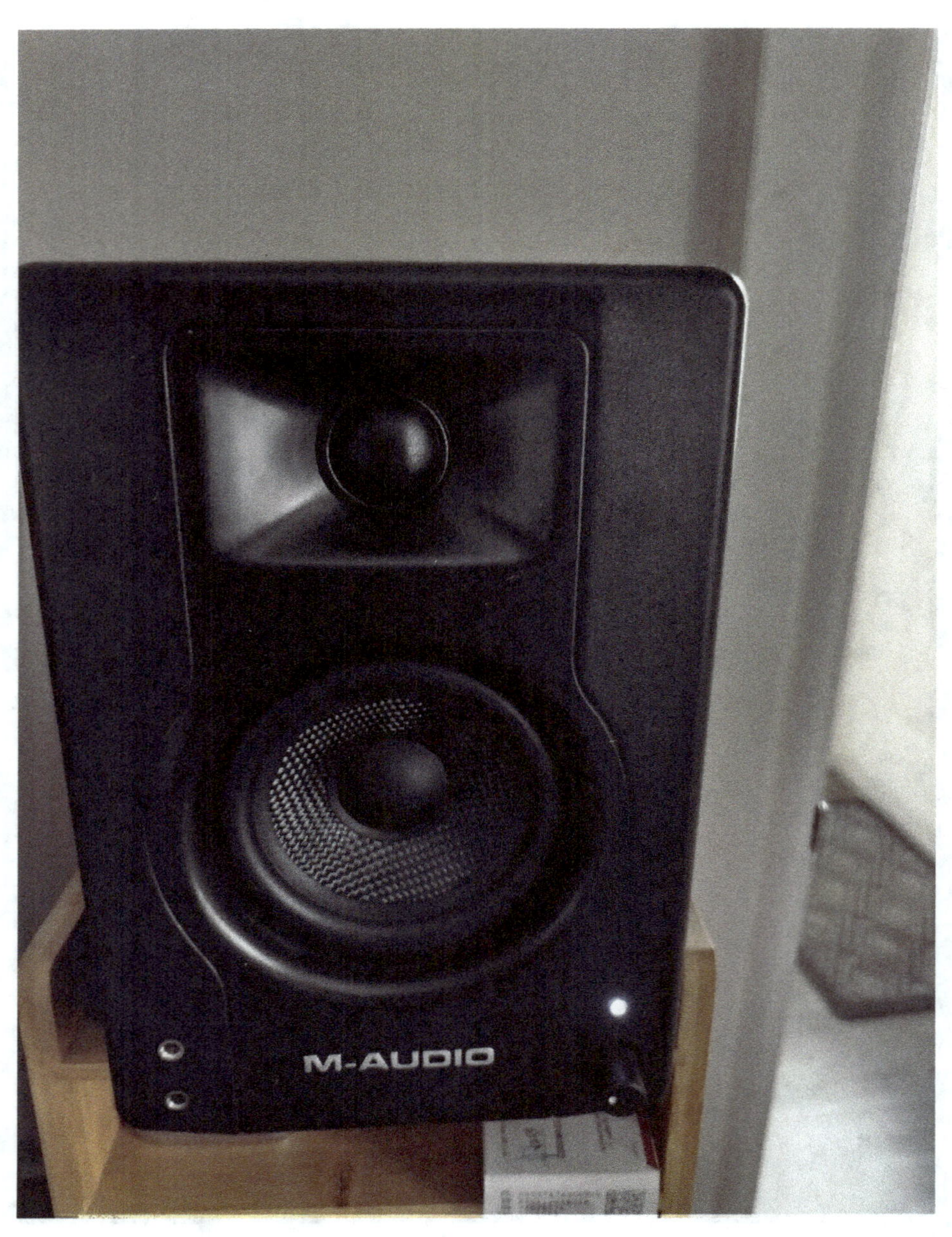

Speaker

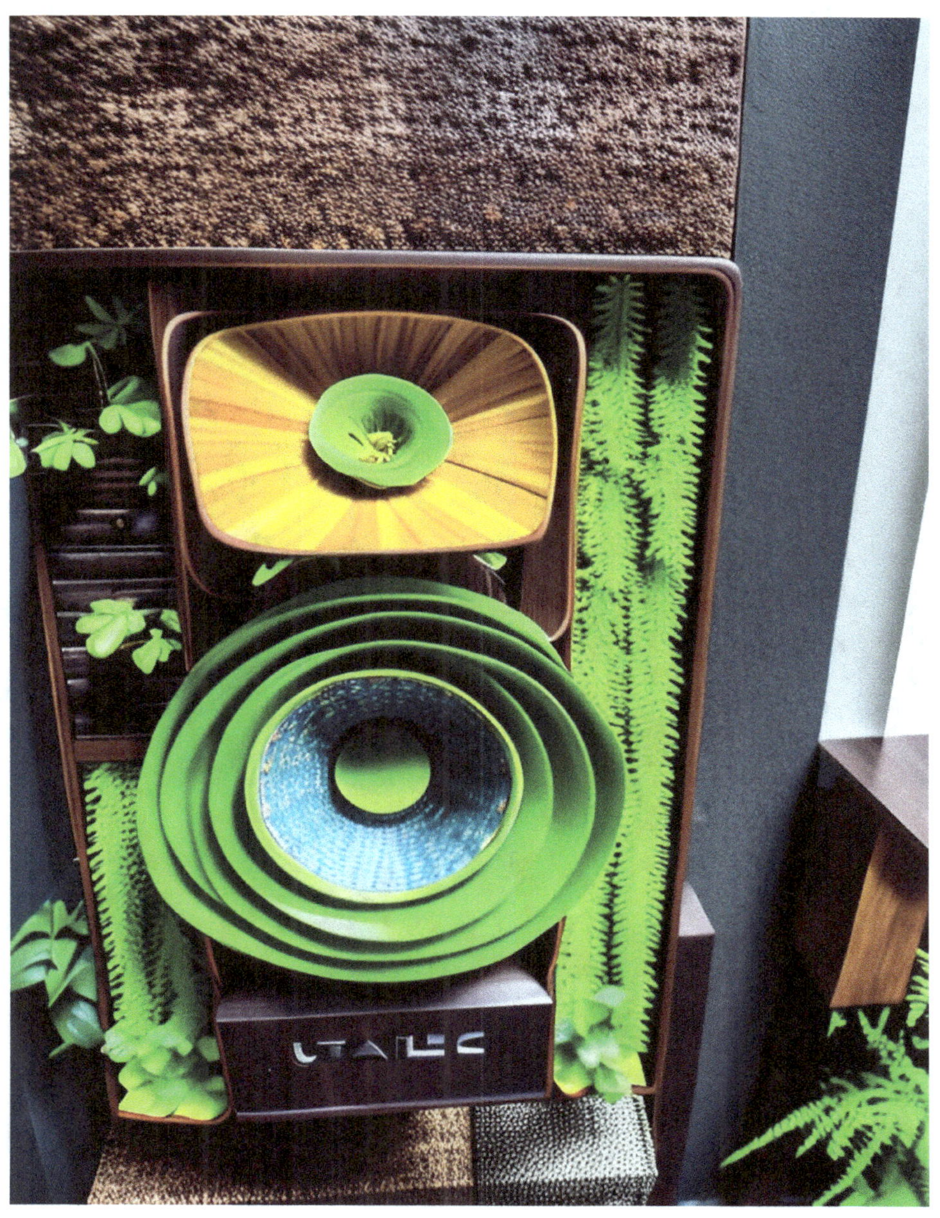

UTAILC

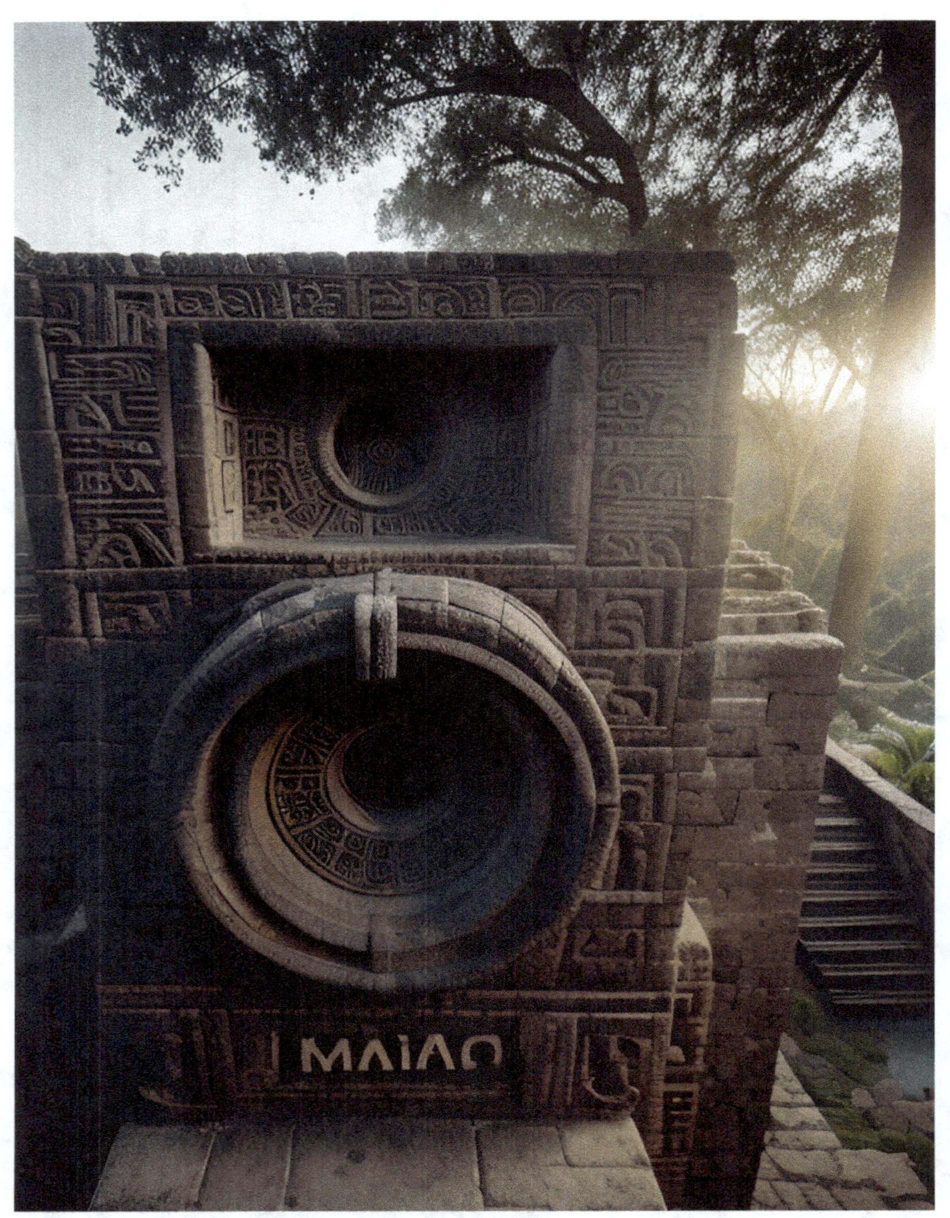

MAIAO

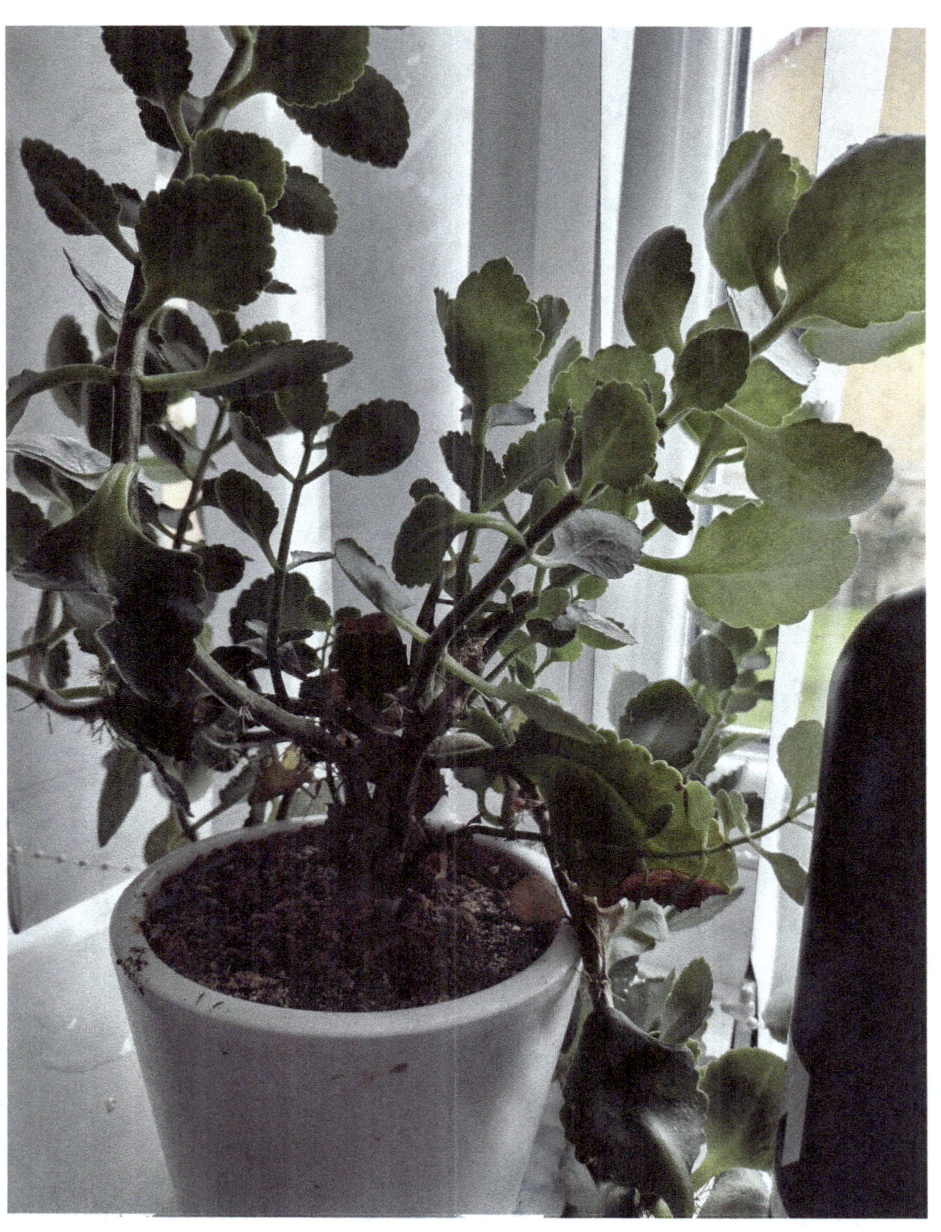

Kitchen plant

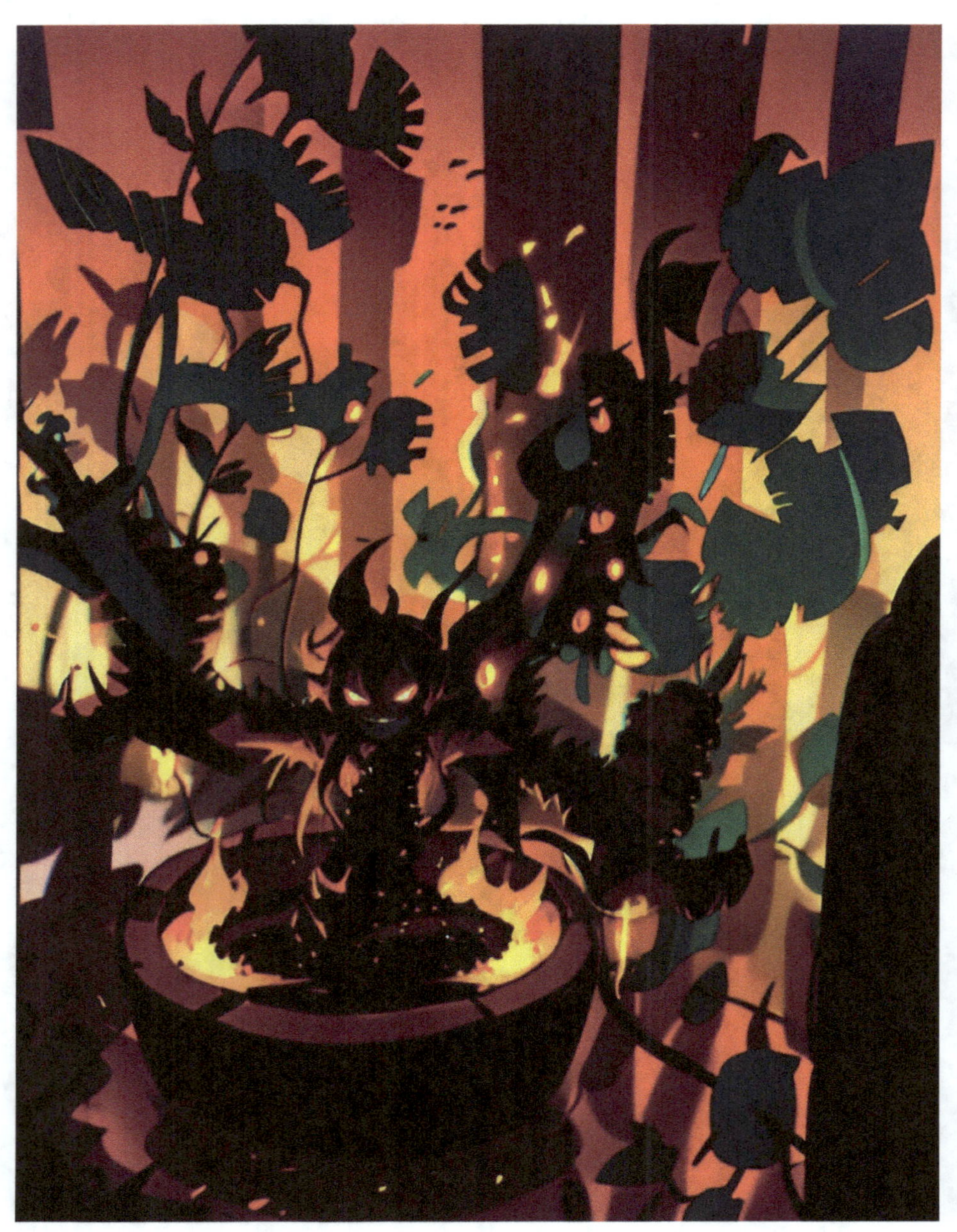

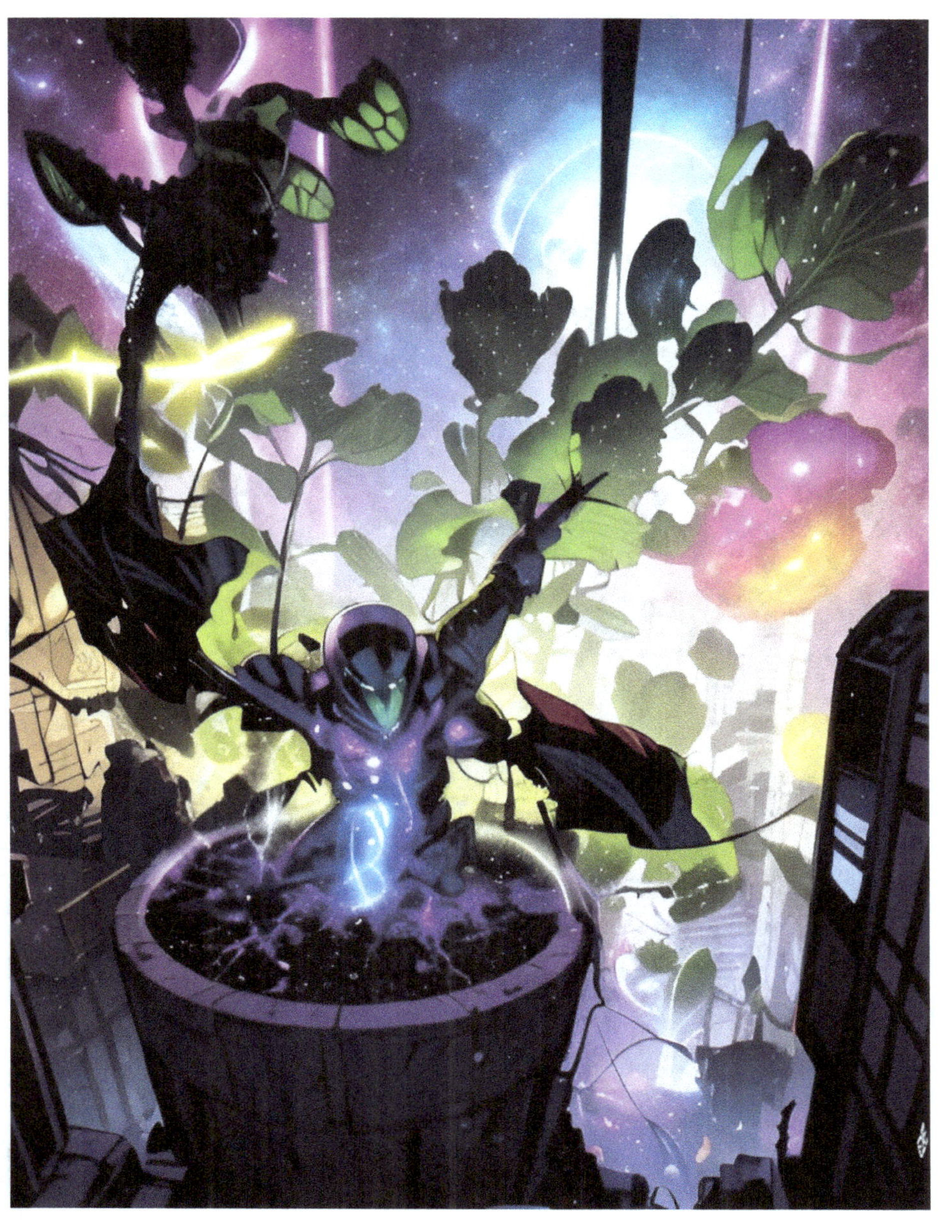

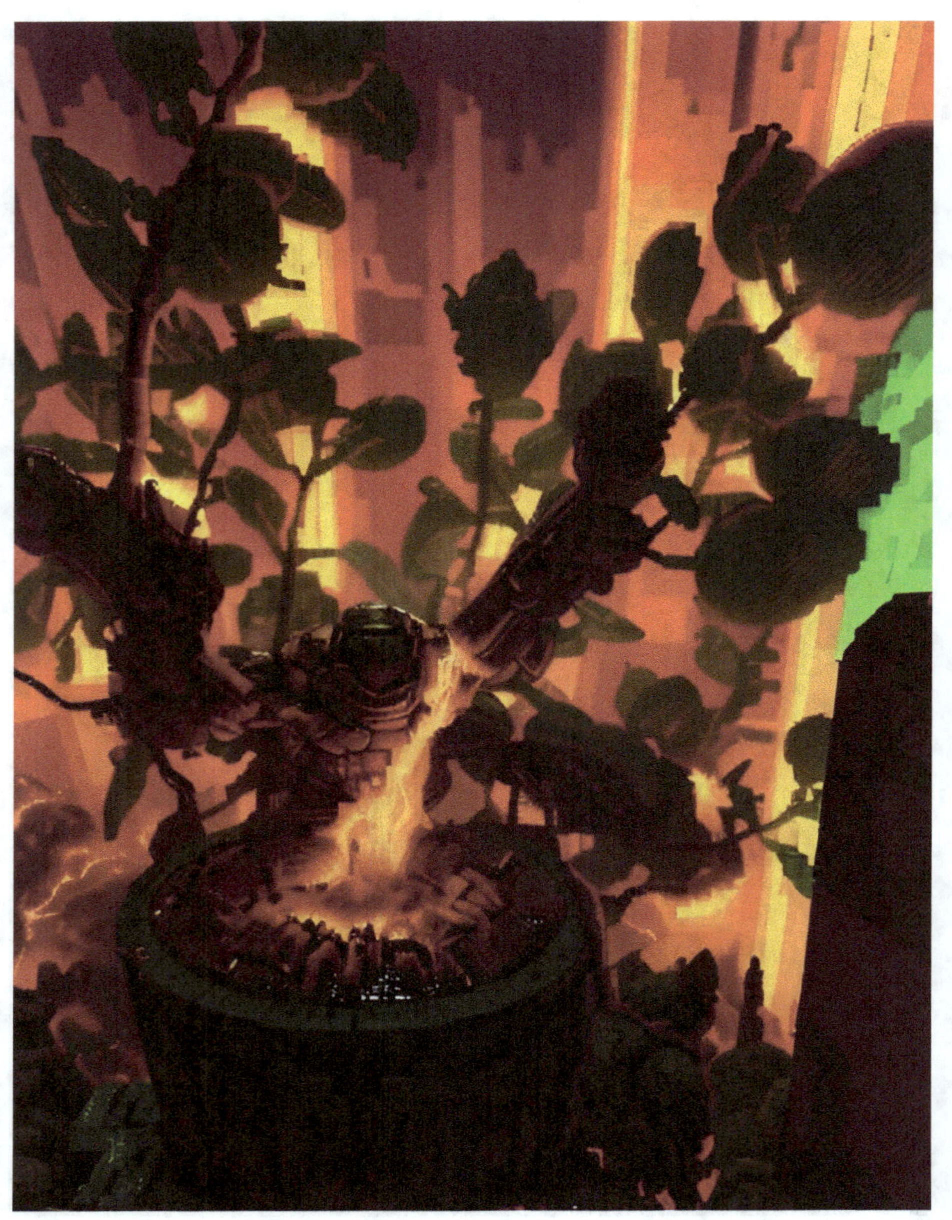

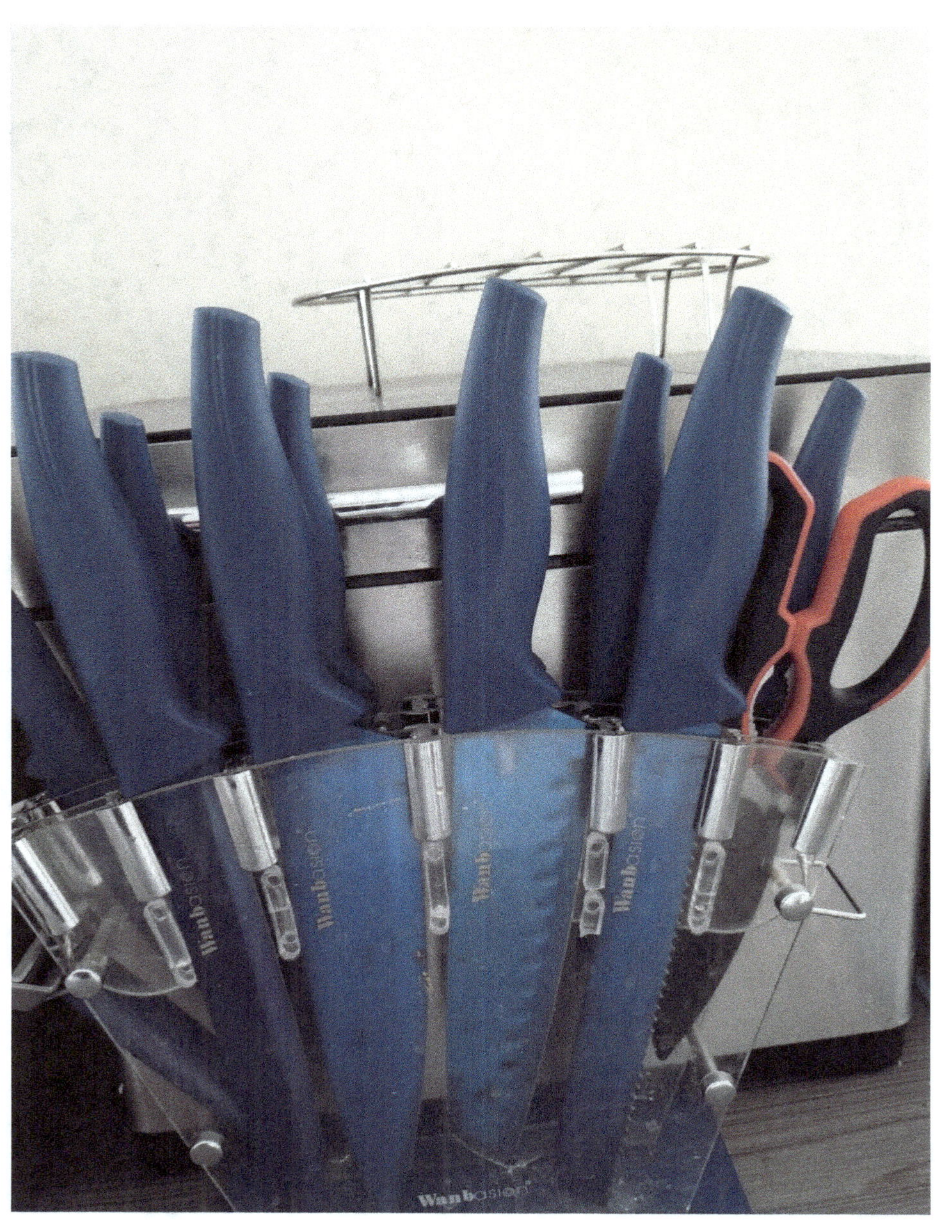

Knives

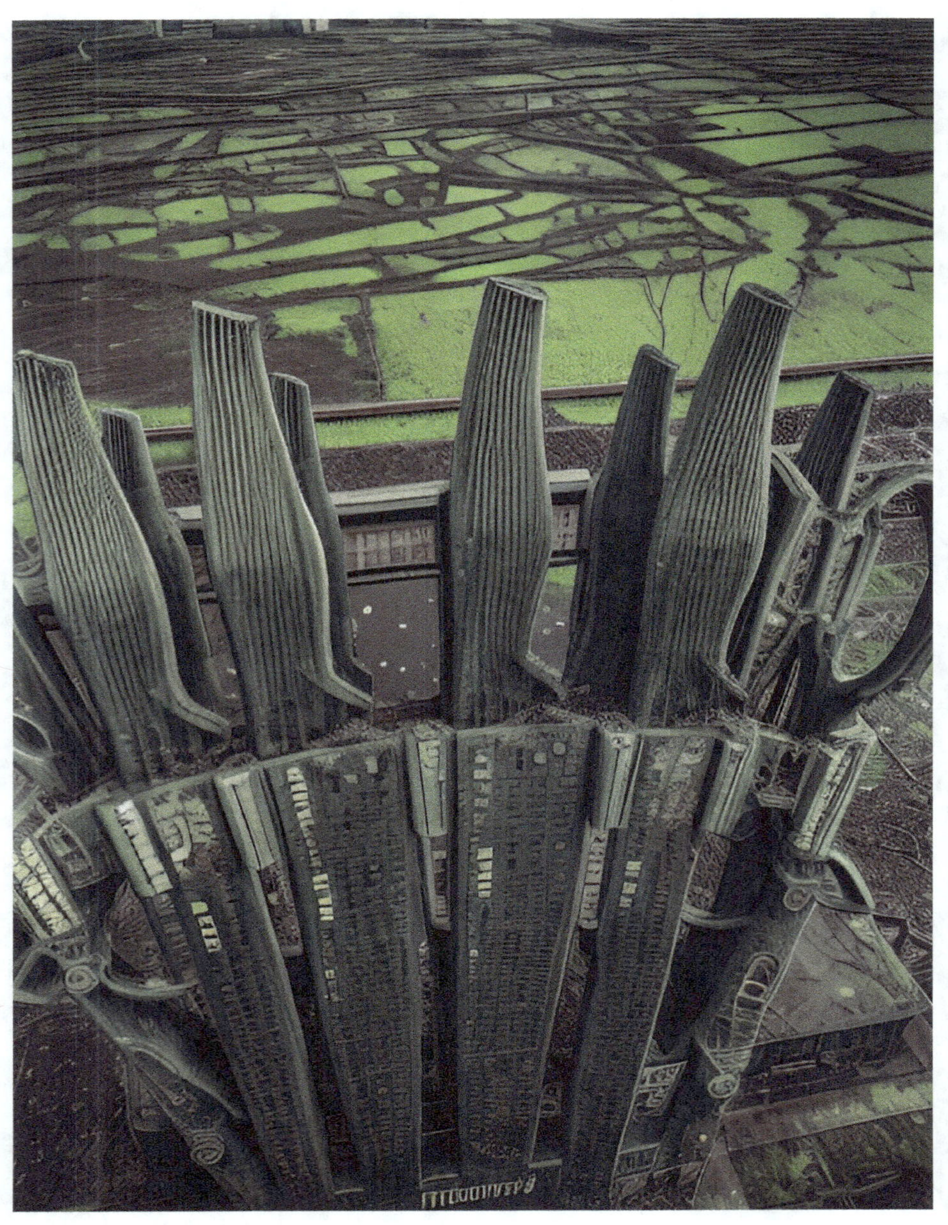

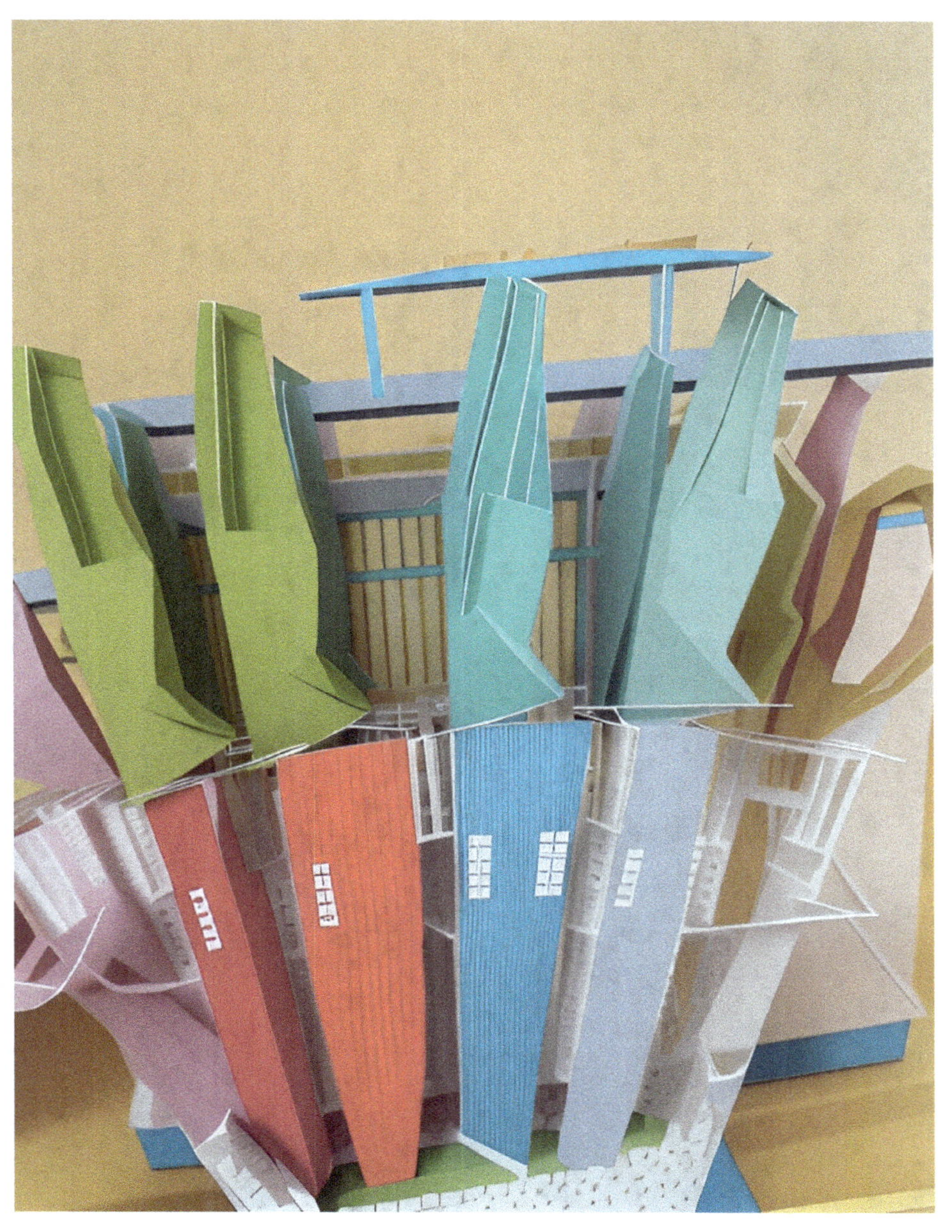

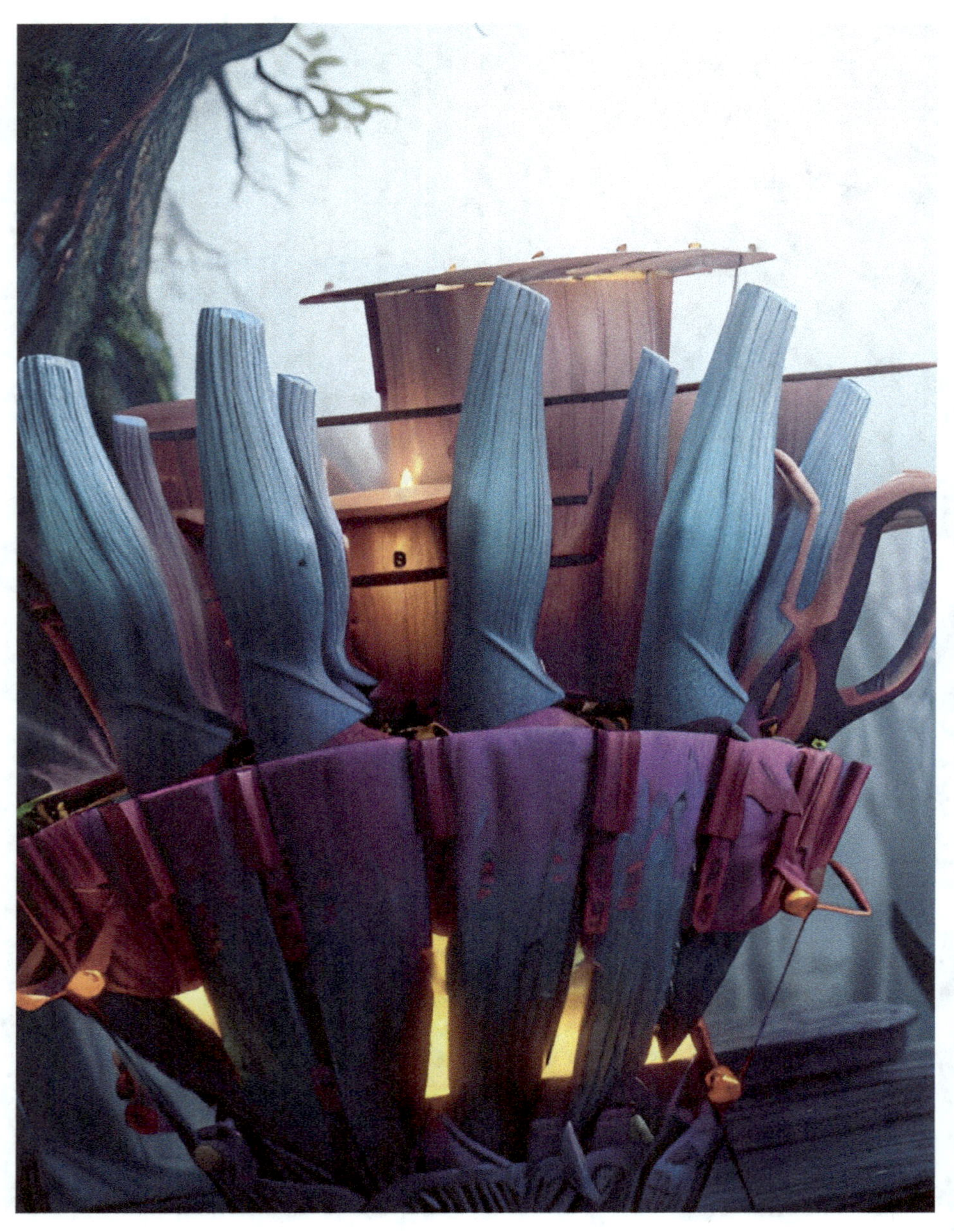

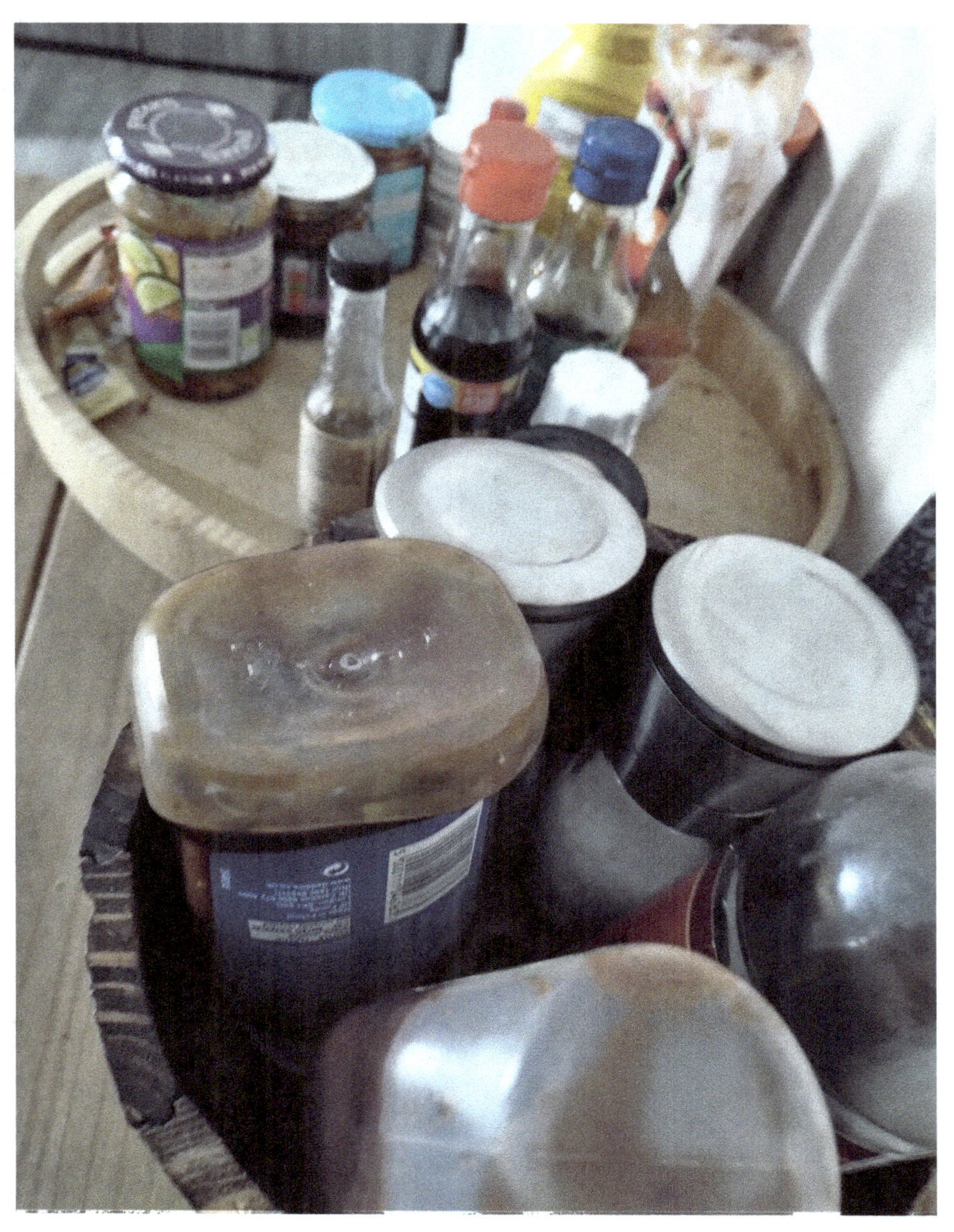

Sauces

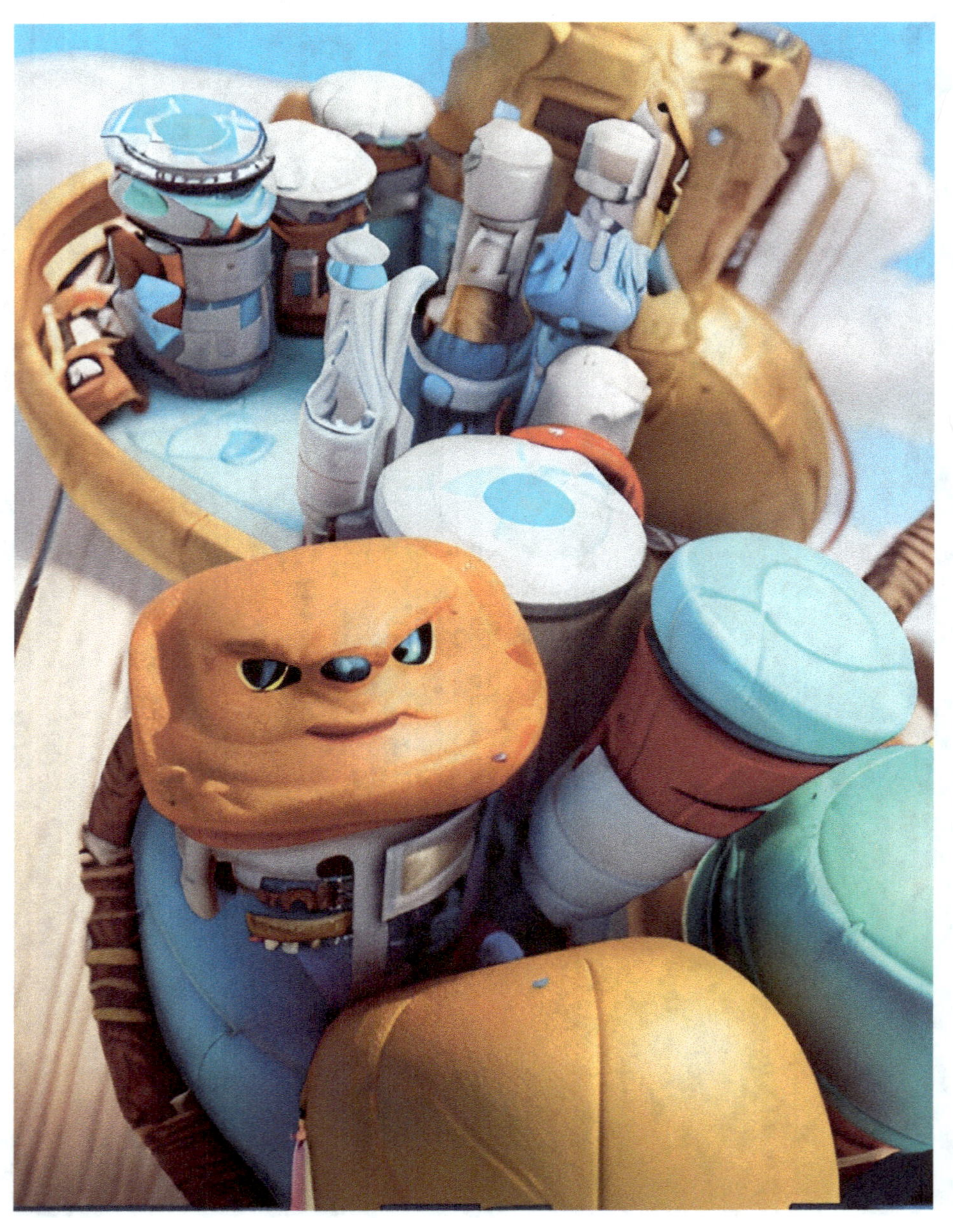

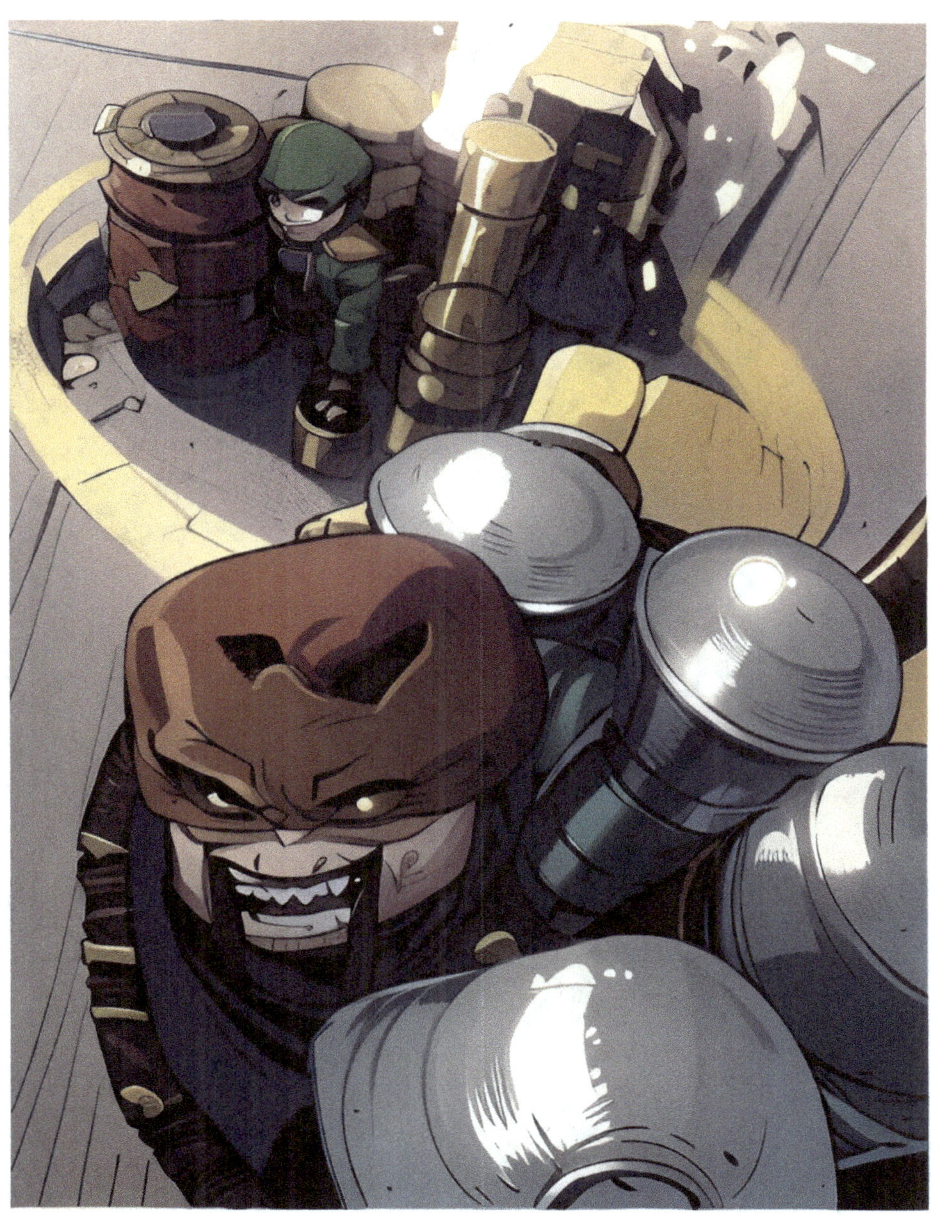

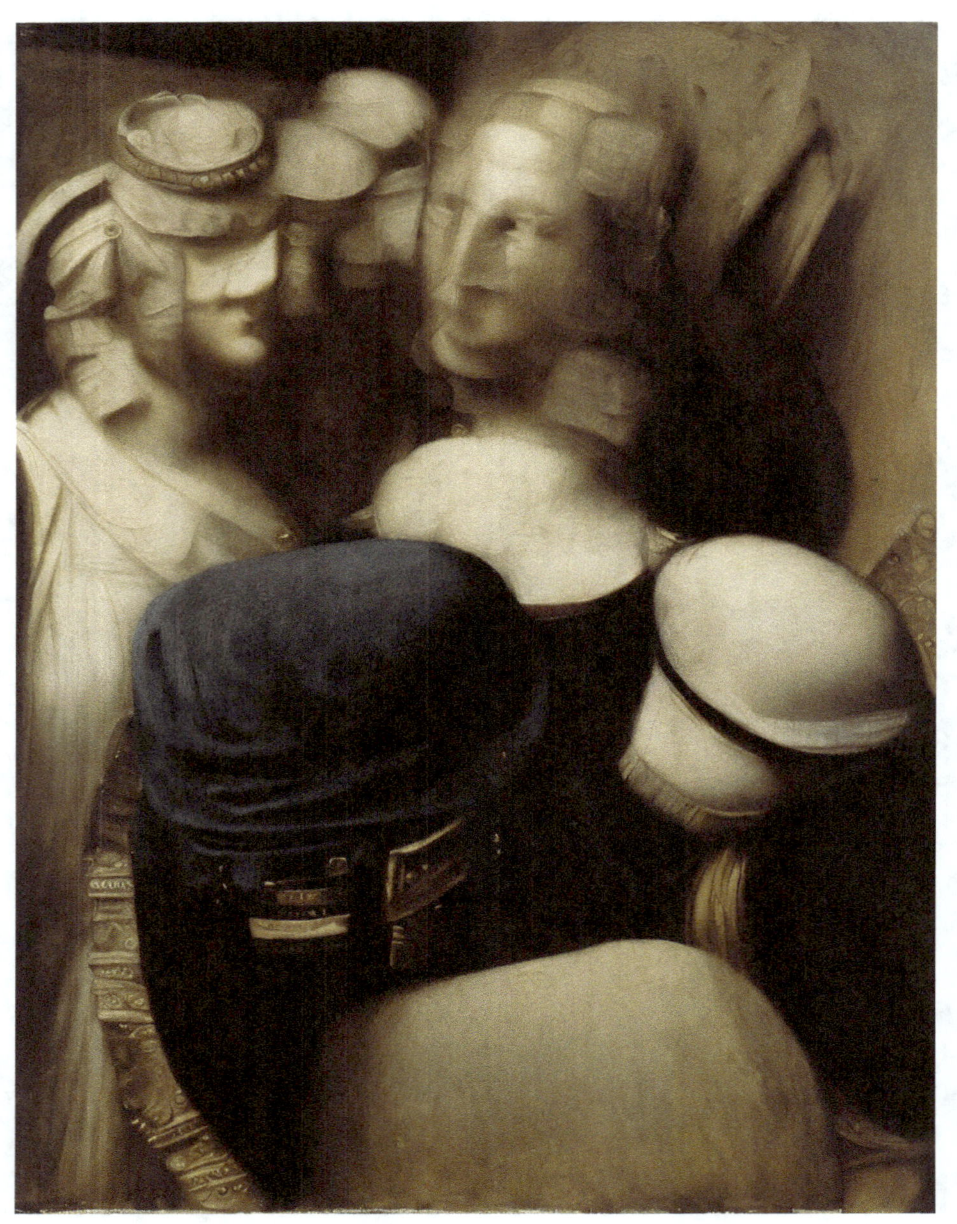

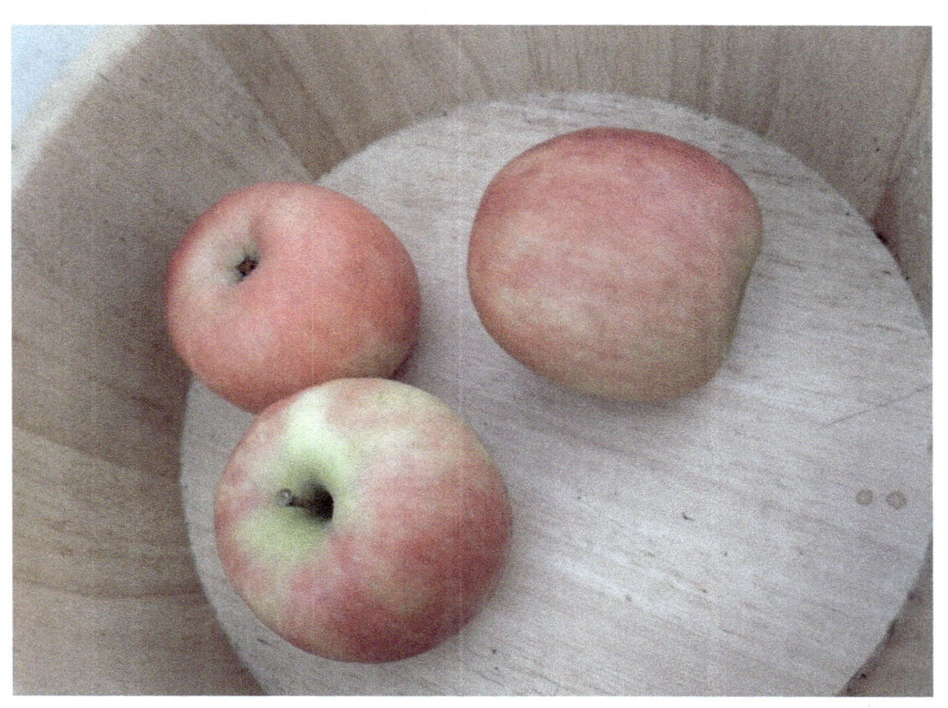

Apples

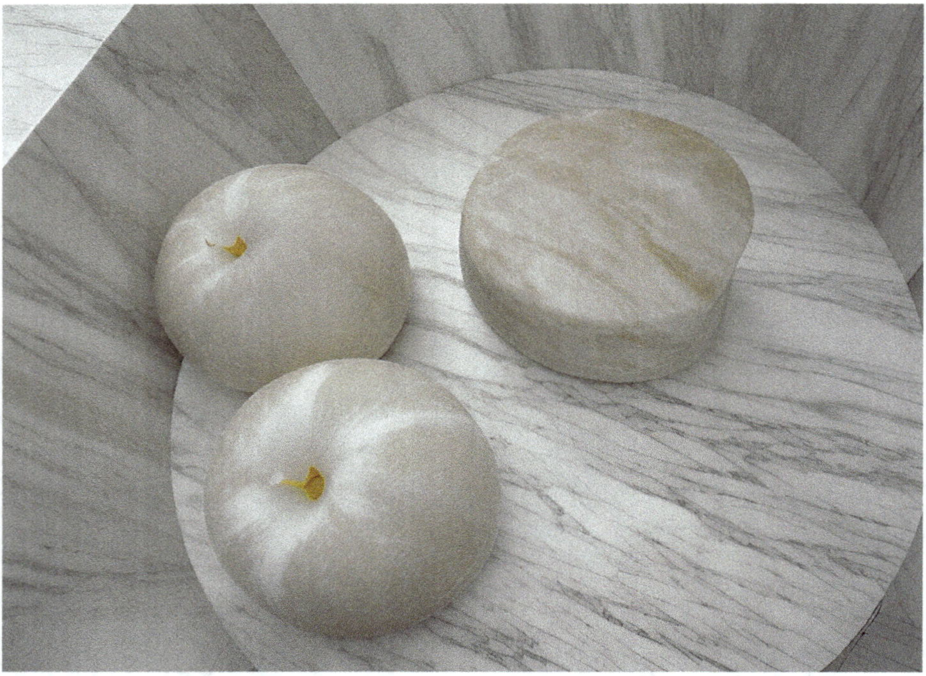

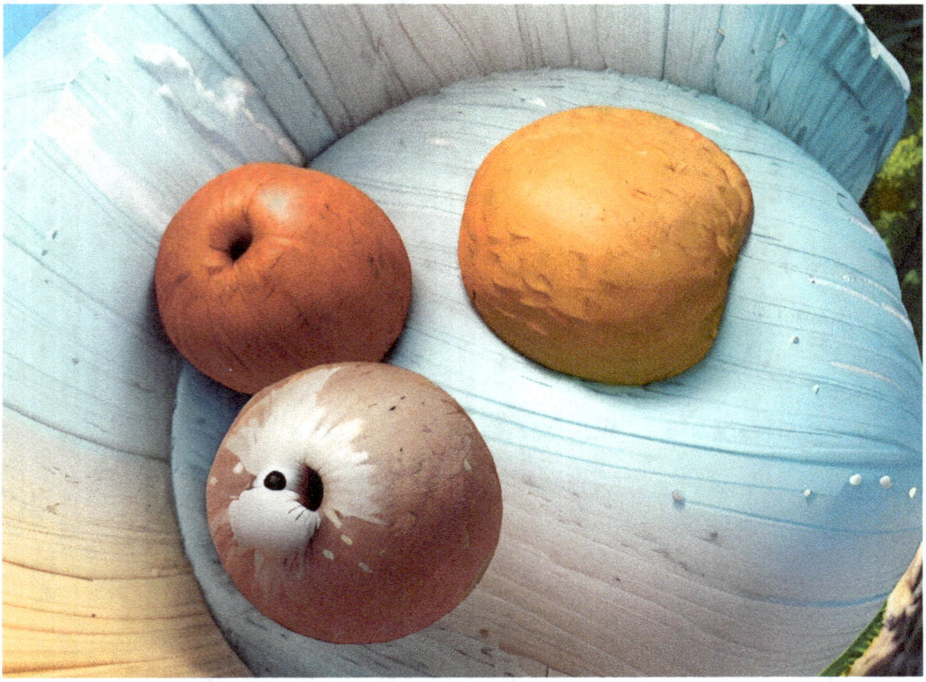

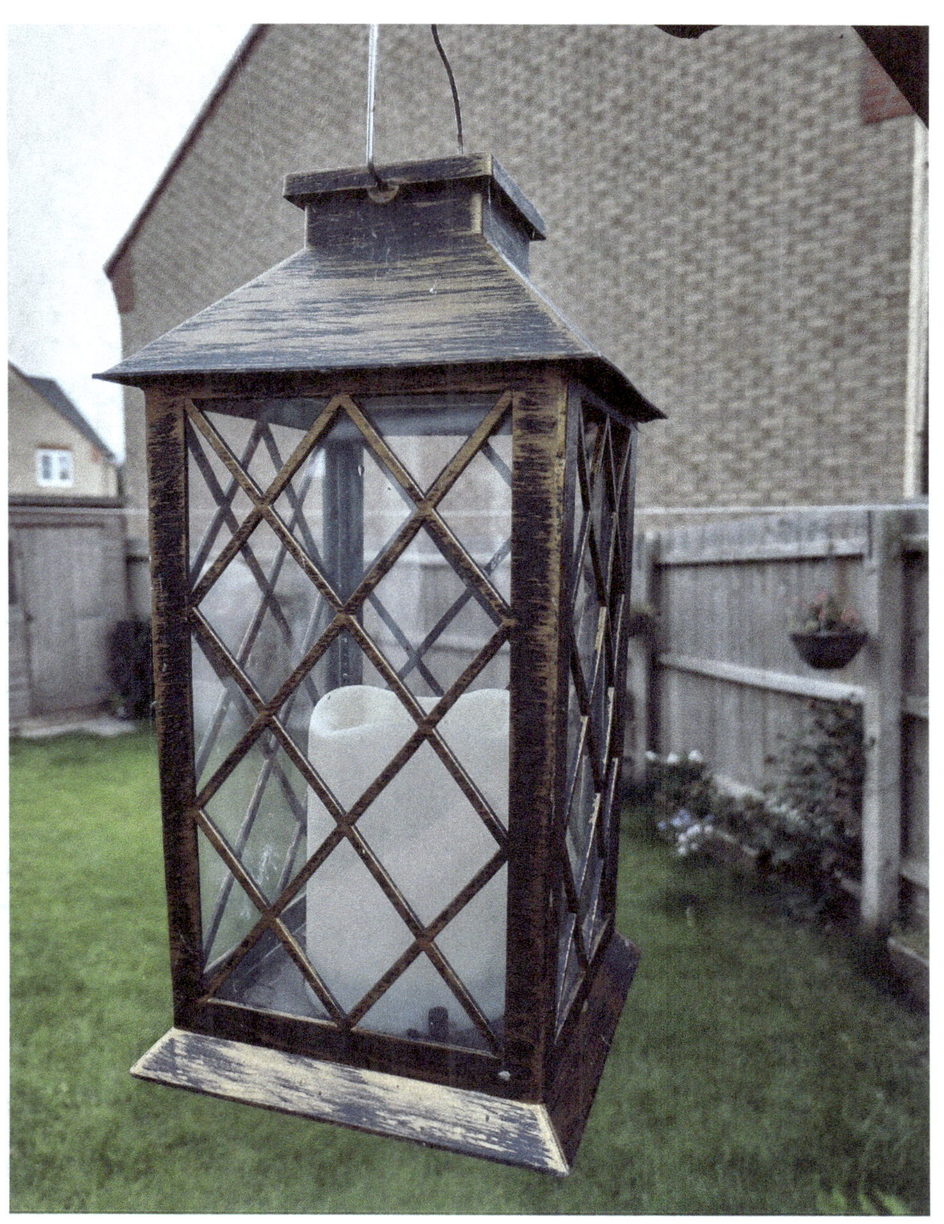

Lantern

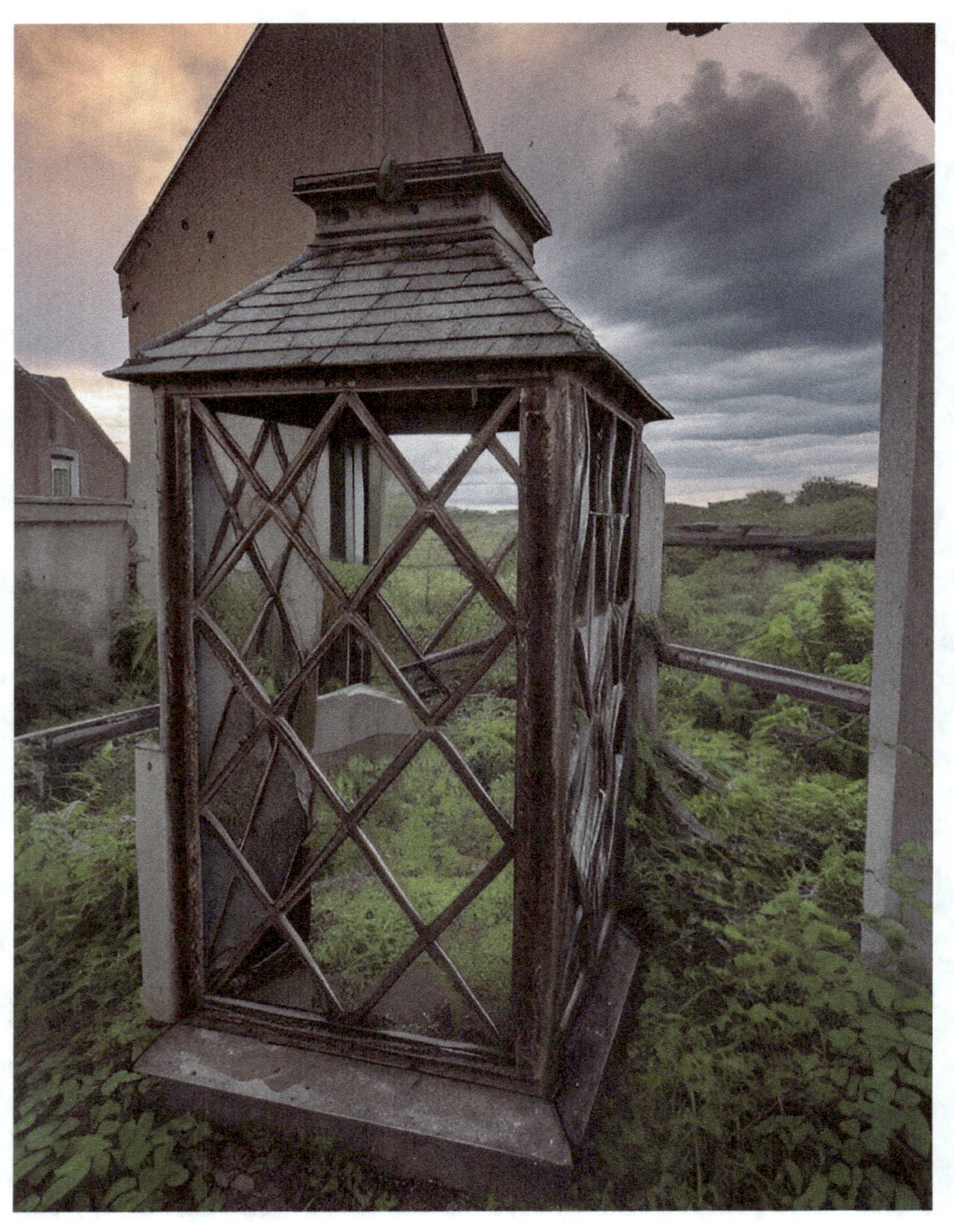

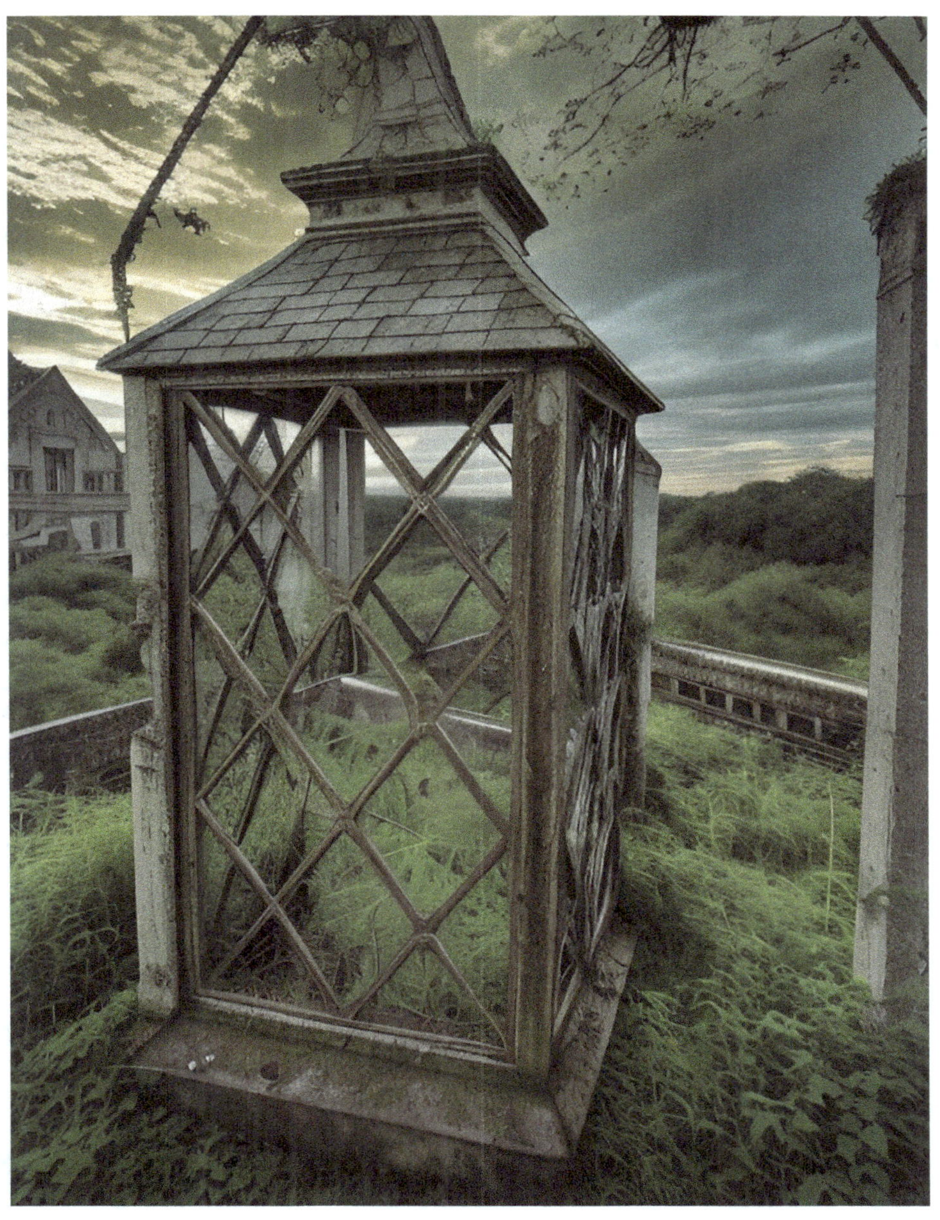

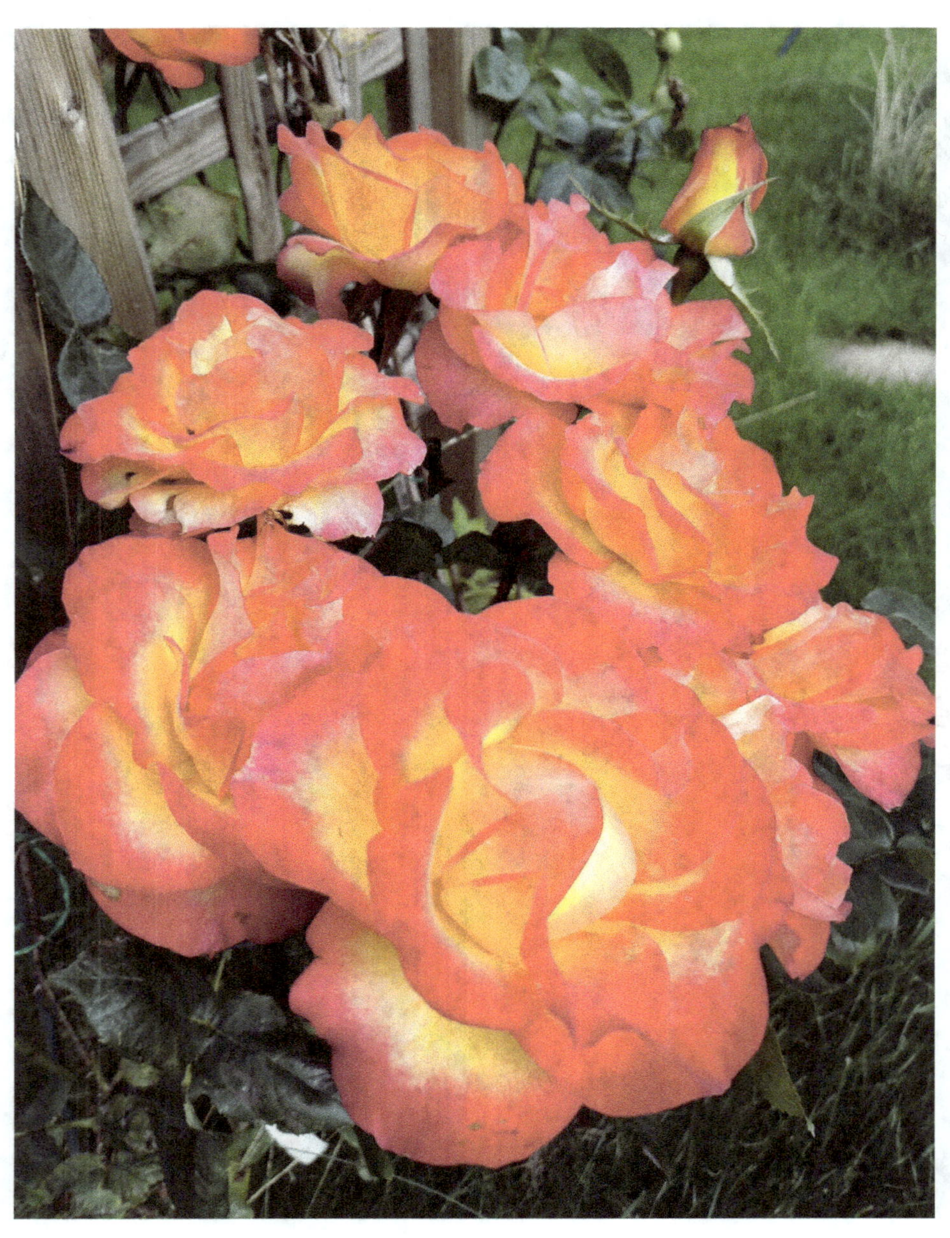

Roses

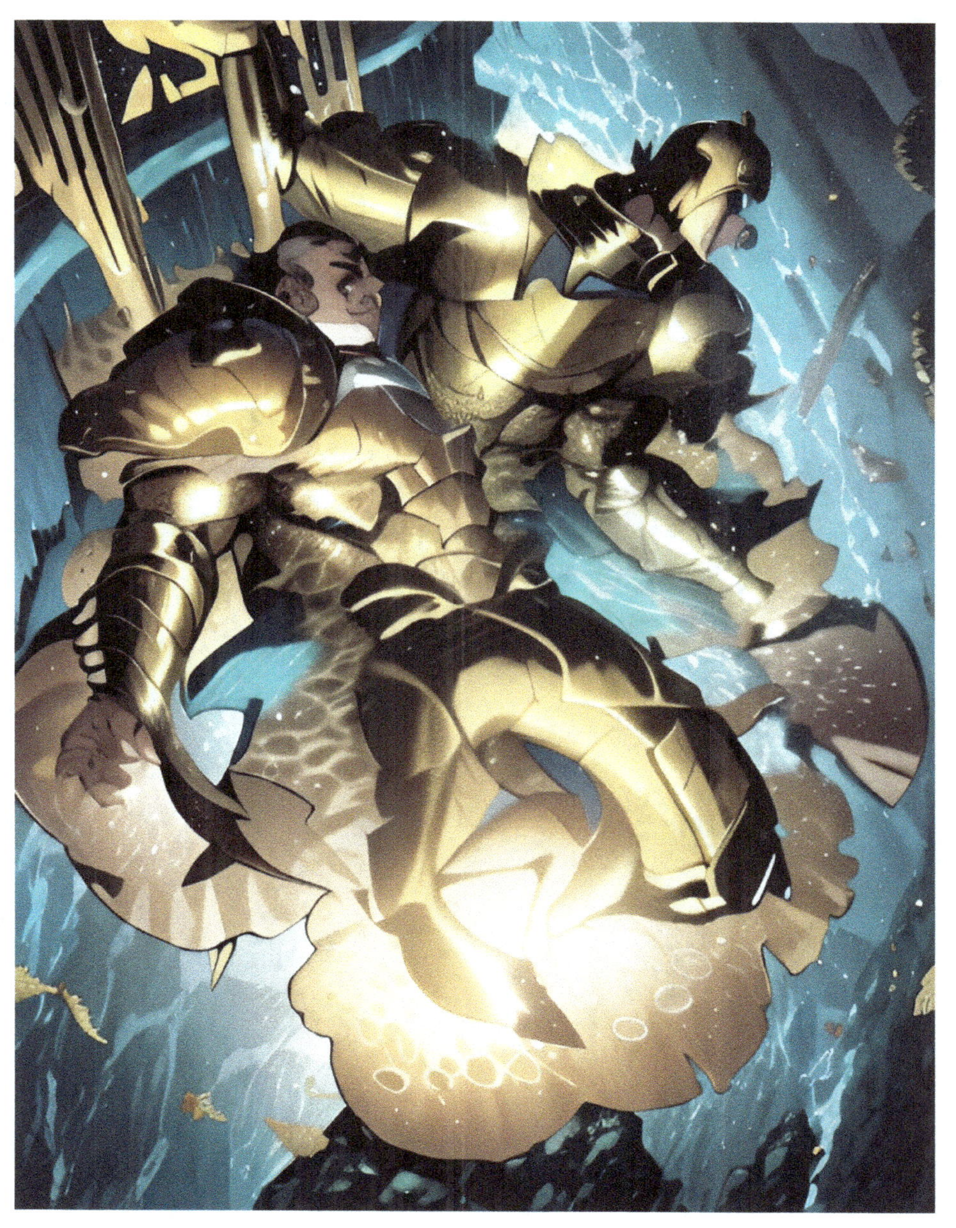

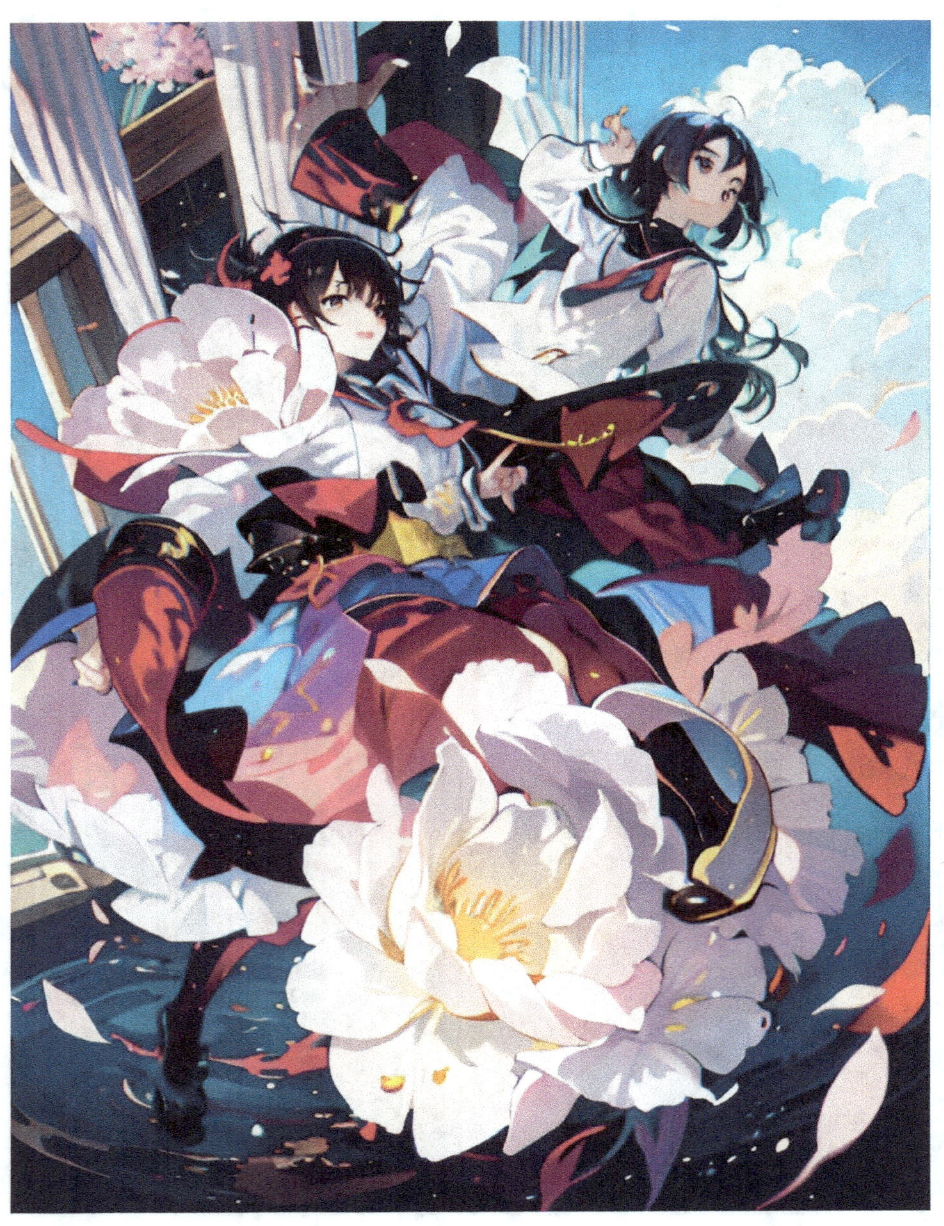

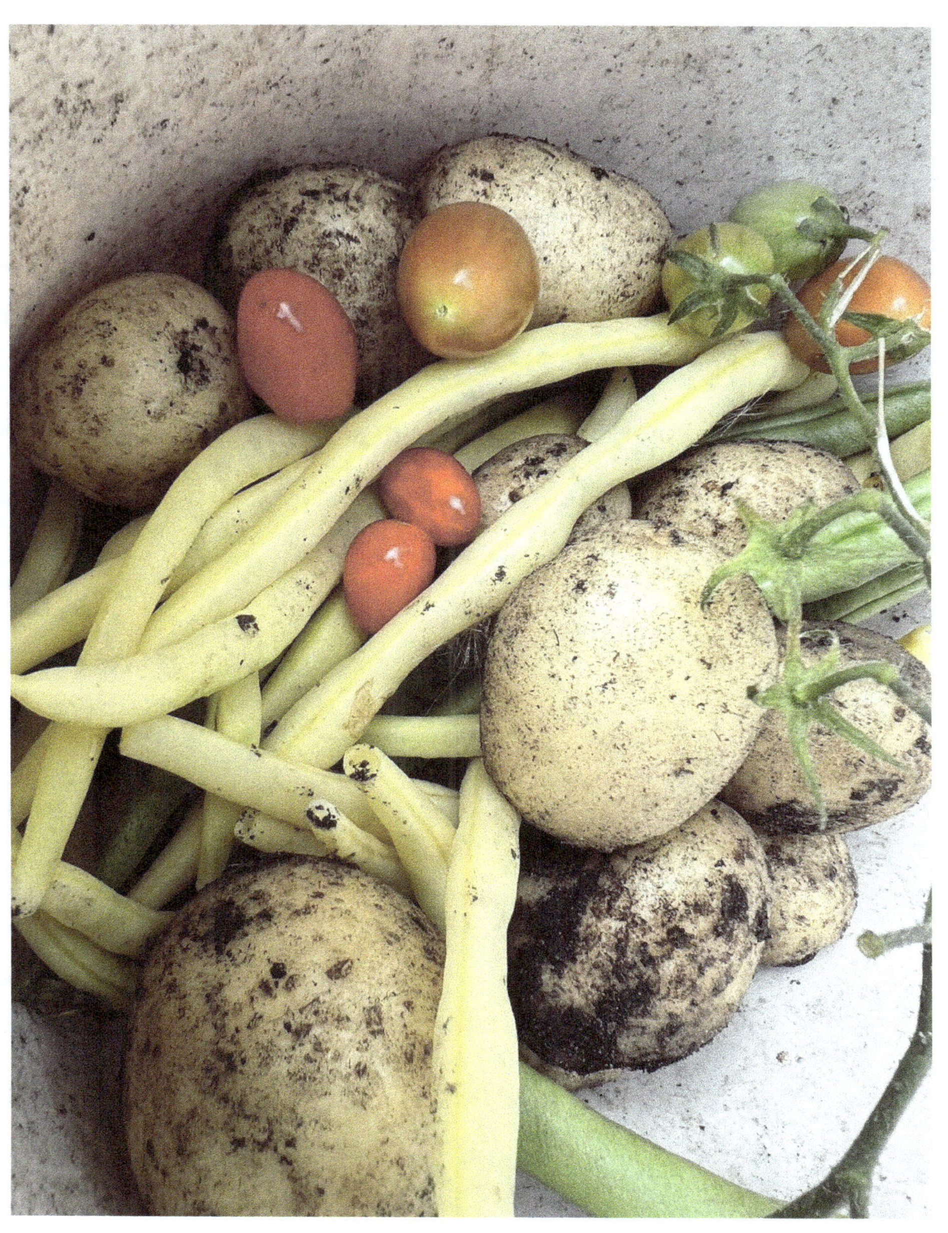

Vegetables

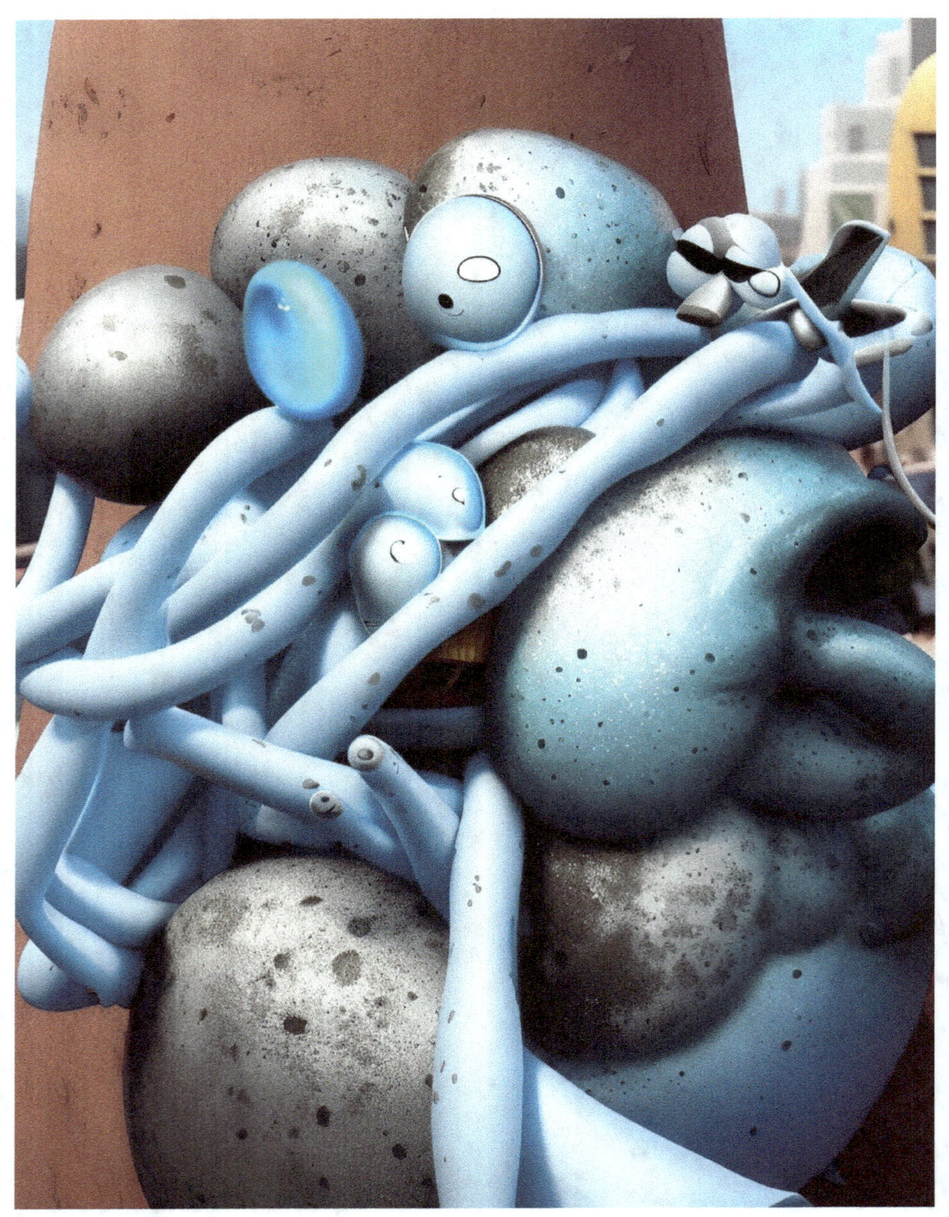

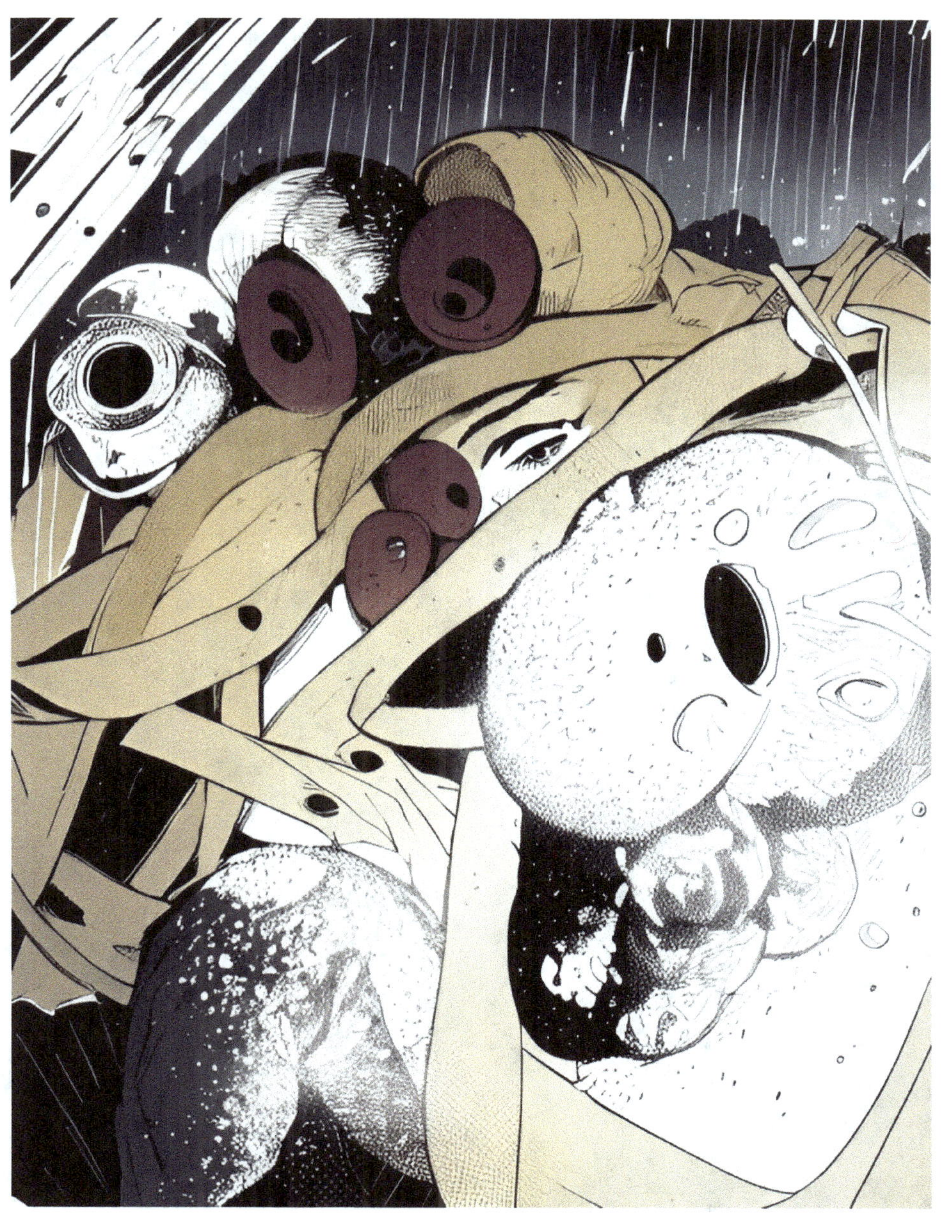

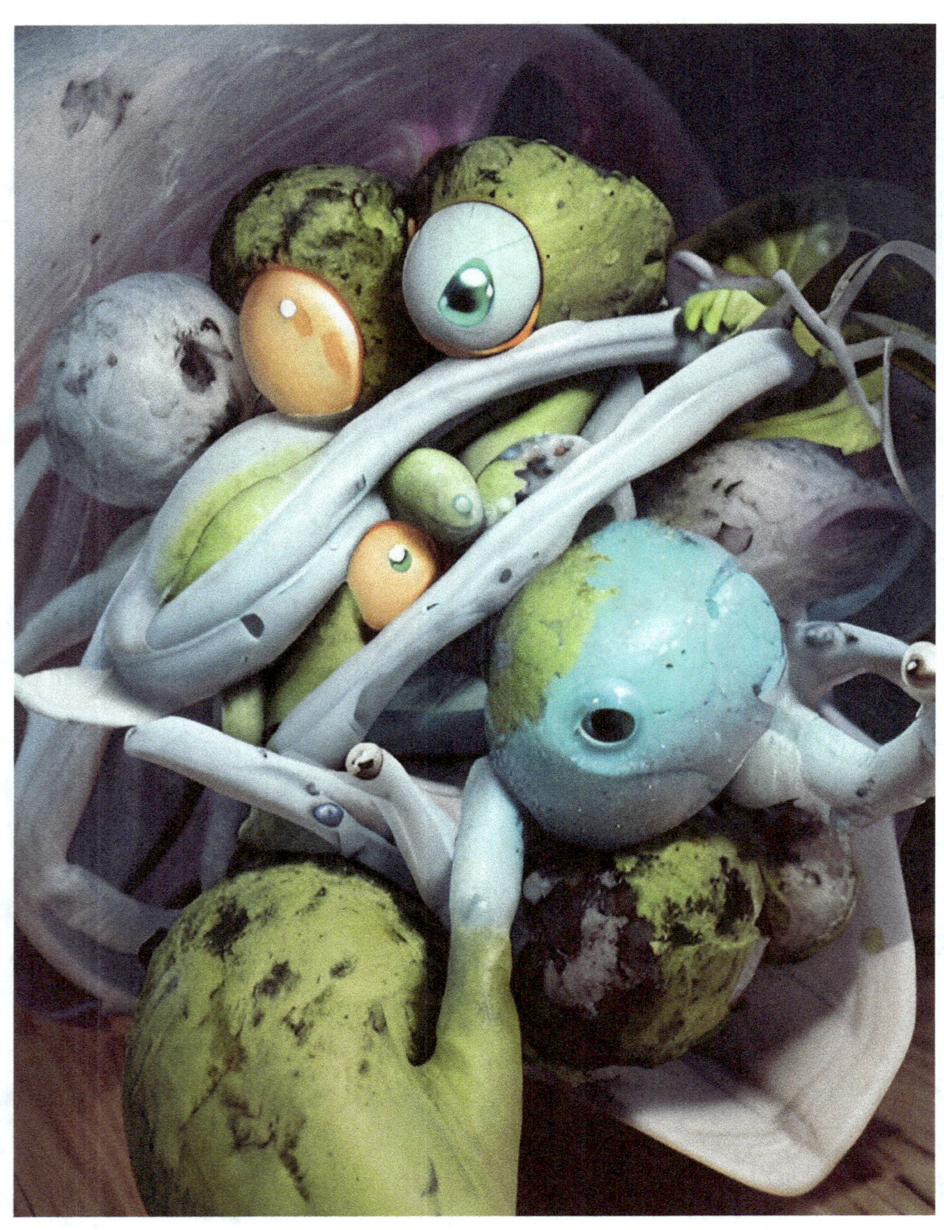

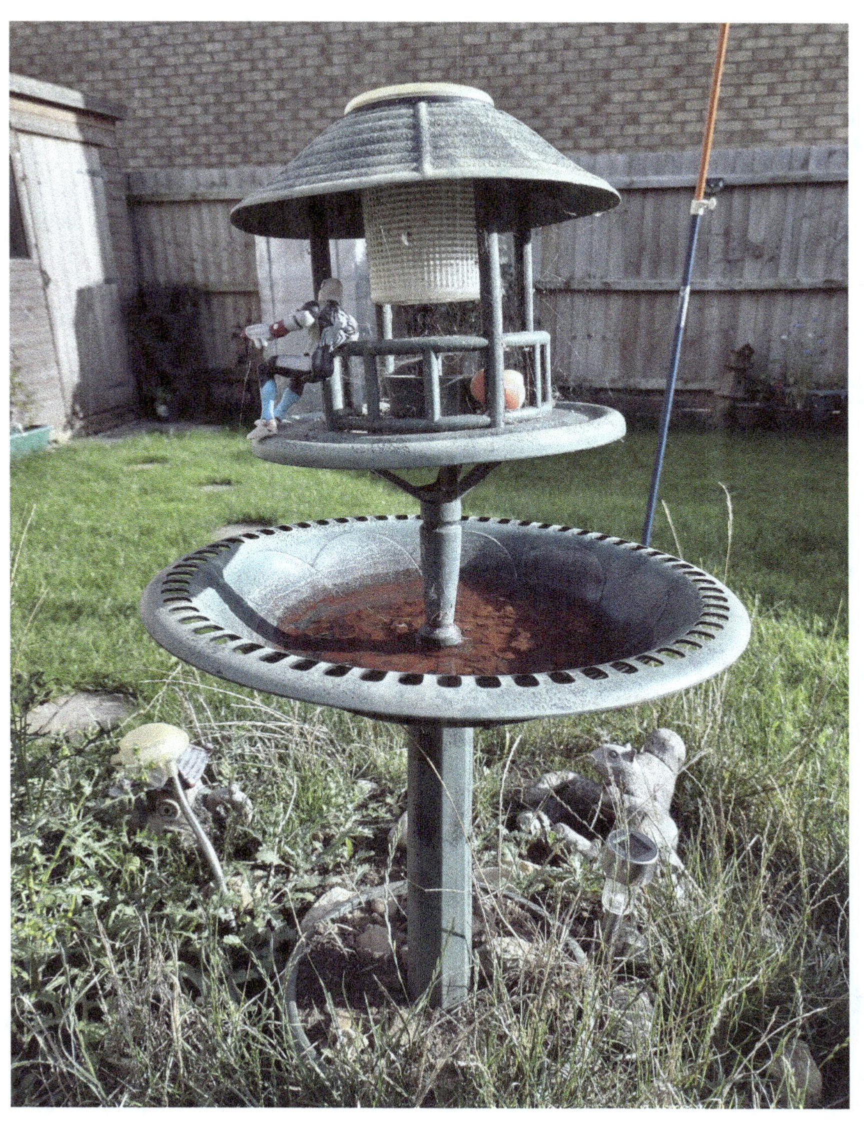

Birdbath

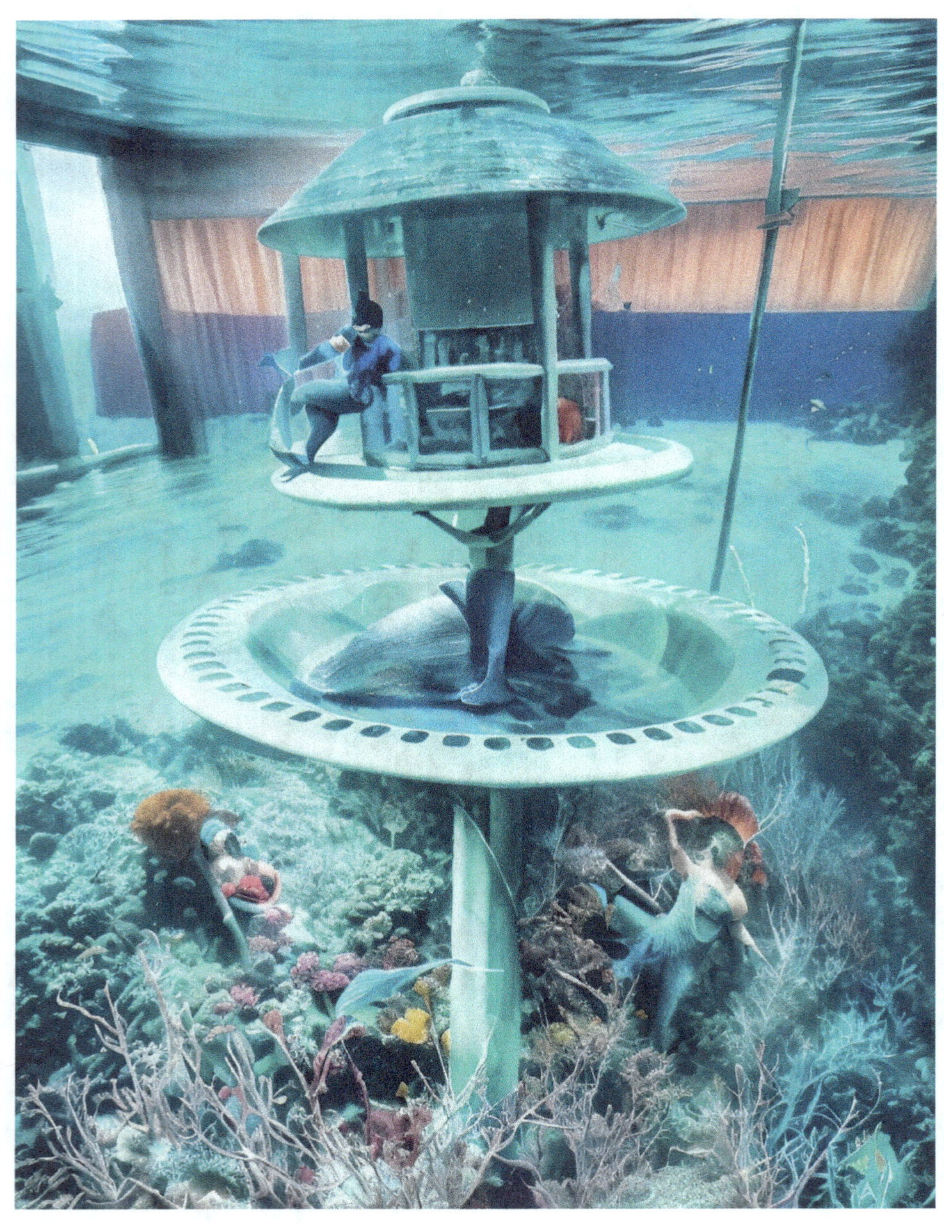

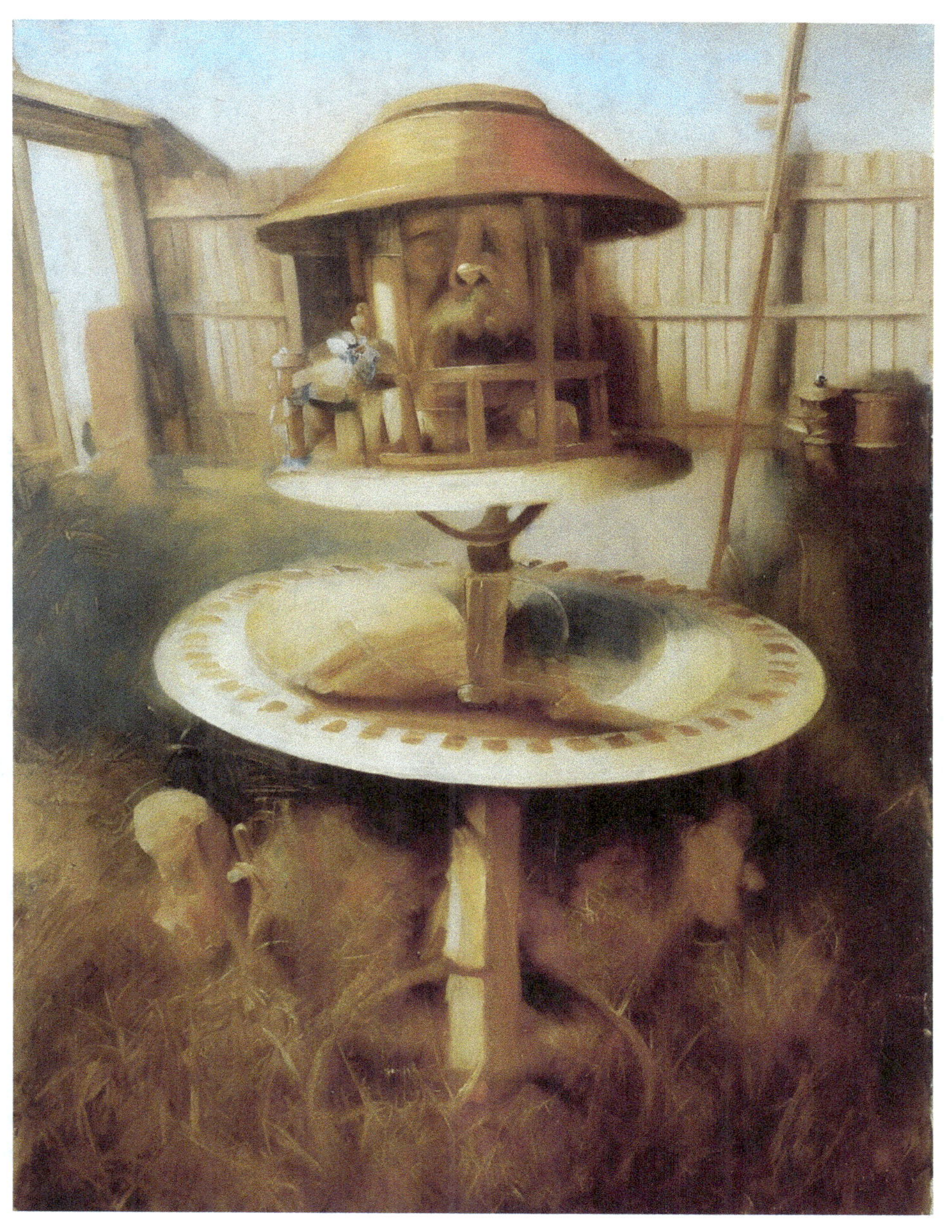

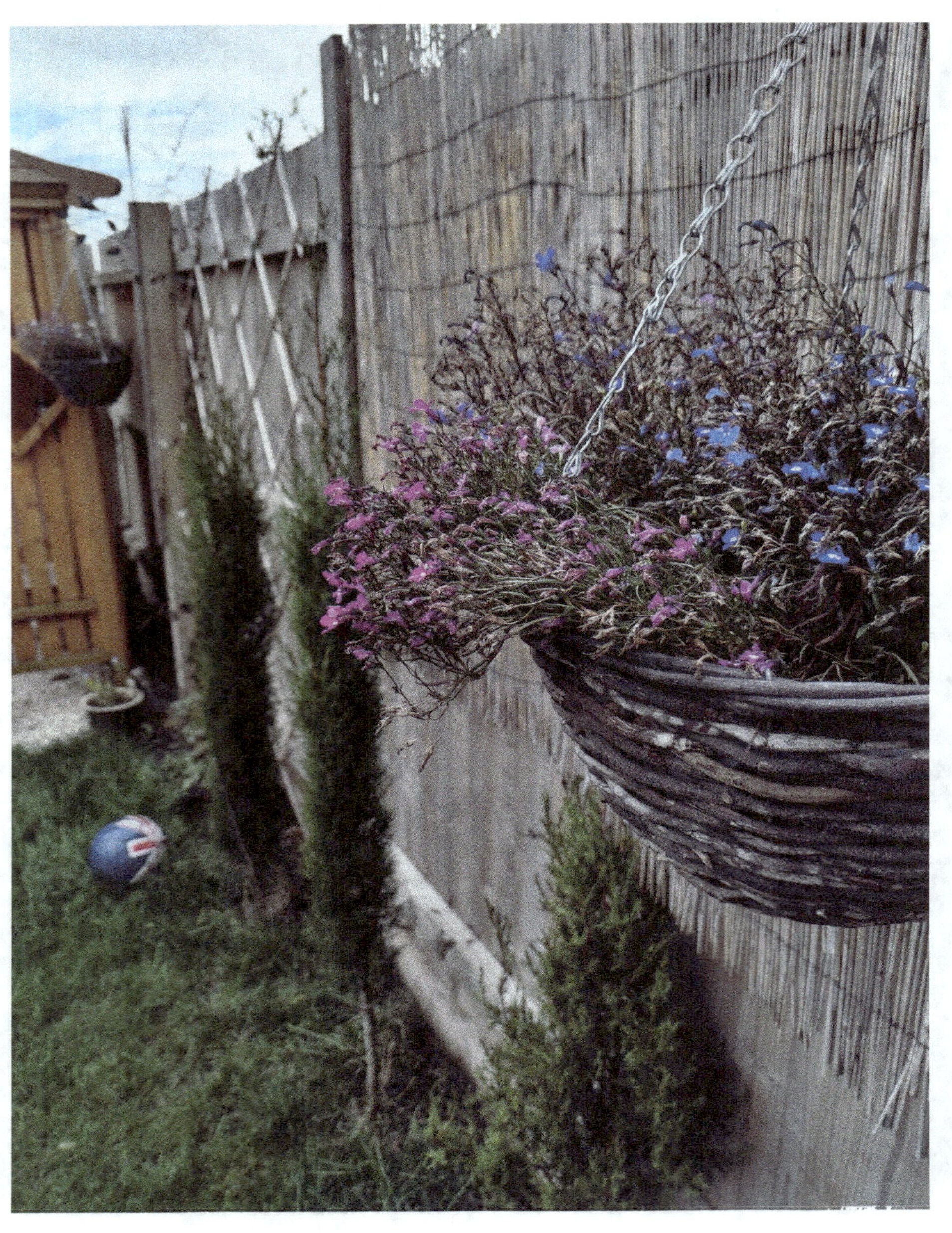

Fence

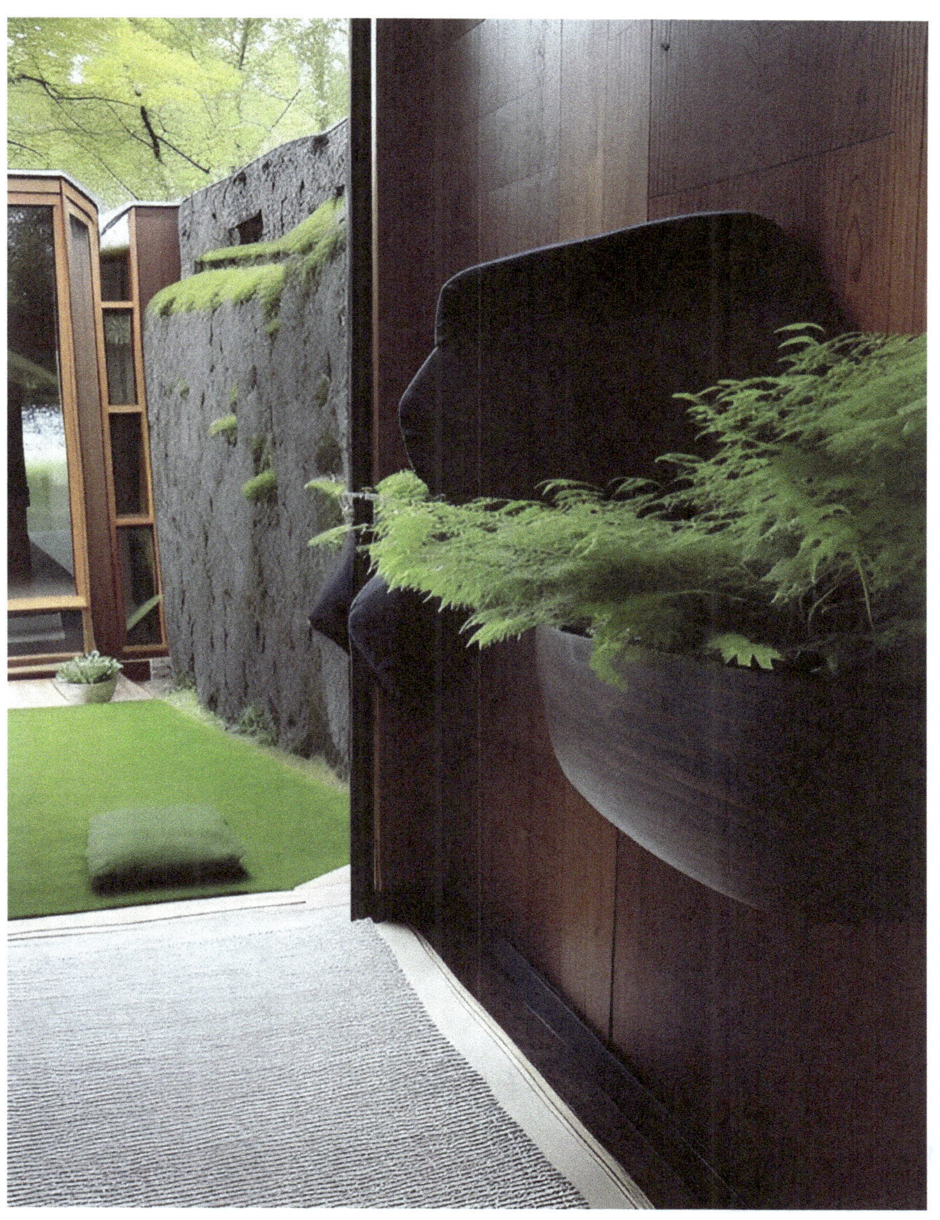

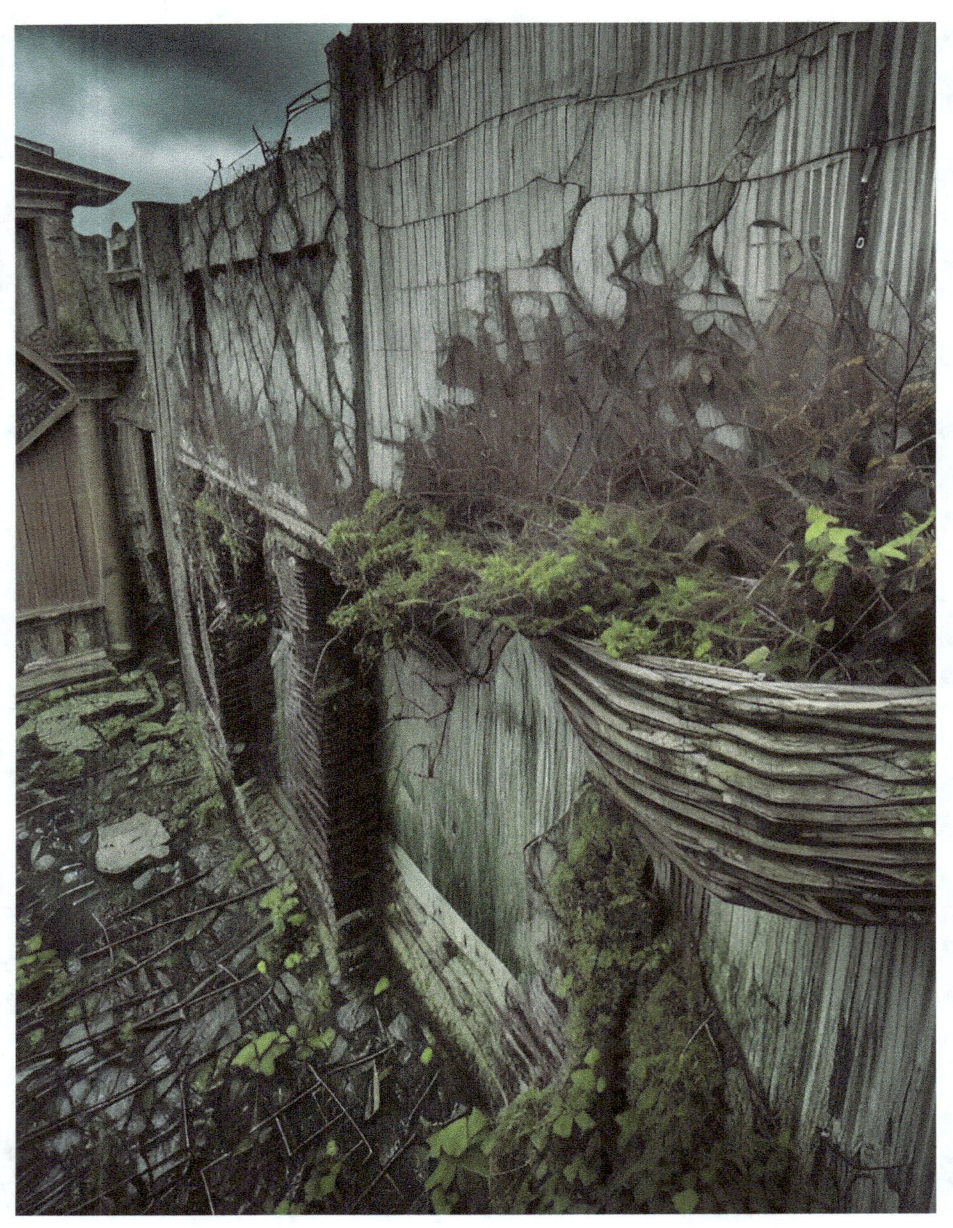

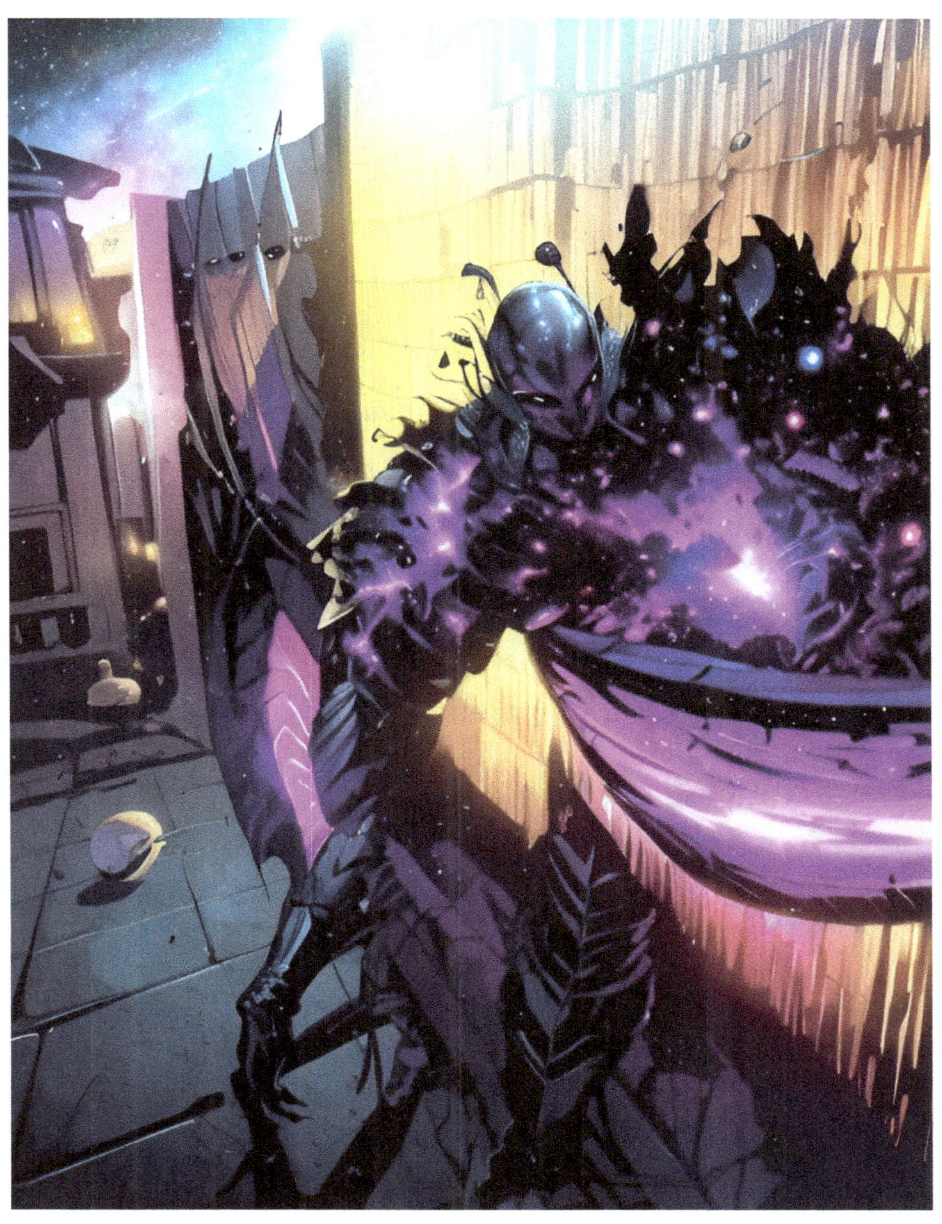

If you enjoyed this book, please let me know

Ant Nottingham
www.darkvillager.com
thedarkvillager@live.co.uk

Many thanks to my brother Robert for the veg photo!

Thanks to my wonderful wife Margie
for your patience and support
X